Machines, Bodies and Invisible Hands

Stefano Fiori

Machines, Bodies and Invisible Hands

Metaphors of Order and Economic Theory in Adam Smith

palgrave macmillan

Stefano Fiori
Department of Economics and Statistics
University of Torino
Torino, Italy

ISBN 978-3-030-85205-4 ISBN 978-3-030-85206-1 (eBook)
https://doi.org/10.1007/978-3-030-85206-1

This Palgrave Macmillan imprint is published by the registered company Springer Nature Switzerland AG.
The registered company address is: Gewerbestrasse 11, 6330 Cham, Switzerland

For Maria Pia

Contents

Abbreviations

Ancient Physics	The History of Ancient Physics (reprinted in Smith 1982a)
HA	The History of Astronomy (reprinted in Smith 1982a)
Edinburgh Review	Letters to the Edinburgh Review (reprinted in Smith 1982a)
IA	Of that Nature of that Imitation which takes place in what are called the Imitative Arts (reprinted in Smith 1982a)
Languages	Considerations Concerning of the First Formation of Languages (reprinted in Smith 1985)
LJ (A)	Lectures on Jurisprudence, Report of 1762–3 (reprinted in Smith 1982b)
LJ (B)	Lectures on Jurisprudence, Report dated 1766 (reprinted in Smith 1982b)
ED	Early Draft of part of *The Wealth of Nations* (reprinted in Smith 1982b)
LRBL	Lectures on Rhetoric and Belles Lettres (reprinted in Smith 1985)
TMS	The Theory of Moral Sentiments (reprinted in Smith 1984)
WN	An Inquiry into the Nature and Causes of the Wealth of Nations (reprinted in Smith 1981)

CHAPTER 1

Introduction

Abstract This book offers an interpretation of how Adam Smith dealt with what he saw as a fundamental problem: an explanation of the economic order in commercial societies of the late eighteenth century.

The thesis put forward is that concepts associated with the invisible hand must be examined as part of a complex process of forming ideas, in which metaphors as well as philosophical analysis play a role.

Metaphors, in particular, are cognitive tools that (at least provisionally) direct research and help identify the causal links that explain phenomena. And Smith used the metaphors of the machine, the body and the invisible hand to explore the nature of social systems, in a setting where market societies were emerging.

Although the three metaphors overlapped in some respects, they exhibited significant differences. Order pre-exists in the machine and in the body, and its component parts perform unchangeable functions, without which the system's functioning is compromised. By contrast, in systems of the "invisible hand" type, the system is self-generating and self-regulating, and coordination between the functions performed by the parties is not predetermined.

Keywords Book's thesis • Metaphorical investigation

S. Fiori, *Machines, Bodies and Invisible Hands*,
https://doi.org/10.1007/978-3-030-85206-1_1

Though this book does not present a systematic account of the work of Adam Smith and its interpretations, it does offer an interpretation of how Smith dealt with what he saw as a fundamental problem: an explanation of the economic order in commercial societies of the late eighteenth century. The main lines of this re-reading of Adam Smith's thought go back to my doctoral dissertation of many years ago and have been further developed in various articles over the years. However, the content of this volume is not a summary of what has already been written, but introduces new content and presents new arguments to support my previous analyses.

In the late eighteenth century, Smith was not the only one who felt the need to explain the formation of modern societies. However, he was probably the author who was best able to express the concept of economic and social order, which—he asserted—should be understood as the unintended coordination of individual behaviors. The image that summarized this perspective is, as is well-known, the invisible hand, a concept that, Vaughn (1989: 170) remarks, has three features: (1) "human action often leads to consequences that were unintended and unforeseen by the actors"; (2) "the sum of these unintended consequences over a large number of individuals or over a long period of time may, given the right circumstances, result in an order that [...] appears as if it were the product of some intelligent planner"; (3) "the overall order is beneficial".

This book's thesis is that concepts associated with the invisible hand must be examined as part of a very complex process of forming ideas, in which metaphors as well as philosophical analysis play a role. Theoretical analysis and metaphorical investigation cannot be clearly distinguished; on the one hand, the conceptual approach of metaphors served as the basis of the theoretical construction, and on the other, philosophical analysis stimulated both the creation of new metaphors and the revitalization of old ones. To understand these phenomena, we will draw on a vast literature that has shown how metaphors play a conceptual role in organizing our ideas about the world, both in daily life and in scientific investigation.

In fact, metaphors are cognitive tools that (at least provisionally) direct research and help identify the causal links that explain complex phenomena. And Smith used the metaphors of the machine, the body and the invisible hand to explore the nature of a particular complex phenomenon: the relationship between individuals and the social system, in a setting where market societies were emerging. The three conceptual metaphors, while exhibiting different characteristics, recur in Smith's system, but none is explicitly indicated as dominant. However, they can be ranged in a logical order, as if some of the problems connected with the use of the metaphor of the machine were better dealt with by using the metaphor of the body and the problems connected with the metaphor of the body were better framed by assuming the perspective of the invisible hand.

As will be shown in Part I of this book, metaphors of the machine had a long tradition, and in the seventeenth century they were used to conceptualize the hierarchical order of the universe and of states. While retaining some aspects of the old metaphor of the machine (especially the idea that the machine is a model of coherence between parts and the whole), Smith revitalized this image. Smith's machine evolves over time; it does not represent a static system. The machine also represents the beauty of order and harmony, and this property, perceived by individuals, triggers behaviors that unintentionally produce beneficial results. However, the machine can only be modified and improved by an outside hand. Thus, its limitation as a metaphor consists in the fact that it is unable to conceptualize the processes of self-adjustment.

The metaphor of the body has some interesting connotations in Smith. In the 1600s, mechanistic philosophy had reduced the body to a machine. However, even in the cultural framework of a dominant mechanism, medical and organic metaphors were used to interpret the physiology of the "body politick" in other than mechanical terms. Smith's metaphor of the body, while reutilizing several arguments from old medical metaphors, emphasizes some properties of living systems that could not be conceptualized using the metaphor of the machine: self-organization and self-preservation.

Lastly, the invisible hand is the metaphor that better represents order as an unplanned result of the behavior of many agents. While with metaphors of the machine and of the body, order is the underlying assumption for analyzing the functions performed by the parts (gears or organs), with the invisible hand order is the result of a process which is arrived at by considering the freedom of movement of the parties (individuals). Order pre-exists in the machine and in the body, and its component parts perform unchangeable functions, without which the system's functioning is compromised. By contrast, in systems of the "invisible hand" type, the system is self-generating and self-regulating, and coordination between the functions performed by the parties is not predetermined.

In short, machine, body and invisible hand can be seen as three theoretical "candidates" that were used as heuristic tools for exploring the causes of the social order's formation and its changes over time.[1] Although they were not only distinct but also competing, so to speak, in Smith's work they overlapped; the beauty of the machine was seen as a factor that set processes in motion that would lead to an unintended order, while the body was used to represent self-organizing properties of systems, an idea that also characterized the model based on the invisible hand.

The invisibility of the "hand" refers to the fact that behind social phenomena there is an organizing force that the literature on Smith has interpreted in various ways. Part II of the volume intends to show how the notion of "invisible" in the late eighteenth century played an important role in various fields of knowledge, especially those such as political economy and the life sciences, whose theoretical foundations were changing radically. What united Smith's economy and the life sciences of the time was the belief that the visible aspects of phenomena (the interdependencies that characterize both economic relations and the various aspects of life) had to be explained by underlying invisible principles of organization. In the seventeenth and early eighteenth centuries, the prevailing idea was that nature would be more intelligible as its visibility increased. Nature would reveal itself in its fullness as closer observation revealed its hidden aspects. Microscopes, telescopes and experiments would make nature increasingly visible, and therefore intelligible. Similarly, from Petty to Quesnay, the anatomy of society and economic interdependencies would have made the nature of economic systems observable, and therefore more understandable. However, in the approach taken by Smith and the life sciences of the late eighteenth century, analysis was not based on the simple visibility of phenomena, even when achieved through appropriate techniques and procedures. It was no longer enough to reduce economic phenomena to "Number, Weight, and Measure", nor to have increasingly accurate taxonomies of living beings. Rather, it was necessary to refer the visible to invisible principles of organization. However, defining these

[1] As for the different sets of metaphors in Smith's work, Cremaschi maintains that "Adam Smith worked with a blissful combination of metaphors [...] that helped in widening the scope of economic theory, imagining counterintuitive connections among separated fields, and shaping new hypotheses to be tested" (Cremaschi, 2002: 89).

principles was formally far from simple. For this reason too, metaphors were used to conceptualize the relationship between perceptible phenomena and the causes that generate them. Invisibility, like the force of gravity, was a kind of experience, a conjecture capable of orienting research and organizing ideas about the phenomena of self-regulation and development. The invisible hand, that is to say the idea that human actions unintentionally produce order and not chaos, to some extent reflected these beliefs.

Lastly, Part III of the book deals with the relationship between the invisible hand and time. Social and economic orders develop over time, and the invisible hand describes how the market's time—ever faster, ever more complex—is at the basis of individuals' inability to predict future scenarios. In other words, this metaphor seems to respond to the problem of how to conceive an order that, by continuously reconfiguring itself, is scarcely predictable. All this implies a temporal dimension, in which the time of the market is integrated into centuries-old historical time. Societies, in fact, tend toward the "natural order", but—says Smith—this takes place irregularly. Modern societies, based on the division of labor, can govern the rhythm of time; they can plan it, compress and organize it, especially in productive activities; but historical time, against which the realization of the "natural order" is measured, cannot be planned. Therefore, considering time in economic thought was a further theoretical challenge; order had to be conceived in dynamic terms, and this made it less predictable.

In conclusion, the volume is based on the idea that one interesting aspect of the metaphor of the invisible hand is its ability to capture the logic of a discourse that pervades much of Smith's work. As a metaphor, it was unable to explain in definitional terms a phenomenon such as the self-regulation of market systems in space and time. However, the hand was able to portray it ostensively. Something similar occurred in the life sciences of that era, for example, in Vitalism. Smith's work can thus hardly be separated from the great cultural events that characterized the era in which he wrote. Accordingly, this book attempts to interpret the history of Smith's thought as an "internal" history that looks at the process of the theory's creation, in relation to the broader sweep of intellectual and scientific history in the seventeenth and eighteenth centuries.

References

Cremaschi, S. (2002). Metaphors in the *Wealth of Nations*. In S. Boehm, C. Gehrke, H. D. Kurz, & R. Sturn (Eds.), *Is There Progress in Economics? Knowledge, Truth and the History of Economic Thought* (pp. 89–114). Edward Elgar.

Vaughn, K. I. (1989). Invisible Hand. In J. Eatwell, M. Milgate, & P. Newman (Eds.), *The New Palgrave. The Invisible Hand* (pp. 168–172). Norton.

PART I

Machines, Bodies and Invisible Hands

CHAPTER 2

Metaphors as Conceptual Tools

Abstract The literature on the cognitive role of metaphors discussed in this chapter shows how scientific theories often develop, not in spite of metaphors, but thanks to them. This literature, although made up of heterogeneous lines of research, formulates a number of ideas that guide the present analysis. One is that metaphors reorganize our ideas about the world, help re-describe it and orient the search for causal links that explain phenomena.

For these reasons, many of our philosophical beliefs depend on how we conceptualize the world out there through metaphors. Complex and unknown events are first analyzed by transferring characteristics of known domains to them, on the basis of analogies.

Keywords Principal subject • Subsidiary subject • Mary Hesse • Theory-constitutive metaphors • Conceptual metaphor

2.1 Metaphors in Philosophy of Science: From Max Black to Thomas S. Kuhn

Around the middle of the twentieth century, several philosophical studies rediscovered metaphor as a conceptual tool.

S. Fiori, *Machines, Bodies and Invisible Hands*,
https://doi.org/10.1007/978-3-030-85206-1_2

Stephen C. Pepper, in *World Hypotheses* (1942), argued that some conceptions that arise from common sense are used to understand other areas of knowledge in terms of description and explanation. Metaphor, in his "root metaphor theory", was seen as an instrument that, by interpreting unknown domains in terms of familiar domains, engenders conceptual "categories":

> A man desiring to understand the world looks about for a clue to its comprehension. He pitches upon some area of commonsense fact and tries if he cannot understand other areas in terms of this one. This original area becomes then his basic analogy or root metaphor. He describes as best he can the characteristics of this area, or, if you will, discriminates its structure. A list of its structural characteristics becomes his basic concepts of explanation and description. We call them a set of categories. In terms of these categories he proceeds to study all other areas of fact whether uncriticized or previously criticized. He undertakes to interpret all facts in terms of these categories. (Pepper, 1942: 91)

A few years earlier, I. A. Richards suggested in *The Philosophy of Rhetoric* that metaphor should be interpreted not as a mere "shifting and displacement of words" (Richards, 1965 [1936]: 94) but as connection between "two *thoughts of different things* active together and supported by a single word, or phrase, whose meaning is a resultant of their *interaction*" (ibidem: 93, emphasis in original). Two components of the metaphor, "tenor" and "vehicle", make this operation possible, where the "tenor" is "the underlying idea or principal subject which the vehicle or figure means" (ibidem: 97). The relationship between tenor and vehicle, therefore, was interpreted as a "co-operation" that "results in a meaning [...] which is not attainable without their interaction" (ibidem: 100).

Max Black developed and modified Richards' ideas in *Metaphor*, an article published in 1954 and later included in his book *Models and Metaphors* (1962). He criticized both the idea that metaphor "is used in place of some equivalent *literal* expression" (Black, 1962: 31, emphasis in original)—Black calls this the substitution view—and the idea that metaphor consists in the presentation of an "underlying analogy" expressed in terms of "condensed or elliptical *simile*" (the comparison view as special case of substitution view) (ibidem: 35). Metaphor, by putting two objects in relation, produces a new meaning that is not identifiable with the literal one. Metaphor cannot be paraphrased, because its translation in literal terms entails a loss of part of the metaphorical meaning. Black, instead of "tenor" and "vehicle", used the expression "principal subject" and "subsidiary subject" (and later, in Black, 1993 [1979]: 27, "primary subject" and "secondary subject") to point out that metaphorical statements regard systems of implications, rather than "things" (ibidem: 44). The statement "Time is Money"[1] invites us to interpret "Time" in terms of "Money" or, more precisely, invites us to compare some details of "Time" in terms of "Money", while other details are not considered. Metaphor reorganizes our ideas about the principal subject (Time), which is seen now in light of the subsidiary subject (Money), because a system of "associated implications" applied to the subsidiary subject is projected upon the principal subject (ibidem: 44). In turn, the subsidiary subject can also be viewed in a new light because of this relationship (Black, 1993 [1979]: 28). A relevant consequence is that metaphors do not illustrate pre-existing similarities but create new ones (Bicchieri, 1988: 104).

Black's interaction view was a watershed in studies on metaphor. Metaphors were viewed as "cognitive instruments" that, for their capacity to organize connections (Black, 1993 [1979]: 37), made it possible to explore characteristics of the world, since implications of the secondary subject could be interpreted as "a *model* of the ascriptions imputed to the primary subject" (ibidem: 30, emphasis in original). In this way metaphors could be considered tools that play an important role in forming scientific theories, and Black's idea that there is an analogy between the use of literary metaphor and the use of models in science was further developed by Mary Hesse, who explained this relation as follows:

> In a scientific theory the primary system is the domain of the explanandum, describable in observation language; the secondary is the system, described either in observation language or the language of a familiar theory, from which the model is taken: for example, "Sound (primary system) is propagated by wave motion (taken from a secondary system)"; "Gases are collections of randomly moving massive particles". (Hesse, 1966: 158–159)

Primary system, to which the "explanandum" corresponds, and secondary system, to which the "explanans" corresponds, are not "irreducible dichotomies". The interactive process that characterizes their relationship implies not only that the primary system is seen through the

[1] Black's original example was "Man is a wolf".

frame and implications of the secondary system but also that the associated ideas of the secondary system are modified in consequence of their assimilation to the primary system. An implication of the interactive process, therefore, is that "the two systems are seen as more like each other; they seem to interact and adapt to one another". If so, opposition between literal and metaphorical dimensions is only pragmatic and means that no sharp line can be drawn between the literal and the figurative (Hesse, 1966: 166; cf. Bicchieri, 1988: 105–106; Bailer-Jones, 2002: 117).

Given these similarities between metaphors and scientific theories, the deductive model of explanation can be interpreted as "metaphoric redescription of the domain of the explanandum" (Hesse, 1966: 171), in which theoretical explanation is characterized by a new vocabulary introduced into the explanans. However, for metaphorical expression to be an explanation, some conditions must be satisfied, and "the criteria of acceptability of metaphoric descriptions of the primary system" must be clarified (Hesse, 1966: 171 and 176).

Richard Boyd's proposal also started from Black's account on metaphor and agreed with the idea that models in science resemble metaphors. His thesis was that there is a type of metaphor which plays an important role in the formation of scientific theories (Boyd, 1993: 481). Metaphors, as in Black's approach, not only make it possible to understand the primary subject in terms of the secondary subject, but also orient scientific investigations, because they encourage identification of new analogies and similarities (ibidem: 489). They provide a new understanding of theoretically relevant features regarding primary and secondary subjects, including as yet undiscovered characteristics of these two domains (ibidem: 481). Since metaphors perform this function, they are constitutive of theories. They are useful tools that introduce a new theoretical terminology for features of the world whose existence is only probable, when formal concepts used to describe causal links among phenomena are not available. Boyd's intention was to go beyond Hesse's idea that the referent of a model or metaphor is the primary subject (Hesse, 1966: 166). Following Kripke and Putnam, he pointed out that the reference for substances, like "water" or "gold", can be preliminarily fixed by ostension, rather than by means of definitional conventions. Our language lacks precision when we refer in this way to certain phenomena or objects, of which we do not know the fundamental properties. However, this operation is useful because it gives us access to those phenomena: "This sort of ostensive reference fixing, then, can be understood as a procedure aimed at accommodation of linguistic usage to as yet undiscovered causal structures" (Boyd, 1993: 492). This operation is performed by theory-constitutive metaphors, that is, metaphors which accomplish "nondefinitional reference fixing" by introducing an ostensive, theoretical terminology (ibidem: 493). The computer metaphor, employed in cognitive psychology, is an example of how metaphors ostensively help to identify properties that have not yet been discovered. This metaphor makes it possible to explore a new, unknown sphere of knowledge, because it leads to investigate a number of similarities and analogies between mind operations and computer computations that have not yet been formally defined. It provides a terminology whereby an investigation can be initiated, and possible causal relations can be sought on the basis of the mind-computer analogy. This makes the research program promoted by theory-constitutive metaphors necessarily incomplete, precisely because the conditions that make it possible to compare human cognition to computer computation is what has to be explored (ibidem: 494).

Theory-constitutive metaphors make linguistically mediated "epistemic access" possible to properties of phenomena to which we refer ostensively. The meaning of the expression "epistemic access" is illustrated by the following examples. The term "red" is a term that identifies the presence of red in many phenomena. By using it, we have an access to these phenomena whereby we can deal with them in many ways. Similarly, the term "DNA" is an epistemic access to DNA (the substance which is the referent of "DNA"). The use of the term "DNA" makes it possible for some practices to take place in the scientific community. For example, it permits "scientists to report to each other the results of studies of DNA", or to discuss theories concerning DNA (ibidem: 505–506).

Thomas S. Kuhn criticized Boyd's notion of "epistemic access". To explain his point of view, he considered Putnam's notion of reference fixing.

> There is something right about Putnam's claim that the referent of "electric charge" is fixed by pointing to the needle of a galvanometer and saying that "electric charge" is the name of the physical magnitude responsible for its deflection. [...] But pointing to a galvanometer needle while supplying the name of the cause of its deflection attaches the name only to the cause of that particular deflection [...]. It supplies no information at all about the many other sorts of events to which the name "electric charge" also unambiguously refers. (Kuhn, 1993: 535)

The problem is that Boyd replaced the notion of "dubbing" with the less clear notion of "epistemic access": "When dubbing is abandoned or shoved aside, the link it provided between language and the world disappears as well" (ibidem: 536). Boyd, Kuhn remarks, tacitly supposes that supporters of a certain theory know to what the terms they use refer, but he is not concerned with how reference is fixed. The relationship between natural kind terms and their reference is complex and cannot merely be given up, nor can it be established, as Putnam supposes, by a single act of ostension. Kuhn presents this concept by an example:

> Exposed to tennis and football as paradigms for the term "game", the language learner is invited to examine the two [...] in an effort to discover the characteristics with respect to which they are alike, the features that render them similar, and which are therefore relevant to the determination of reference. As in the case of Black's interactive metaphors, the juxtaposition of examples calls forth the similarities upon which the function of metaphor or the determination of reference depend. (Ibidem: 537)

In this perspective, metaphor can be viewed as "a higher-level version of the process by which ostension enters into the establishment of reference for natural-kind terms". While the latter aim at fixing the salient features, that is, the similarities, through which terms apply to nature, metaphors remind us that other features could be highlighted and that languages can "cut up" the world in many ways (ibidem: 537). In the scientific domain, metaphors establish links between scientific language and the world (ibidem: 539). Scientific models also perform this function, and as for Bohr's atom model, they do not need to be completely interpreted in literal terms, because the interactive process which governs both metaphors and models is a process of creation of similarities, as Black showed (ibidem: 538).

This view is related to the concept of scientific paradigm. Paradigms and metaphors used in scientific discourses change, and with them also change "the corresponding parts of the network of similarities" (ibidem: 539). Only with Copernicus was Mars conceptualized as a planet and ceased to be considered an object of a different nature. This occurred because metaphors associated with paradigms, and the network of analogies to which they referred, radically modified scientific discourse. Paradigms are incommensurable, but this does not mean that comparisons among different theories are impossible, because adopting one type of paradigm entails a comparison among theories. By contrast, terms drawn from one theory cannot be applied to another one. The word "flogiston" cannot be translated in modern chemical terms because it refers to a set of analogies and concepts that are not included in subsequent approaches. In conclusion, theories are comparable, but incommensurable, since the reference of the terms adopted in alternative theories is differently fixed and is related to the structure of these theories. Theoretical terms cannot be taken in isolation, because their meanings emerge from the semantic field of which they are part. For this reason, there is no superior, neutral vocabulary that can include and translate the terms adopted by two different paradigms, whose succession cannot be interpreted in cumulative terms.[2]

2.2 Alternative Philosophical Approaches to Metaphors: Donald Davidson, Richard Rorty and John Searle

Against Black, Lakoff and others, Donald Davidson expressed the idea that metaphors have no metaphorical meaning. They simply "mean what the words, in their literal interpretation, mean" (Davidson, 1978: 32). Metaphors cannot be paraphrased not because, as Black maintained, paraphrase entails the loss of the cognitive content, but because what the metaphor says is literal. What distinguishes metaphors from literal statements is how terms are used. In metaphor, this use "is something brought off by the imaginative employment of words and sentences and depends entirely

[2]Many metaphors have been used in economic thought in the course of time (Mirowski, 1989; Henderson, 1994; Hodgson, 1999: 60–83), and some scholars have tried to interpret this use in light of what has been suggested by Black, Hesse and Boyd. McCloskey (1998), in contrast with the "methodology of positive economics", has identified some traits of the rhetoric of economics. One thesis she puts forward is that analogy pervades economics, even when economists do not have explicit analogical intentions. Expressing ideas in terms of supply and demand curves, games theory and the invisible hand means unconsciously resorting to metaphors. Klamer and Leonard argued that "economics *is* metaphorical". Following Boyd, they maintained that, in addition to pedagogical and heuristic metaphors, there are "constitutive metaphors", that is, metaphors that "determine what makes sense and what does not; they will determine, among other things, the effectiveness of pedagogical and heuristic metaphors" (Klamer & Leonard, 1994: 40). Lewis (1999) also adopted the critical realisms approach encapsulated in Boyd's perspective, and maintained that metaphors play a "fundamental role" in the development of models. By contrast, Lagueux (1999: 5) remarks that "almost all metaphors used in economics are dead metaphors which no longer work as metaphors".

on the ordinary meanings of those words and hence on the ordinary meanings of the sentences they comprise" (ibidem: 33). Black's interaction view is wrong because it does not clarify why the special content of metaphor, which would be lost in literal paraphrase, cannot be made explicit (ibidem: 44). If metaphor does not convey any special message or meaning, then the mistake of those who support the interaction view is that they think that thoughts induced by that metaphor are contents of the metaphor. By contrast, these thoughts do not depend on metaphor (ibidem: 45).

Richard Rorty explicitly followed Davidson in his analysis of metaphor, and similarly criticized Black and Hesse. The meaning associated with metaphor is literal (Rorty, 1987: 284), since metaphor does not introduce a new language. By contrast, it utilizes tools provided by the current language. This does not mean that metaphors are useless instruments. In scientific discourses they help in forming new theories, because they increase our ability to discover more about the world, although they do not provide additional knowledge. This also occurs in everyday life, where metaphors help to develop more complex and accurate ideas about values, religion and tradition. In short, they increase our ability to deal with many problems, but they do not improve our cognitive ability (ibidem: 285). They invite us to discover analogies and similarities, and to acquire new knowledge, but as such they do not possess cognitive content (ibidem: 290).

Hesse (1987), by contrast with Rorty (and Davidson), replied that all language is metaphorical. In accordance with Wittgenstein's notion of family resemblances, she argued that

> *all* applications of general terms, however apparently literal, depend on perceptions of similarities between their referents. In learning a language, we learn to structure our perceptions of similarity, so that the general terms of that language implicitly classify the furniture of the world in conformity with the classification of our culture. (Hesse, 1987: 311, emphasis in original)

Different languages and theories entail different kinds of classification, and metaphor "is only a complex extension of the same process into novel and striking contexts" (ibidem: 311).

John Searle also opposed the concept of metaphorical meaning. The main problem he aimed to investigate consists of explaining how metaphors work. This subject is pragmatic in nature and focuses on the difference between what words mean literally and what the speaker means and tries to communicate. This difference depends not on the fact that metaphor yields a change of meaning, in some way attributable to a change of meaning of its lexical elements (Searle, 1993 [1979]: 90), but on the fact that "the speaker means something different by them" (ibidem: 90). More formally, if the speaker says that "S is P" ("sentence meaning") and means metaphorically that "S is R" ("the speaker's utterance meaning"), the problem consists in finding principles that connect and distinguish "sentence meaning" and "speaker's utterance meaning".

Moreover, Searle criticized the views that consider metaphorical utterances in terms of both comparison (or similarity) and interaction.

As regards comparison theories, Searle observed that they erroneously assume that metaphorical statements are reducible to statements of similarity (ibidem: 91). At most, the simile might work as a tool for understanding what the speaker means metaphorically. The wrong idea consists in explaining metaphor as a "relation between references" (ibidem: 94), that is, as an actual comparison between two existing objects. When we say "Sally is a block of ice", we are no more comparing two existing and distinct entities than when we say "Sally is a dragon". Moreover, if we say "Richard is a gorilla", we attribute to Richard certain, presumed characteristics of gorillas (their being fierce and violent) that ethology considers false; nonetheless the statement is true because it aims at saying something about Richard, not about gorillas. As a consequence, a metaphorical statement can be true even when comparison is false (ibidem: 92).

As regards the interaction view, Searle states that it correctly assumes that the process through which we produce and understand metaphors does not involve references, but the set of beliefs, associations and imagery associated with references. Interaction theories are incorrect in that they locate this relation at the level of the sentence, not at the level of the utterance. That is, they try to explain metaphors in terms of interaction between metaphorical expressions and the literal context in which they occur. Searle criticized: (i) the idea that there is a distinction between expressions used literally and expressions used metaphorically and (ii) the idea that the metaphorical meaning depends on some peculiar feature of a sentence. In his words, "the most serious objection to the semantic interaction view [is] that, even where the metaphorical occurrence is within the context of literal occurrences, it is not in general the case that the metaphorical speaker's meaning is a result of any interaction among these elements of the sentence in any literal sense of 'interaction'" (ibidem: 94).

In a pragmatic understanding of the mental and semantic process of encoding/decoding metaphors, Searle defines eight principles that ensure that the speaker's utterance is taken metaphorically and that the hearer recognizes that the utterance is meant metaphorically, and not literally. These principles are shared by the speaker and the hearer and consist in patterns of inference which allow speaker and hearer to understand metaphors.

2.3 From Conceptual Metaphor Theory to Recent Studies

Metaphors, Lakoff and Johnson maintain, are not mere linguistic phenomena, but the substance of thought:

> The concepts that govern our thought are not just matters of the intellect. They also govern our everyday functioning, down to the most mundane details. Our concepts structure what we perceive, how we get around in the world, and how we relate to other people. Our conceptual system thus plays a central role in defining our everyday realities. If we are right in suggesting that our conceptual system is largely metaphorical, then the way we think, what we experience, and what we do every day is very much a matter of metaphor. (Lakoff & Johnson, 1980: 3)

Metaphors determine and organize our perception of the world, and systematically structure everyday activity, by conceptualizing "one mental domain in terms of another" (Lakoff, 1993: 203). An example is the conceptual metaphor "ARGUMENT IS WAR" that deals with some properties of the topic "argument" in terms of properties of the topic "war". A consequence of the use of this metaphor is that interlocutors are seen as opponents, discourses are defined in terms of strategies, verbal confrontations are conceived in terms of positions to defend, or alternatively to attack. This process "can be understood as a mapping (in the mathematical sense) from a source domain ["war", in this case] to a target domain ["argument", in this case]", where "entities in the domain of [argument] correspond systematically to entities in the domain of [war]" (ibidem: 206–207). In addition, metaphorical mappings are not isolated but are organized hierarchically in many, interacting levels (ibidem: 222).

Another example of metaphorical mapping which structures our experience is "TIME IS MONEY". Time in our culture is conceived as a limited resource, and a "valuable commodity" (Lakoff & Johnson, 1980: 8), and words like *budget*, *spend*, *invest*, *profit* and *loss* are economic concepts by means of which "time" is mapped. A set of correspondences, therefore, are established (Lakoff & Johnson, 1999: 163–164):

Money	→	Time
The User Of The Money	→	The User Of Time (The Agent)
The Purpose That Requires The Money	→	The Purpose That Requires Time
The Value Of The Money	→	The Value Of The Time
The Value Of The Purpose	→	The Value Of The Purpose

"Time is money", "time is a limited resource" and "time is a valuable commodity" are related concepts that form a system of subcategories under a general category which connects time to value.

Time, in this context, is conceptualized as a thing (money) that, since it is spent, borrowed, wasted and flows, can be expressed in quantitative terms. As a "thing", time is related to a number of other metaphors. When we say "time flows", we implicitly represent time as a river and communicate this conceptual metaphor with expressions such as "flow of money" or "cash flow". Metaphors which represent time in terms of money, and money in terms of a river are "ontological metaphors", that is, metaphors which take shape from our experiences with tangible things, and that make it possible to deal with abstract concepts in terms of "entities and substances" (Lakoff & Johnson, 1980: 25–26). As a defined entity, time can be represented in terms of "location", for example, when a point of time is reduced to a point in space ("I'll see you *at* four") (T. L. Brown, 2003: 36). The consequence is that we use many spatial terms in order to represent and describe time: "Future times are in front of the observer, past times are behind, and the passage of time is continuous and one-dimensional" (ibidem: 36).

Spatialization of time is an example of how "orientational metaphors" work. This kind of metaphor, with which one represents some domains in terms of up-down, in-out, front-back, central-peripheral, is based on bodily experiences of spatial orientation and is embodied in social and cultural contexts. For example, the experience of verticality is used to metaphorically conceptualize various conditions of everyday life, such as those regarding happiness, social or professional status, in terms of "happy is up; sad is down", "high status is up; low status is down", where the general principle underlying these conceptual metaphors is "more is up". But metaphors are also containers which exhibit in/out orientation, because we image certain events as objects that contain something. Classical philosophical "categories" also reflect this function. The principle "If X is in container A and container A is in container B, then X is in container B" is the same principle of syllogistic reasoning. The most famous syllogism "Socrates is a man/All men are mortal/Therefore, Socrates is mortal" can be reformulated as "If X is in category A, and A is in category B, then X is in category B", where the category is used as a container (Lakoff, 1993: 212–213). The idea of applying the conceptual metaphor theory, not only to everyday life, but also to philosophy, was developed by Lakoff and Johnson in *Philosophy in the Flesh* (1999), a book in which the two authors consider (1) how metaphors are at the basis of many abstract concepts, and (2) how the mind is embodied in neural structures.

1) Many abstract ideas, such as events, causation, time, the self, mind and morality, are conceptualized by means of metaphors, and "When philosophers construct their theories of being, knowledge, mind, and morality, they employ the very same conceptual resources and the same basic conceptual system shared by ordinary people in their culture" (Lakoff & Johnson, 1999: 338).

An example among others is Descartes' notion of mind. This concept is based on a set of correspondences fixed by the "Knowing Is Seeing" metaphor, where the elements of the visual domain (such as, Object seen, Person who sees, Light, Physical Viewpoint) are projected on elements which belong to the domain of philosophical knowledge (such as, respectively, Idea, Knowing an Idea, "Light"of reason, Mental Viewpoint). Thus, mind is conceived as a container for ideas, perception is represented as a person who does the receiving, imagination is personified, and so on (ibidem: 393–395).

Abstract ideas are at the basis of many disciplines, not only philosophy. Lakoff and Núñez (Lakoff & Núñez, 2000; Núñez, 2008) have shown how even mathematical tools (from infinitesimal calculus to logic, from projective geometry to transfinite arithmetic) can be explained by means of conceptual metaphor theory (Núñez, 2008: 342). Many cognitive mechanisms, such as those employed in spatial relations, bodily orientations, grouping and manipulation of objects, are at the basis of mathematical ideas. Thus, for example, the mathematical concept of class refers to the familiar conceptualization of the practice of collecting objects in a delimited space, the mathematical concept of recursion derives from the conceptualization of the practice of repeating an action, and so on (Núñez, 2008: 343). Mathematical concepts are operational thanks to the embodied mind, and are metaphorical in nature, like many other concepts of everyday life. Since mathematics is grounded on bodily experience "Human mathematics is not structured after objectively pre-existing, external timeless mathematical entities or eternal mathematical truths" (Núñez, 2008: 357). However, this does not mean that mathematics is based on subjective judgments, or is a matter of mere social agreement. Rather than being rejected, the concept of mathematical truth must be profoundly revised, as regards the fact that a statement is true if our understanding of that statement accords with our bodily experience.

2) As cognitive science has shown, our thought is unconscious in the sense that it arises from neural activities independently of our awareness. A number of neural structures by which we codify the world are triggered automatically, without noticeable effort (Lakoff & Johnson, 1999: 10–11).

Concepts emerge from the brain's neural networks, and "reason", the capacity to organize concepts, depends on perception, motion, emotion and other bodily capacities (ibidem: 17). In this specific sense, our categories are embodied and unconscious. Studies of neural modeling help in understanding how conceptual reasoning makes use of the sensorimotor system, and clarify how some kinds of concept such as color concepts, basic-level concepts and spatial-relational concepts are shaped (ibidem: 22–23).

Brain science and neural computation are the new frontiers of the research on metaphor. Thought is physical in that concepts are "computed" by physical brain structures. In the neural theory of language, developed by Lakoff with Jerome Feldman since 1988, neuronal groups are modeled as "nodes", where each neuron works in different neural groups (Kövecses, 2010: 87). From this perspective, a role is played by mirror neurons, that is, those neurons that make it possible to understand meanings of action (e.g., picking up a glass), because the brain relates observed movements (someone who picks up a glass) to our own analogous movements (Rizzolatti & Sinigaglia, 2006: 3). Meanings of "physical concepts" are, therefore, "mental simulations" which take shape from activation of specific groups of neurons. On the basis of these findings, the neural theory of language suggests that "the neural circuitry characterizing the meaning of 'grasp' is the neural circuitry in the mirror neurons that are activated when imagining either performing or perceiving grasping" (Lakoff, 2008: 19). The meaning processed by the neuronal activity, therefore, is at the origin of the formation of metaphorical patterns such as those associated with "grasping concepts". In this way, this approach provides a plausible approximation of how neural groups engender computations that are at the basis of conceptual metaphors and give shape to our inferences.

2.4 Adam Smith on Metaphors, Rhetorical Discourse and Analogies

Usually the use of metaphors, in both scientific and philosophical discourses, is independent of the way in which authors evaluate their usefulness, sometimes with complex theories. However, one may wonder what Smith's view was on this issue, since he dealt with it at least partially in his LRBL. Howell (1975: 42) praised the originality of Smith's rhetorical theory and maintained that "it took the position that the new rhetoric must define its function as broadly communicative rather than narrowly persuasive". Although some scholars (Purcell, 1986) do not share this interpretation, Trincado (2019: 127) recently argued that in order for Smith's theory of rhetoric to be correctly evaluated, it must be considered in relation to his general interpretation of social systems. This is true because Smith's theory of rhetoric is a theory of communication that is explained in the light of the concept of sympathy, a notion that in the TMS accounts for how relationships between individuals arise. This aspect emerges in a famous passage from the LRBL, where Smith points out that what the Greeks and Romans called "figures of speech" possess no intrinsic beauty per se:

> the case is far otherwise. When the sentiment of the speaker is expressed in a neat, clear, plain and clever manner, and the passion or affection he is poss(ess)ed of and intends, *by sympathy*, to communicate to his hearer, is plainly and cleverly hit off, then and then only the expression has all the force and beauty that language can give it. It matters not the least whether the figures of speech are introduced or not. {When your Language expresses perspicuously and neatly your meaning and what you would express, together with the Sentiment or affection this matter inspires you with, and when this Sentiment is nobler or more beautifull than such as are commonly met with, then your Language has all the Beauty it can have, and the figures

> of speech contribute or can contribute towards it only so far as they happen to be the just and naturall forms of Expressing that Sentiment.} They neither add to nor take from the beauty of the expression. When they are more proper than the common forms of speaking then they are to be used but not otherwise. They have no intrinsick worth of their own. That which they are often supposed to have is entirely derived from the expression they are placed in. (LRBL i.v. 57: 26, emphasis in original)

Although "figures of speech" have a subordinate role compared to ordinary language (the latter could do without them), they are not mere decoration of language. They possess a certain beauty, but this depends solely on their ability to communicate feelings (see Bazerman, 1993: 178). Only if they turn out to be "naturall forms of Expressing [a certain] Sentiment" can they help language carry out its communicative function. With regard to the *figurae verborum* and the *figurae sententiarum*, Smith states that they:

> give no beauty of their own, they only are agreable and beautifull when they suit the sentiment and express in the neatest manner the way in which the speaker is affected. When the common form of speech well enoug(h) describes the thing we want to make known or sufficiently communicates our sentiments, yet perhaps it does not express clearly and with sufficient life the manner we ourselves regard it. If in this case the fig(urative) way of speaking is more suited to our purpose, then it surely ought to be used preferably to the other. (LRBL i. 73–74: 33)

Rhetorical figures can express something more than and different from ordinary language, although they are subordinate to it. They are described as "exceptions" to grammatical rules, and this seems to assign them a special place in the economy of discourse. Although their function is limited, they enhance the expressive capacity of speech, and due to this characteristic, they can in certain circumstances even replace the "common form of speech". In this perspective, it is not surprising that metaphors can be used appropriately, especially if they possess the "due strength of expression to the object to be described" (LRBL i. 66: 29. See McKenna, 2006: 89, and Kennedy, 2017: 47).

The scheme used by Smith when describing the forms of speech refers to themes developed in the TMS, especially with regard to relationships that are established on a moral level between individuals, thanks to participation in the feelings of others. As is well known, this occurs if there is a sympathetic relationship between the spectator and the observed individual. However, in the TMS, communication between an individual who experiences a feeling or an emotion and a spectator who "by sympathy" identifies with his/her situation is not limited to verbal expression alone. First, Smith clarifies, we need to conceive of "what we ourselves should feel in the like situation" (TMS I.i.I.2: 9), because it is this condition that allows us to participate in the emotional experiences of others. The ability to place oneself "in the like situation" implies that mental analogies are elaborated that allow us to place ourselves in others' situation, even though we cannot live their experience.

Smith as well as other Scottish philosophers of the time considered analogies and the identification of similarities to be important tools of knowledge, not only on the psychological and moral level. According to Hume, in cases concerning relations of ideas, moral reasoning or matters of fact, the relations of cause and effect are deduced from experience, and not on the basis of a priori reasoning: "Reason can never shew us the connexion of one object with another" (Hume, 1985 [1739–40]: 140), and strictly speaking, experience cannot tell us anything about the present. Experience can inform us about the past, but nothing rules out that the cause-effect relationships of nature can change over time. Consequently, the information provided by experience is only probable. However, Hume continues:

> In reality, all arguments from experience are founded on the similarity, which we discover among natural objects, and by which we are induced to expect effects similar to those, which we have found to follow from such objects. (Hume, 2007 [1748]: 26)

The origin of our inferences must be sought in "custom or habit", that is, in that principle that makes us expect that similar causes observed in the past will generate similar events in the future (Hume, 2007 [1748]: 32). The appearance of analog reasoning is clarified as follows:

> If sometimes we ascribe a continu'd existence to objects, which are perfectly new to us, and of whose constancy and coherence we have no experience, 'tis because the manner, in which they present themselves to our senses, resembles that of constant and coherent objects; and this resemblance is source of reasoning and analogy, and leads us to attribute the same qualities to the similar objects. (Hume, 1985 [1739–40]: 259)

Analogy as a tool of investigation works even when it is imperfect and is used to extend causal relationships from a known domain to a less known one (ibidem: 259). For example, observations about blood circulation in an animal can be extended "to all animals".

Sometimes analogy precedes metaphor and the understanding of the metaphor depends on it. Other times it is the metaphor that "prompts the recognition of an analogy" (Bailer-Jones, 2002: 114), and consequently makes it possible to investigate an unknown domain starting from a known domain.[3] Hume, while not mentioning metaphor, describes this kind of process when he notes:

> When we have lived any time, and have been accustomed to the uniformity of nature, we acquire a general habit, by which we always transfer the known to the unknown, and conceive the latter to resemble the former. (Hume, 2007 [1748]: 126)

In Smith, relationships of similarity are the basis of analogies and shade into metaphors. In the *History of Astronomy*, the analogy between machines and scientific systems ("Systems in many respects resemble machines") immediately develops into metaphors: "A machine is a little system", "A system is an imaginary machine" (HA IV.19: 66). Furthermore, Smith affirms that analogy is at the basis of the abstraction processes that allow us to conceptualize characteristics shared by many objects, through language. At the origins of language, a specific name used for a particular object was later used to denote a class of objects with common characteristics, because "It was impossible that those savages could behold the new objects, without recollecting the old ones; and the name of the old ones, to which the new bore so close a resemblance" (Languages 1: 204). Even the formation of adjectives required a process of abstraction, since in order to conceive words like "green, blue, and red", first the "resemblances and dissimilitudes" of the qualities of color had to be observed (Languages 7: 206).

[3] According to Perelman and Olbrechts-Tyteca (1969: 403), "Any analogy [...] turns into metaphor quite spontaneously". Cohen (1993: 35–36) remarks that the lack of a clear distinction between metaphor and analogy dates back to classical Greece, and etymologically the meaning of metaphor entails the use of analogy. Klamer and Leonard (1994: 35) maintain, "Analogy is an expanded metaphor; more precisely, analogy is sustained and systematically elaborated metaphor".

However, analogies must be used with caution, since the network of similarities they identify is not always founded in reality. They are a particular source of error when they are based on ignorance. Many of those who thought to identify imaginative similarities between different fields such as painting, poetry, music, architecture, beauty and virtue, in fact produced only "lucubrations", due to the fact that they "were acquainted with the one art, but ignorant of the other". Despite this error, their weak analogy became "the great hinge upon which every thing turned" (HA II.12: 47).

While aware of the dangers, Smith, the Scottish philosophers and scientists attached great importance to analogical reasoning, provided it was based on a large number of experiences (see Thomson, 1965: 223–224). Lord Kames, not very differently from Hume, expressed himself in these terms:

> Analogy is one of the most common sources of reasoning; the force of which is universally admitted. The conviction of every argument founded on analogy, arises from this very sense of uniformity. Things similar, in some particulars, are presumed to be similar in every particular. (Kames, 1751: 305)

Almost 50 years later John Millar (1803: 138–9), a student of Smith, correlated the use of analogy with the dissemination of useful knowledge. For him it is the multiplication of analogies, not arbitrary but stimulated by experience, that fosters "new inventions and discoveries", and therefore the development of society.

The development of these ideas had lasting philosophical and scientific consequences. As Olson (1975, chap. 1) observes, one of these was that British scientists in the mid-nineteenth century were influenced by the pervasive idea in the Scottish philosophy of common sense that analogies and models play a significant role in the development of scientific theories. As for Smith, the most important analogies he used were encapsulated in metaphors. Of these, the machine, the body and the invisible hand were the most relevant from a conceptual point of view.

References

Bailer-Jones, D. (2002). Models, Metaphors and Analogies. In P. Machamer & M. Silberstein (Eds.), *The Blackwell Guide to the Philosophy of Science* (pp. 108–127). Blackwell.

Bazerman, C. (1993). Money Talks: The Rhetorical Project of the *Wealth of Nations.* In W. Henderson, T. Dudley-Evans, & R. Backhouse (Eds.), *Economics and Language* (pp. 173–199). Routledge.

Bicchieri, C. (1988). Should a Scientist Abstain from Metaphor? In A. Klamer, D. N. McCloskey, & R. M. Solow (Eds.), *The Consequences of Economic Rhetoric* (pp. 100–114). Cambridge University Press.

Black, M. (1962). *Models and Metaphors. Studies in Language and Philosophy.* Cornell University Press.

Black, M. (1993 [1979]). More About Metaphor. In A. Ortony (Ed.), *Metaphor and Thought* (2nd ed., pp. 19–41). Cambridge University Press.

Boyd, R. (1993). Metaphor and Theory Change: What Is "metaphor" a Metaphor for. In A. Ortony (Ed.), *Metaphor and Thought* (2nd ed., pp. 481–532). Cambridge University Press.

Brown, T. L. (2003). *Making Truth: Metaphor in Science.* University of Illinois Press.

Cohen, B. I. (1993). Analogy, Homology, and Metaphor in the Interaction Between the Natural Sciences and Social Sciences, Especially Economics. In N. de Marchi (Ed.), *Non-Natural Science: Reflecting on the Enterprise of More Heat than Light. History of Political Economy* (pp. 7–44) Annual Supplement to volume 25.

Davidson, D. (1978). What Metaphors Mean. *Critical Inquiry, 5*(1), 31–47.

Henderson, W. (1994). Metaphor and Economics. In R. E. Backhouse (Ed.), *New Directions in Economic Methodology* (pp. 343–367). Routledge.

Hesse, M. (1966). *Models and Analogies in Science.* University of Notre Dame Press.

Hesse, M. (1987). Unfamiliar Noises: Tropical Talk: The Myth of the Literal. *Proceedings of the Aristotelian Society*, Supplementary Volumes, *61*, 297–311.

Hodgson, G. M. (1999). *Evolution and Institutions. On Evolutionary Economics and the Evolution of Economics.* Edward Elgar.

Howell, W. S. (1975). Adam Smith's Lectures on Rhetoric: An Historical Assessment. In A. S. Skinner & T. Wilson (Eds.), *Essays on Adam Smith* (pp. 11–43). Clarendon Press.

Hume, D. (1985 [1739–40]). *A Treatise of Human Nature*, E. G. Mossner (Ed.). Penguin Books.

Hume, D. (2007 [1748]). *An Enquiry Concerning Human Understanding*, P. Millican (Ed.). Oxford University Press.

Kames, L. H. H. (1751). *Essays on the Principles of Morality and Natural Religion.* Fleming.

Kennedy, G. (2017). *An Authentic Account of Adam Smith.* Palgrave Macmillan.

Klamer, A., & Leonard, T. C. (1994). So What's an Economic Metaphor? In P. Mirowski (Ed.), *Natural Images in Economic Thought* (pp. 20–51). Cambridge University Press.

Kövecses, Z. (2010). *Metaphor. A Practical Introduction* (2nd ed.). Oxford University Press.

Kuhn, T. S. (1993 [1979]). Metaphor in Science. In A. Ortony (Ed.), *Metaphor and Thought* (2nd ed., pp. 533–542). Cambridge University Press.

Lagueux, M. (1999). Do Metaphors Affect Economic Theory? *Economics and Philosophy, 15*, 1–22.

Lakoff, G. (1993). The Contemporary Theory of Metaphor. In A. Ortony (Ed.), *Metaphor and Thought* (2nd ed., pp. 202–251). Cambridge University Press.

Lakoff, G. (2008). The Neural Theory of Metaphor. In R. W. Gibbs Jr. (Ed.), *The Cambridge Handbook of Metaphor and Thought* (pp. 17–38). Cambridge University Press.

Lakoff, G., & Johnson, M. (1980). *Metaphors We Live By*. University of Chicago Press.

Lakoff, G., & Johnson, M. (1999). *The Philosophy in the Flesh. The Embodied Mind and Its Challenge to Western Thought*. Basic Books.

Lakoff, G., & Núñez, R. (2000). *Where Mathematics Comes From: How the Embodied Mind Brings Mathematics into Being*. Basic Books.

Lewis, P. (1999). Metaphor and Critical Realism. In S. Fleetwood (Ed.), *Critical Realism in Economics. Development and Debate* (pp. 83–101). Routledge.

McCloskey, D. (1998). *The Rhetoric of Economics* (2nd ed.). University of Wisconsin Press.

McKenna, S. J. (2006). *Adam Smith. The Rhetoric of Propriety*. State University of New York Press.

Millar, J. (1803). *An Historical View of the English Government* (Vol. IV). Printed for J. Mawman.

Mirowski, P. (1989). *More Heat than Light. Economics as Social Physics: Physics as Nature's Economics*. Cambridge University Press.

Núñez, R. (2008). Conceptual Metaphor, Human Cognition, and the Nature of Mathematics. In R. W. Gibbs Jr. (Ed.), *The Cambridge Handbook of Metaphor and Thought* (pp. 339–362). Cambridge University Press.

Olson, R. (1975). *Scottish Philosophy and British Physics 1750–1880. A Study in the Foundation of the Victorian Scientific Style*. Princeton University Press.

Pepper, S. C. (1942). *World Hypotheses: A Study in Evidence*. University of California Press.

Perelman, C., & Olbrechts-Tyteca, L. (1969). *The New Rhetoric. A Treatise on Argumentation*. University of Notre Dame Press.

Purcell, W. M. (1986). A Reassessment of Adam Smith's Lectures on Rhetoric and Belles Lettres. *Central States Speech Journal, 37*(1), 45–54.

Richards, I. A. (1965 [1936]). *The Philosophy of Rhetoric*. Oxford University Press.

Rizzolatti, G., & Sinigaglia, C. (2006). *So quel che fai. Il cervello che agisce e i neuroni specchio*. Raffaello Cortina.

Rorty, R. (1987). Unfamiliar Noises: Hesse and Davidson on Metaphor. *Proceedings of the Aristotelian Society*, Supplementary Volumes, *61*, 283–296.
Searle, J. R. (1993 [1979]). Metaphor. In A. Ortony (Ed.), *Metaphor and Thought* (2nd ed., pp. 83–111). Cambridge University Press.
Thomson, H. F. (1965). Adam Smith's Philosophy of Science. *Quarterly Journal of Economics, 79*(2), 212–233.
Trincado, E. (2019). *The Birth of Economic Rhetoric. Communication, Arts and Economic Stimulus in David Hume and Adam Smith.* Palgrave Macmillan.

CHAPTER 3

The Metaphor of the Machine

Abstract The metaphor of the machine, and the metaphor of the clock in particular, was used in the seventeenth century to interpret both nature and the hierarchical features of the political body. In addition, another metaphor—the balance—was used in the same period and in the early decades of the eighteenth century to conceptualize equilibrium in economic and political spheres. Mandeville, among others, seemed to reuse the ideas embodied in it.

When Smith introduced the metaphor of the machine, the novelty was that this image ceased to represent static order, because—he maintained—machines evolve. Moreover, he showed that the beauty of order embodied in the machine could trigger behaviors which produce unintended outcomes. Despite these characteristics, this metaphor was not fully able to illustrate how economic order emerges.

Keywords Metaphor of the machine • Balance • Mandeville • Beauty of order • Economic system as machine

S. Fiori, *Machines, Bodies and Invisible Hands*,
https://doi.org/10.1007/978-3-030-85206-1_3

3.1 Mechanical Metaphors of Order in the Seventeenth Century

The use of the metaphor of the machine in the seventeenth century was closely related to the spread of mechanical philosophy. In this approach the universe was seen as a machine, and bodies were metaphorically compared to automatons. However, these ideas went beyond mechanism and pervaded a number of philosophical approaches. One of them was Hobbes' approach. As is well known, in the introduction to *Leviathan*, Hobbes reduced bodies to machines and, in particular, argued that hearts, nerves and joints are nothing more than springs, strings and wheels. In terms of the interactive theory of metaphor, it is noteworthy that this reduction entailed giving machines an important feature of bodies: life. In fact, "automata", that is, "engines that move themselves by springs and wheels as doth a watch", resemble living beings because they exhibit an "artificial life".[1]

Given this premise, the Leviathan, a "Commonwealth, or State", was also conceived as a machine, an "artificial man" whose parts are held together by "pacts and covenants" (Hobbes, 1996 [1651]: 7). The mechanical metaphor, therefore, worked on both the micro- and the macro-level. On the micro-level, it dealt with natural body in terms of machine by fixing a set of correspondences between the two domains. On the macro-level, a macro-structure, the "body politic" (i.e., the Leviathan), was conceptualized in terms of micro-structure (the natural body), which in turn was viewed as an automaton.

The model of the machine played a fundamental role in the works of Descartes, Borelli, Boyle, Huygens, Malpighi, Leibniz and many others. Descartes argued that there is no difference between artificial and natural artifacts. The human body is but "a statue or machine made of earth", similar in many respects to machines built by man which "have the power to move of their own accord in many different ways", like "clocks, artificial fountains, [and] mills" (Descartes, 1985 [1662]: 99). Malpighi considered the body to consist of tiny, invisible machines (Clément, 2003: 2), and in turn Hooke (1665: in *Preface*, unnumbered page [but 25]) was of the opinion that "small Machines of Nature", observable with the

[1] In Max Black's terms, this is a consequence of the fact that metaphor allows us not only to conceive the "principal subject" in terms of the "subsidiary subject", but also to conceptualize the "subsidiary subject" in consequence of its interaction with the "principal subject".

microscope, cause natural phenomena. Lastly, Pascal maintained that human beings behave as automata when their behavior is governed by habit, but—unlike Descartes—he believed that this does not happen when they use reason (Pascal, 1995 [1670]: 148–149).

Among the mechanical metaphors, one was particularly successful: the metaphor of the clock. The mechanical clock appeared between the end of the thirteenth and the beginning of the fourteenth centuries, but practitioners and scholars developed an interest in its production only during the Scientific Revolution (Cipolla, 1996: 29). In this period, the metaphor of the clock was employed as a model for interpreting the natural world because of its capacity to make natural phenomena intelligible. In 1605 Kepler abandoned the idea that a "soul" causes planetary motion and argued that "the machine of the universe is not similar to a divine animated being, but similar to a clock" (quoted in Shapin, 1996: 33). Descartes also adopted this metaphor to illustrate the mechanical structure of nature (Descartes, 1985 [1647]: 288). Movements and functions of the body cannot be explained by resorting to a "vegetative or sensitive soul" because, he argued, they "follow from the mere arrangement of the machine's organs every bit as naturally as the movements of a clock or other automaton follow from the arrangement of its counter-weights and wheels" (Descartes, 1985 [1662]: 108).

Mechanism had many adherents, and, under the influence of Descartes, Fontenelle (1998 [1686]: 64) pointed out that the universe resembles a watch. Hooke (1665: 133–134) illustrated some natural processes of corruption and regeneration by describing a clock that, after stopping, starts working again, and compared insects to "little *Automatons*" and "Watches" made of "several materials" (ibidem: 193–194). In turn, Boyle compared nature to the famous Strasbourg cathedral clock and viewed the universe as a "great Automaton"

> or self-moving engine, wherein all things are performed by the bare motion (or rest), the size, the shape, and the situation, or texture of the parts of the universal matter it consists of [...] So that the world being but, as it were, a great piece of clockwork, the naturalist, as such, is but a mechanician; however the parts of the engine, he considers, be some of them much larger, and some of them much minuter, than those of clock or watches. (Boyle, *The Excellency of Theology Compared with Natural Philosophy*, quoted in O. Mayr, 1986: 56)

Cosmos is a perfect "engine" that cannot have formed spontaneously (Boyle, 1772a [1666]: 48), and God continuously intervenes to perpetuate its order:

> this most potent Author, (if I may so speak) Opificer of the world, hath not abandoned a master-piece so worthy of Him, but does still maintain and preserve it, so regulating the stupendiously swift motions of the great globes, and other vast masses of the mundane matter, that they do not, by any notable irregularity, disorder the grand system of the universe, and reduce it to a kind of chaos, or confused state of shuffled and depraved things. (Boyle, 1772b [1690]: 519)

In reaction to Scholasticism, this kind of approach conveyed the idea that the hidden structure of nature could be made visible, and its movements intelligible. Discoveries achieved by microscope, telescope and anatomical studies strengthened this conviction. If human art, thanks to technological developments, could force nature to follow artificial courses, then nature could be fully understood, because its forces, no longer mysterious, were handled, dominated and organized (see Sect. 6.1). Two arguments were derived from the metaphor of the clock as a tool for interpreting the world.

The first argument was that if the world is like a clock and exhibits regular patterns of movement, then its functioning is revealed by the study of mechanical forces that work inside this machine and convey motion by means of wheels and springs. A long process of secularization of science originated from this perspective, because it implied that nature could be studied by regarding its own laws, without referring to occult forces.

The second argument, which legitimized the "argument from design", was that if the clock has been built by a clockmaker, the universe has been created by an intelligent agent. This simple conviction was summarized by Malebranche, who maintained: "When I see a *Watch*, I have reason to conclude, that there is some Intelligent Being, since it is impossible for Chance and Hap-hazard to produce, to range and posture all its Wheels" (Malebranche, 1700 [1674–5]: 51, emphasis in original). This perspective led to a view of the universe, and other "machines" like the political body, as hierarchical structures which respond to centralistic commands of authority because, as Leibniz asserted, God is an "architect and monarch". Leibniz criticized Cartesian mechanism: perception is not deducible from mechanical reasons, because analyzing the parts of the machine does not reveal how perception is produced (Rescher, 1991, § 17: 83). In a sense, however, nature is more mechanical than artificial machines.

> Each organic body of a living being is a kind of divine machine or natural automaton which infinitely surpasses all artificial automata. For a machine made by human artifice is not a machine in each of its parts. For example, the tooth of a brass wheel has parts or pieces which to us are no longer artificial things, and no longer have something recognizably machine-like about them, reflecting the use for which the wheel is intended. But the machines of nature, namely living organisms, are still machines even in their smallest parts, *ad infinitum*. It is this that constitutes the difference between nature and artifice, that is, between divine artifice and ours. (Rescher, 1991, § 64: 221)

Leibniz described a deterministic world, and in the last few years of his life, in a famous controversy, he defended the idea that God created a perfect world which does not request continuous Divine intervention, against the view put forward by Samuel Clarke, a disciple of Newton, that God, as omnipotent Being, intervenes periodically in the world. Plants and animals, he maintained, come from seeds "in which there was undoubtedly some *pre-formation*" (Rescher, 1991, § 74: 242, emphasis in original), and body and soul, as expressions of the pre-established harmony, are like two clocks perfectly regulated to the same time (see O. Mayr, 1986: 71).

The clock, as a metaphor of the body politic, conveyed the idea that social and political order was static, in that each part of society and the State had its assigned place. Hobbes, in *De Cive*, maintained that to understand how the State works, it is necessary to consider its parts separately, as it is necessary to examine each part of a clock to discover its functions, because "a thing is best known from its constituents" (Hobbes, 1998 [1642]: 10). On the other hand, the State is an "artificial man", and "the *sovereignty* is an artificial *soul*, as giving life and motion to the whole body" (Hobbes, 1996 [1651]: 3, emphasis in original). Therefore, in Hobbes' celebration of human art, the metaphor of the clock performed a dual function. It suggested a model for knowledge (the clock like any other artifact has to be analyzed in its components) and illustrated the hierarchical structure of the State as an artifact, whose movements emanate from a decisional center: the monarch.

From the end of the seventeenth century, the use of the metaphor of the machine, especially as an expression of the mechanical philosophy, began to decline. The idea that natural and political systems are organized structures, although still associated with the image of the machine as a model of coordination, was less and less frequently expressed by referring to "springs", "wheels" and "strings" as components that make a complex system work. In some cases, the image of the machine was used to describe not mechanical but biological processes that lead to the death of bodies. Thus Moyle (1969 [ca 1699]: 225) could maintain that "politic orders were the great springs and wheels" and at the same time declare that "as all natural bodies are born with seeds of dissolution in their own frame, so these great artificial bodies, commonwealths, are founded with such original flaws in their first constitution, as, in some periods of time, corrupt and dissolve them".

The metaphor of the clock, like other mechanical metaphors, in addition to being less often used, acquired new meanings. Locke (1997 [1690]: 299) remarked that animals are similar to clocks, with the difference that animals change their own organization over time, and their movements are produced by internal forces, while the machine is put into motion by external forces. The concept of order also started to be represented by nonmechanical metaphors in the eighteenth century, and the image of "balance" (introduced in phrases like "balance of power", "checks and balances", etc.) was used to conceptualize self-regulating properties of systems (see O. Mayr, 1986, chap. 7). Despite its decline, the metaphor of the machine did not disappear, although in many cases it became a mere commonplace. In the eighteenth century, it was used by Wolff, Voltaire and Diderot. La Mettrie, while rejecting Cartesian dualism between body and soul, compared the human body to a watch in *L'homme machine* (1748). King Frederick II, "the Great", of Prussia (1712–1786) shared the mechanical and deterministic conception of the State, and supported an authoritarian, centralistic conception of order, according to which the prince is the head or heart of the body, and the organization of the State is comparable to that of a clock (O. Mayr, 1986: 107–109).[2] Mechanical images also appeared in Rousseau, but in reference to society organized according to the common will of the people, and not as the Hobbesian "artificial man". Condillac was convinced that systems—including the universe—are machines or clocks set in motion by a first

[2] Rothschild (2001: 67) maintains that Smith refers to Frederick the Great in *The Theory of Moral Sentiments*, when he introduces the "man of system", who arranges individuals as "the different pieces upon a chess-board".

cause (Condillac, 2014 [1749], chap. 17). He also argued that the State is a machine that the "magistrate", as an enlightened "mechanic", had to govern not simply by exerting his authority but by knowing the complex interdependences which shape society as an "artificial body" (Condillac, 2014 [1749], chap. 15). Condillac's metaphor reflected a new political awareness which partially modified the old image of political power, because it described a political power that was less authoritarian and better able to take political and social dynamics into account.

Traditional metaphors of the machine and of the body gradually acquired new meanings (Anonymous, 1997: 1845). As Boyd points out, metaphors not only re-describe a domain in terms of another one (heuristic function) but also perform a "pedagogical" function when they explicate concepts already expressed in nonmetaphorical formulations (Boyd, 1993: 485). This means that, on the one hand, they help to conceptualize domains that are not fixed in definitional terms, while, on the other, they are reshaped and acquire new meanings over time thanks to new perspectives suggested by theoretical discourses. But the demarcation line between heuristic and pedagogical metaphors can be uncertain, when old metaphors, subsequently revitalized, engender new conceptualizations. In Moyle's writings, where heuristic and pedagogical metaphors appear, the metaphor of the machine conveyed not the image of an established, authoritarian order, but that of a balanced political power. The "true Constitution of the Government" in Sparta, he maintained, was a "great Machine", characterized by "a proper Distribution of Power into several Branches", where "each grand Branch was a Check upon the other; so that not one of them could exceed its just Bounds, but was kept within the Sphere in which it was circumscribed by the Original Frame" (Moyle, 1727 [1698]: 59–60). In short, preservation of "liberty" required a "due Ballance in Property, Power and Dominion" (ibidem: 50). This change in the meaning of the metaphor of the machine led to the decline of this image in philosophical discourses. The machine originally evoked to represent hierarchical, political order was not fit to conceptualize either political or economic liberty (O. Mayr, 1986, chap. 6), because, as Smith was to show in the late eighteenth century, the machine, as an image of pre-established order, was not able to represent the formation of social order as a consequence of free individuals' behaviors and choices.

Lastly, Hume expounded alternative arguments in favor of both mechanical and organic metaphors in *Dialogues Concerning Natural Religion*. In this work Cleanthes, an empirical theist, maintained that the "world" is "nothing but one great machine, subdivided into an infinite number of lesser machines" (Hume, 2007b [1779]: 19), while Philo, a skeptic, compared the universe to "animal bodies":

> If the universe bears a greater likeness to animal bodies and to vegetables, than to the works of human art, it is more probable, that its cause resembles the cause of the former than that of the latter, and its origin ought rather to be ascribed to generation or vegetation than to reason or design. (Ibidem: 52)

Organic, nonmechanical metaphors occurred frequently in the eighteenth century. From Quesnay to Adam Smith and Alexander Hamilton, the metaphorical field of the body was reinvented (Anonymous, 1997: 1845–1846), and many authors referred to it when they compared natural and political bodies by means of medical metaphors (see Chap. 4, and Part II of this volume).

3.2 From the Mercantilists' Balance of Trade to Mandeville's Notion of Order

In addition to "machine" and "body", another term was used in the seventeenth century to metaphorically represent equilibrium in the economic and political spheres: "balance". This word comes from late Latin (*bilanx*) and denotes an apparatus for weighing (Onions, 1973). "The balance was physically and metaphorically the model of intelligibility" in the Scientific Revolution (Machamer, 1998: 58), and it was used in many fields of knowledge. Influenced by Archimedean tradition, Galileo in *De Motu* (1590) dealt with problems of falling and floating bodies as balance problems and showed how "the motion of bodies moving naturally can be reduced to the motion of weights on a balance" (Galilei, 1960 [1590]: 259/38, quoted in Machamer, 1998: 58). Moreover, in *Dialogo* (1632), it was the metaphor of balance that "provided Galileo the means by which to think about motion and the relativity of perceived motion" (Machamer, 1998: 62).

The concept of balance, as a synonym of a system's order, was used to conceptualize the notion of circulation of money, a concept inspired by Harvey's notion of blood circulation as a zero-sum game, where the volume of blood is fixed (Eriksen, 2017). The word "balance" also appeared in phrases like "balance of trade" and "balance of power". "Balance of trade" was mentioned in the early years of the seventeenth century in the writings of Malynes, Misselden, Bacon and Mun.[3] According to Finkelstein (2000: 90), this notion derived from the Italian discovery of double-entry bookkeeping, but—as we have just mentioned—the real origin of this term was probably associated with the image of scales (Davidko, 2013: 93–94). This image, which conveyed an idea of equilibrium as the mean between two extremes, was simpler than the metaphor of machine, because it represented neither complex systems nor the principle of hierarchical coordination among parts of a system. Misselden had this meaning in mind when, with an analogy, he described the balance of trade:

> a paire of Scales of Ballance, is an invention to shew us the waight of things, whereby we may discerne the heavy from the light, and how one thing differeth from another in the Scale of waight: So is also this *Ballance of Trade*, an excellent and politique Invention, to shew us the difference of waight in the *Commerce* of one Kingdome with another: that is, whether the Native Commodities exported, and all the forrraine Commodities Imported, doe ballance or overballance one another in the *Scale of Commerce*. (Misselden, 1623: 116-117, emphasis in original)

The use of the image of balance, however, was in a sense surprising, since the mercantilist recommendation to preserve a positive balance of trade implied a permanent imbalance in which exports exceeded imports (Finkelstein, 2000: 90; Magnusson, 2015: 108–111).[4] The balance had to be unbalanced, and this implied that international trade had to be characterized as disequilibrium among countries, rather than as equilibrium between equal weights in the scale. However, this was only one part of the reasoning, because some mercantilists perceived imbalance as dangerous, when merchants erected barriers against competitors. In this case, it was preferable to restore a system of counterweights. Malynes illustrated this problem and maintained that merchants

[3] For an analysis of the genesis of this term, see Finkelstein (2000: 89–90), and Magnusson (2015: 107–108).

[4] "If the Native commodities exported doe waigh downe and exceed in value the forraine Commodities imported, it is a rule that never faile's, that then the Kingdome growe's rich, and prosper's in estate and stocke: because the overplus thereof must needs come in, in treasure. But if the Forraine Commodities imported, doe exceed in value the Native Commodities exported, it is a manifest signe that then trade decayeth, and the stocke of the Kingdome wasteth apace: because the overplus must needs goe out in treasure" (Misselden, 1623: 117).

are like a Commoditie weighed in a Ballance, that hath but one end, where there can be no Counterpoize, and then it seemes to bee great weight, although it be never so light. So that this ingrossing of Trade into few mens hands, hath caused our home Trades to decay, our Manufactures to decrease. (Malynes, 1622: 54)

The idea of balance between two (or more) forces was used to examine political order since the sixteenth century. Hume, who knew this tradition of political thought, was of the opinion that the concept of "balance of power" could be traced back to Greek civilization: "In all the politics of GREECE, the anxiety, with regard to the balance of power, is apparent, and is expressly pointed out to us, even by the ancient historians" (Hume, 1985d [1777]: 332–333). As Thucydides showed, "after the decline of ATHENS, when the THEBANS and LACEDEMONIANS disputed for sovereignty, we find, that the ATHENIANS (as well as many other republics) always threw themselves into the lighter scale, and endeavoured to preserve the balance" (ibidem: 333). Walter Moyle (1969 [ca 1699]: 244) described a similar mechanism in republican Rome: "But although there was no counterpoise in the laws to balance the regal authority, yet the liberty seems to have been in a great measure supported by the mere weight of the people, whose property was the noblest root of liberty". And Jonathan Swift in 1701 analytically described how to conceive the equilibrium engendered by the principle of the balance of power:

The true Meaning of a Balance of Power, either without or within a State, is best conceived by considering what the nature of a Balance is. It supposes three Things. First the Part which is held, together with the Hand that holds it; and then the two Scales, with whatever is weighed therein. Now consider several States in a Neighborhood. In order to preserve Peace between these States, it is necessary they should be formed into a Balance, whereof one or more are to be Directors, who are to divide the rest into equal Scales, and upon Occasions remove from one into the other, or else fall with their own Weight into the Lightest. So in a State within itself, the Balance must be held by a third Hand; who is to deal the remaining Power with utmost exactness into the several Scales. Now, it is not necessary that the Power should be equally divided between these three; for the Balance may be held by the Weakest, who by his Address and Conduct, removing from either Scale, and adding of his own, may keep the Scales duly pois'd. (Swift, 1701: 5-6)[5]

[5] On the conceptual history of the notion of "checks and balances", see Wootton (2006). See also O. Mayr (1986, chap. 9).

Mercantilist ideas of the favorable balance of trade slowly declined during the seventeenth century, and this decline became apparent in the 1690s, in consequence of the formulation of theories on free trade (Magnusson, 2015: 124). Gradually, other concepts and metaphors came on the scene to represent social and economic order that, now, was conceived as a result of complex, self-organizing processes, and not as a simple system of counterweights. In 1720, in *The System or Theory of Trade of the World*, Isaac Gervaise proposed a model of self-regulating order that replaced the old idea of static equilibrium associated with the image of scales (see O. Mayr, 1986: 165–169).[6] However, it was Hume that developed the idea that the balance of trade maintains itself in equilibrium automatically, thanks to a mechanism—the specie-flow—that ensures that each nation attracts the appropriate quantity of money. For this purpose, he drew an analogy between flows of money and water. If hypothetically in Great Britain 4/5 of money disappeared, the price of commodities and labor proportionally would decrease. As a result, money would be attracted from other countries, and the previous level of prices restored, provided that no barrier obstructs money flow. This process is similar to water that flows in two containers, since "All water, whenever it communicates, remains always at a level" (Hume, 1985c [1777]: 312. See Wennerlind, 2006: 60–62, and Schabas, 2001).

Mandeville conceived social order in terms of a balance between two (only apparently) opposed inclinations: vice and virtue. In his view, vice makes virtue possible, and virtue supports vice. Vices and virtues are forces that, rather than being in conflict, act as counterweights which, by interacting, favor the formation of social order and promote the progress of society. Mandeville provided many examples of such counterweights. "Chastity—he argued—may be supported by Incontinence, and the best of Virtues want the Assistance of the worst of Vices" (Mandeville, 1924c [1724]: 100). If so, this means that women can safeguard their honor and virtue, because men, by following their vices, can turn to prostitutes to

[6] His idea was that temporary deviations from the "balance" of currency, as this balance is determined by the "Proportion of Poor and Rich" in a country, could be automatically resolved, because if "Labour draws the Denominator of the World [i.e., currency], also the Denominator draws Labour from the World; so that if the particular Denominator of any Nation, be greater than its just Proportion, it will draw from the other Nations a Portion of Labour, proportion'd to its Excess; and if its Denominator be less than its just Proportion, it will draw a Portion of Gold and Silver, proportion'd to what it wants of its just Proportion" (Gervaise, 1954 [1720]: 7).

satisfy their sexual appetites. Not only vice and virtue, but also different kinds of vice can cooperate. In fact, two vices like avarice and prodigality are in equilibrium, because the former provides resources to the latter, and "Tho' these two *Vices* appear very opposite, yet they often assist each other" (ibidem: 101; emphasis added).

Human inclinations mix, but do not lose their specific traits. An analogy illustrates this idea: "I would compare the Body Politick [...] to a Bowl of Punch. Avarice should be the sow'ring, and Prodigality the Sweetning of it". Moreover, punch contains "water" (i.e., "Ignorance, Folly and Credulity") and "brandy" (i.e., "Wisdom, Honour, Fortitude and the rest of the sublime Qualities of Men"). These ingredients, if tasted separately, apparently cannot produce a "tolerable Liquor", "[y]et Experience teaches us, that the ingredients I named judiciously mixt, will make an excellent Liquor" (ibidem: 105–106). Harmony of liquor, therefore, depends on the interaction of very different flavors (sour and sweet) and substances (water and brandy). This view culminates in another analogy which envisages harmony more clearly as a result of opposite substances that neutralize each other, and which in some respects recalls the old metaphor of counterweights:

> [I] shall only add, that I look upon Avarice and Prodigality in the Society as I do upon two contrary Poysons in Physick, of which it is certain that the noxious qualities being by mutual mischief corrected in both, they may assist each other, and often make a good Medicine between them. (Ibidem: 106)

Passions and human inclinations have to be harnessed by the "skillful politician", who behaves as a physician and knows that "Contraries are best cured by Contraries" (Mandeville, 1924b [1723]: 321).[7]

Hume, about 20 years later, in an essay in which he alludes to Mandeville's conception of luxury, drew alternative conclusions. Not only did he develop a different (metaphorical and theoretical) approach to social order as self-regulating process, but he also reconsidered the role of the statesman, viewed as an actor who intervenes in social, complex

[7] Hayek (1978: 259), following Rosenberg (1963), maintained that in Mandeville the role of government consists in a function aimed at establishing the general rules of the game, and not at producing a direct intervention. Hirschman (1977: 18) appropriately pointed out that the "Skilful Management of the Dextrous Politician" is "a necessary condition and agent for the turning of 'private vices' into 'publick benefits'".

systems. First, he analyzed the idea of balance of passions: "To say, that, without a vicious luxury, the labour would not have been employed at all, is only to say, that" vicious luxury is a remedy to some "defects in human nature", "as one poison may be an antidote to another. But virtue, like wholesome food, is better than poisons, however corrected" (Hume, 1985b [1777]: 279). Governance of human passions requires an accurate strategy that is not based on exploitation of opposed human inclinations. The logic of counterweights, which holds that a vice had to be opposed to another vice to neutralize it, does not work. It is true that "two opposite vices in a state may be more advantageous than either of them alone; but let us never pronounce vice in itself advantageous" (ibidem: 280). This implies that the "magistrate" should direct his intervention with precision by choosing the lesser of two evils:

> Very often he can only cure one vice by another; and in that case he ought to prefer what is least pernicious to society. Luxury, when excessive, is the source of many ills; but is in general preferable to sloth and idleness, which would commonly succeed in its place, and are more hurtful both to private persons and to the public. (Hume, 1985b [1777]: 280)

By contrast with Hume, Mandeville's work is pervaded by the idea that passions neutralize each other. Fear is the "Passion that is rais'd in us when we apprehend that Mischief is approaching us [...] so that some other Passion must be able to overcome this Fear, and the most contrary to it is Anger" (Mandeville, 1924c [1724]: 200–202). In turn, the "Fear of Death" is tamed by "Pride", and this helps the "Politician" to reach his ends because "Without Vices the Excellency of the Species would have ever remain'd undiscover'd" (Mandeville, 1924a [1723]: 334). Also in this circumstance, Hume seems to reject Mandeville's approach. The politician in promoting the progress of society does not rely on the balance of opposing passions but encourages those passions which may be most useful to public welfare. When necessary, it would be good that the state relies on "passion for public good" of citizens, "But as these principles are too disinterested and too difficult to support, it is requisite to govern men by other passions, and animate them with a spirit of avarice and industry, art and luxury" (Hume, 1985a [1777]: 262–263).

* * *

Adam Smith did not use the metaphor of balance and like Hume tried to identify self-regulating properties of complex systems. As it will be shown in the next section, Smith redefined the mechanical metaphor, although he preserved the traditional idea that coordination among parts is a property of machines. Whereas in the seventeenth century, the machine provided an image of static order, in Smith this same metaphor provided the image of an order that evolves and becomes more efficient over time.

3.3 The Metaphor of the Machine and the Beauty of Order in Adam Smith

Many scholars have pointed out that, according to Smith, when individuals evaluate philosophical theories, institutions and human artifacts, they also formulate aesthetic judgments, because systems of this kind, if well organized, express a certain beauty. Few, however, have pointed out that in Smith this view is based on the metaphor of the machine. He employed this metaphor to represent one property of systems: the capacity to produce agreeable or desirable effects as a result of the harmonious interaction of their components. However, Smith did not provide a set of systematic correspondences between the machine and other domains, as did mechanical and corpuscular philosophy, where single parts of the machine were analytically compared to parts of other systems. The metaphor applied to many spheres such as the physical universe, human society, scientific systems, languages, arts and the division of labor and suggested, but did not develop, a conceptual view about the nature of these systems.

In the TMS, the universe is described as an "immense" and "great" "machine", whose "various appearances" hide "secret wheels and springs" (TMS I.i.4.2: 19). Thanks to the intervention of the benevolent "divine Being", it "produce[s] the greatest possible quantity of happiness" (TMS VI.ii.5: 236). Society, too, "appears like a great, an immense machine, whose regular and harmonious movements produce a thousand agreeable effects" (TMS VII.iii.I.2: 316). Since harmony is a source of beauty, society-machine can be compared to the technical products of "human art".

> As in any other beautiful and noble machine that was the production of human art, whatever tended to render its movements more smooth and easy, would derive a beauty from this effect, and, on the contrary, whatever tended to obstruct them would displease upon that account. (Ibidem: 316)

The harmony of machines created by human art—that is, the coherence between their internal organization and the ends they accomplish—exhibits two characteristics. It is source of both utility, because utility depends on machine's capacity to render "movements more smooth and easy", and beauty (TMS IV.I.1: 179). It is noteworthy that this aesthetic dimension of machines was not emphasized in mechanical metaphors of the seventeenth century.

Smith maintains that beauty of harmony rather than utility explains why individuals appreciate machines, and in this he differs from his contemporary, David Hume, who thought that utility is per se a source of pleasure (see J. R. Harrison, 1995: 101–105; Wight, 2014: 229–31). A man who buys an expensive watch is not attracted by the utility of that object, if he does not use it to keep better time than other people, "What interests him is not so much the attainment of this piece of knowledge [exact time], as the perfection of the machine which serves to attain it" (TMS IV.I.5: 180), where this "perfection" is presumably a source of aesthetic appreciation. Similarly, what pleases people who buy superfluous objects "is not so much the utility, as the aptness of the machines which are fitted to promote it" (TMS IV.I.6: 180). Wealth in general is metaphorically viewed as a fragile, beautiful and scarcely useful machine (TMS IV.I.8: 182–183). The capacity of the machine of wealth to produce an end through the harmonious interaction of its components is the source of its beauty, and ultimately the beauty of the wealth-machine induces man, as the figure of a "poor man's son" shows (TMS IV.I.8: 181–182), to strive to obtain more wealth. In society, where everyone observes the condition of others, the spectator's admiration for "the condition of the rich and the great" is a powerful incentive to be industrious and to become rich and admired. But it is wealth as "ingenious and artful adjustment of those means [the 'means of happiness' which constitute wealth] to the end for which they were intended, that is the principal source of his admiration" (TMS IV.I.8: 182).

Although admiration for the rich derives from admiration for the means-ends coherence of the machine of wealth, this beautiful coherence does not guarantee its owner real happiness. The "poor man's son" sacrifices his tranquility to become richer and richer, but once he becomes old and sick, he will discover that "wealth and greatness are mere trinkets of frivolous utility" (TMS IV.I.8: 181). The argument of nature's deception, whereby society unintentionally increases general welfare, while individuals do not because they sacrifice their tranquility in search of illusory wealth, focuses on the idea that people are induced to be industrious because

> [w]e naturally confound [the poor, real, satisfaction produced by things possessed by the rich] in our imagination with the order, the regular and harmonious movement of the system, the machine or oeconomy by means of which it is produced. The pleasures of wealth and greatness, when considered in this complex view, strike the imagination as something grand and beautiful and noble, of which the attainment is well worth all the toil and anxiety which we are so apt to bestow upon it. (TMS IV.I.9: 183)

In short, the harmonic and functional organization of machines is a technical and aesthetic property (i.e., the beauty of order) which connotes wealth and makes it possible to reinterpret motives which direct human behavior. In particular, nature's deception would not be conceivable without the influence exerted on individual behaviors by the beauty of order. In this sense, the metaphor of the machine, by illustrating this property, contributes to developing some ideas on how wealth increases in a framework in which an unintentional social order takes shape.

The beauty of order is a property metaphorically shared by domains other than wealth. The "love of system" associated with the "regard to the beauty of order, of art and contrivance" (TMS IV.I.11: 185) characterizes our appreciation for institutions which promote "public welfare". For the patriot who intends to improve public institutions, "sympathy" for the happiness of others is often not a sufficient motivation to act. Public welfare is achieved because the pleasure engendered by observing the perfection of a political system prompts the preservation of political order. The "perfection of police, the extension of trade and manufactures, are noble and magnificent objects [...] They make part of the great system of government, and the wheels of the political machine seem to move with more harmony and ease by means of them, and we are uneasy till we remove any obstruction that can in the least disturb or encumber the regularity of its motions" (ibidem: 185).

This conception leads to several conclusions:

1. A well-organized political machine exhibits a means-ends coherence because thanks to "the connexions and dependencies of its several parts", it procures public "advantages" and increases people's "happiness" (TMS IV.I.11: 186).
2. This coherence is beautiful, and "We take pleasure" (ibidem: 186) in it.
3. The beauty of a coherent, institutional order is a source of actions to remove "any obstruction" that disturbs the harmony of the political

machine. In this way, the beauty of institutional order promotes public happiness more efficaciously than "sympathy" addressed to another's happiness ever could (TMS IV.I.11: 185). This result is not a consequence of the benevolent regard for others, rather it is an unintended outcome, because the primary end of a patriot's behavior is establishing the harmony of the political machine, while public happiness is only a by-product of that behavior.[8] The unintentional increase of "public welfare", in this and in other circumstances, is triggered by human sensitivity to the beauty of machines and in particular is the consequence of the appreciation of the "great system of government" which induces individuals to preserve the machine of political order, although they follow an end differing from that they aim directly to achieve.

4. The increase in well-being described in the TMS is similar to the one illustrated by the metaphor of the invisible hand of the WN, where the individual by "pursuing his own interest [...] frequently promotes that of the society more effectually than when he really intends to promote it" (WN IV.ii.9: 456).
5. Unintentional outcomes are engendered because men are not forward-looking in their actions, and they simply "sometimes seem to value the means more than the end" (TMS IV.I.11: 185). And the "economy" is a machine (TMS IV.I.9: 183) which connects means (related to the search for increase of private revenue) to ends (the increase of the wealth of society).
6. In this perspective, "machine" and the "invisible hand" are metaphors that attempt to represent similar, complex events.

3.4 Scientific Systems, Language, Workshop and Economic System as Machines

The metaphor of the machine as representation of coherently connected parts that achieve a given end is also applied to theoretical systems. Since nature "seems to abound with events which appear solitary and incoherent", the task of philosophy (i.e., science) is to provide "invisible chains

[8] As is well known, also in the WN public welfare is achieved more effectively by following private interests than by means of benevolence. One can adopt an intentional, benevolent behavior, but the increase of wealth is an unintended outcome which depends on complex events.

which bind together all these disjointed objects" and introduce "order into this chaos of jarring and discordant appearances" (HA II.12: 45–46). Scientific theories are "imaginary machines" (Cremaschi, 1984: 50–56) whose evolution over the course of time can be examined on the basis of their capacity "to soothe the imagination, and to render the theatre of nature a more coherent, and therefore a more magnificent spectacle" (HA II.12: 46):

> Systems in many respects resemble machines. A machine is a little system, created to perform, as well as to connect together, in reality, those different movements and effects which the artist has occasion for. A system is an imaginary machine invented to connect together in the fancy those different movements and effects which are already in reality performed. The machines that are first invented to perform any particular movement are always the most complex, and succeeding artists generally discover that, with fewer wheels, with fewer principles of motion, than had originally been employed, the same effects may be more easily produced. The first systems, in the same manner, are always the most complex, and a particular connecting chain, or principle, is generally thought necessary to unite every two seemingly disjointed appearances: but it often happens, that one great connecting principle is afterwards found to be sufficient to bind together all the discordant phaenomena that occur in a whole species of things. (HA IV.19: 66)

Like machines which progressively reduce their "wheels of motion", from antiquity to Isaac Newton, astronomical systems progressively reduced the number of "connecting principles" needed to explain the variety of celestial phenomena, and gradually resolved any incoherencies that emerged as a result of more accurate observations. This process culminates in the Newtonian theory,

> a system whose parts are all more strictly connected together, than those of any other philosophical hypothesis. Allow his principle, the universality of gravity, and that it decreases as the squares of the distance increase, and all the appearances, which he joins together by it, necessarily follow. (HA IV.76: 104)

The Newtonian theory is not only a meaningful piece of the history of astronomy, whose description concludes Smith's narrative, but also an approach that, through its method, allows us to interpret the history of astronomy. The idea that science should resort to one or few connecting principles in order to explain a variety of phenomena more efficiently is what Newton prescribed as the correct method for science in the first two *Rules for the Study of Natural Philosophy*:

> No more causes of natural things should be admitted than are both true and sufficient to explain their phenomena [Rule 1] [...] Therefore, the causes assigned to natural effects of the same kind must be, so far as possible, the same [Rule 2]. (Newton, 1999 [1687]: 440-441)

What Smith apparently does is to construct a history in which methods of astronomical theories gradually approximate Newton's method for the study of natural philosophy. Newton's recommendation to reduce the number of causes necessary to explain natural phenomena is reformulated by Smith as the criterion which explains the tendency of astronomical systems to reduce their connecting principles over time. Therefore, Newton's theory appears in two ways: as one phase of the history of astronomy and as a theory whose rules establish the criterion for interpreting that history.

In a hypothetical line whose extremes are a system with many connecting principles, and a system with one or few connecting principles, the Aristotelian system—with its 56 celestial spheres (HA IV.9: 59)—is close to the first, extreme pole. It can thus be considered as a cumbersome machine opposed to Newton's system:

> [I]n Nat(urall) Phil(osophy) or any other Science of that Sort we may either like Aristotle go over the Different branches in the order they happen to cast up to us, giving a principle commonly a new one for every phaenomenon; or in the manner of Sir Isaac Newton we may lay down certain principles known or proved in the beginning, from whence we account for the severall Phenomena, connecting all together by the same Chain.—This Latter which we may call the Newtonian method is undoubtedly the most Philosophical, and in every scien(c)e w(h)ether of Moralls or Nat(urall) phi(losophy) etc., is vastly more ingenious and for that reason more engaging than the other. It gives us a pleasure to see the phaenomena which we reckoned the most unaccountable all deduced from some principle (commonly a well known one) and all united in one chain, far superior to what we feel from the unconnected method where everything is accounted for by itself without any referen[e]ce to the others. (LRBL II.133: 145-146)[9]

[9] These sentences, in truth, show another dimension of the Newtonian method: the didactic method. Smith illustrates two didactic methods. The first, similar to the Newtonian method, is based on "one or a very few principles by which we explain the severall Rules, or

Lastly, the same perspective is adopted to illustrate the evolution of language, which in many respects evolves by improving like machines and systems:

> [L]anguage becomes more simple in its rudiments and principles, just in proportion as it grows more complex in its composition, and the same thing has happened in it, which commonly happens with regard to mechanical engines. All machines are generally, when first invented, extremely complex in their principles, and there is often a particular principle of motion for every particular movement which it is intended they should perform. Succeeding improvers observe, that one principle may be so applied as to produce several of those movements; and thus the machine becomes gradually more and more simple, and produces its effects with fewer wheels, and fewer principles of motion. (Languages 41: 223)

However, the metaphor of the machine does not fit well with language, because the "simplification of machines renders them more and more perfect", while the "simplification of the rudiments of languages renders them more and more imperfect, and less proper for many of the purposes of language" (Languages 42: 224; see Trincado, 2019: 125–126). By contrast, real machines are characterized by increasing simplification (i.e., reduction of cog-wheels and "principles of motion") and efficiency (see Dascal, 2006: 107–108).

In summary, Smith revitalizes the metaphor of the machine. Although it still symbolizes order and coherence of the parts, the image of the mechanism is freed from the idea of static perfection, inherent in the seventeenth-century metaphor of the clock, because Smith's machine evolves and improves over time. What matters, now, is not only the harmony of the machine, but how harmony (the coherence among the parts which yields the desired result) is achieved.

The metaphor of the machine-system exhibits the features of Black's "interactive metaphor" (1962, chap. 3), since the "principal subject" (e.g., "system") and the "subsidiary subject" (e.g., "machine") shed light on each other. The machine—with its "wheels" and "principles of motion"—reorganizes the view of (theoretical) systems, and

Phaenomena, connecting one with the other in a natural order". The second, similar to the Aristotelian method, and followed by Virgil, implies that "we beginn with telling that we are to explain such and such things and for each advance a principle either different or the same with those which went before" (LRBL II.132: 145).

systems—with their "connecting principles" whose number is increasingly reduced—reorganize the view of machines, which become tools that evolve according to Newtonian principles. Indeed, Smith makes the interaction between the two terms (system and machine) even more explicit by means of two types of metaphor which, respectively, reverse the "principal" and the "subsidiary" subjects. The first type of metaphor, which implies that systems are viewed as (imaginary) machines, is represented by the sentence "A system is an imaginary machine" (HA IV.19: 66). The second type of metaphor is "A machine is a little system" that connects "different movements and effects" (ibidem: 66). In this case, the coherence of parts of the system and the movements that it engenders is the property selected to illustrate the nature of machine.

The idea that machines change over time by acquiring further internal coherence and efficiency is what Smith illustrates in the opening pages of the WN, where he describes how inventions and innovations—considered as machines—contribute to reorganizing labor.

> In the first fire-engines, a boy was constantly employed to open and shut alternately the communication between the boiler and the cylinder, according as the piston either ascended or descended. One of those boys, who loved to play with his companions, observed that, by tying a string from the handle of the valve, which opened this communication, to another part of the machine, the valve would open and shut without his assistance, and leave him at liberty to divert himself with his play-fellows. (WN I.1: 20)

After the intervention of the young workman, the machine works—so to speak—with "fewer principles of motion", and it is more efficient because it performs his function by saving labor. This innovation is a consequence of the division of labor in factories that reduces labor to simple operations.

Machines, like the steam engine made more efficient by a simple string, become simpler and simpler, and this influences their cost:

> all such improvements in mechanicks, as enable the same number of workmen to perform an equal quantity of work, with cheaper and simpler machinery than had been usual before, are always regarded as advantageous to every society. A certain quantity of materials, and the labour of a certain number of workmen, which had before been employed in supporting a more complex and expensive machinery, can afterwards be applied to aug-

ment the quantity of work which that or any other machinery is useful only for performing. (WN II.2: 287)

The transition from more complex (i.e., intricate) to simpler machines involves a transition from more expensive to cheaper machines.[10] Therefore, the same principle of efficiency seems to characterize many objects (real machines, scientific systems and languages) which appear similar in light of a metaphor which connects them and provides a provisional framework for investigating theoretical problems related to these similarities.

However, the introduction of innovations only limitedly rests on the specialization of the process of manufacture. Machines basically improve as a result of the social division of labor and of the formation of new employments in society:

> Many improvements have been made by the ingenuity of the makers of the machines, when to make them became the business of a peculiar trade; and some by that of those who are called philosophers or men of speculation, whose trade it is, not to do any thing, but to observe every thing; and who, upon that account, are often capable of combining together the powers of the most distant and dissimilar objects. (WN I.9: 21)

The capacity of philosophy (i.e., science) to connect distant or "disjoined" objects analyzed in the *History of Astronomy* now is considered in light of the concept of the social division of labor, a framework which illustrates new aspects of the metaphor of machines. Smith does not perceive qualitative differences between the division of labor in factory and in society.[11] Transition from the micro-universe of the workshop to the macro-universe of the market, where the division of labor among employments prevails, does not exhibit a qualitative change. What changes is only the scale of the phenomenon:

[10] Of course, efficient machines can be expensive, and usually they "replace the capital laid out upon it, with at least the ordinary profits" (WN I.x.b: 118).

[11] Marx (1976, chap. 14), in commenting on Smith, remarks that "in spite of the numerous analogies and links connecting them, the division of labour in the interior of a society, and that in the interior of a workshop, differ not only in degree, but also in kind" (Marx, 1976: 474). Specialized workers in factories are not independent laborers, because "the specialized worker produces no commodities" (ibidem: 475).

> What takes place among the labourers in a particular workhouse, takes place, for the same reason, among those of a great society. The greater their number, the more they naturally divide themselves into different classes and subdivisions of employment. More heads are occupied in inventing the most proper machinery for executing the work of each, and it is therefore more likely to be invented. (WN I.8: 104)

The metaphor of the machine, as a coordinated system which exhibits increasing efficiency, is applied to the division of labor both in factories and in society, with the consequence that the economy improves the more it becomes like a well-organized machine.

The market becomes more efficient not only because the division of labor expands but also because individuals improve their capacity to be persuasive. Persuasion is an ability that precedes exchanges, because the "real foundation" of the "disposition to barter" is the "principle to perswade" (Smith LJ(B) 221: 493; see Fiori, 1992; Walraevens, 2010). Addressing others' desires in exchange, in order to obtain some advantages, is a persuasive argument:

> Whoever offers to another a bargain of any kind, proposes to do this. Give me that which I want, and you shall have this which you want, is the meaning of every such offer; and it is in this manner that we obtain from one another the far greater part of those good offices which we stand in need of. (WN I.ii: 26)

It is the search for persuasion that induces individuals to address not benevolence but the self-interest of "the butcher, the brewer, or the baker". The practice of convincing others to share our opinion is a skill, which individuals acquire and improve over time, and requires a sort of specialization.

> This being the constant employment or trade of every man, in the same manner as the artizans invent simple methods of doing their work, so will each one here endeavour to do this work in the simplest manner. That is bartering, by which they adress themselves to the self interest of the person and seldom fail immediately to gain their end. (LJ(A) vi.57: 352)

The analogy between individuals who invent persuasive new arguments in bartering, and artisans who "invent simple methods of doing their work", evokes the metaphor of systems that like machines simplify over time by reducing their connecting principles. Inventions of this kind are possible because individuals, by focusing their attention on specific operations, specialize in their work. The logic of machines is that the more they simplify their structure, the more they perform complex and efficient operations (Aspromourgos, 2012: 482 and 486). Machines are originally intricate tools that by simplifying their structure perform more complex tasks. Simplicity is a characteristic of many objects: theoretical systems which reduce their connecting principles; languages which improve their "rudiments and principles"; practices, such as the use of persuasion to encourage exchanges; new methods introduced by artisans in their activity; real machines which become "cheaper" and more efficient; and labor in factories which, reduced to "simple", basic operations, increase productivity.

Labor exhibits some of the features of a machine because both of them simplify and increase productivity, and this renders workers and machines similar and interchangeable: "as the operations of each workman are gradually reduced to a greater degree of simplicity, a variety of new machines come to be invented for facilitating and abridging those operations" (WN II: 277). Machines facilitate and replace labor, and a "man educated at the expence of much labour and time to any of those employments which require extraordinary dexterity and skill, may be compared to one of those expensive machines" (WN I.x.b: 118). Thus, and not only as a result of the division of labor in factories, simple workers can be easily replaced by machines because they have some traits in common (see Aspromourgos, 2009: 139), while specialized workers can be considered similar to complex and expensive machines (WN II.i. 17: 282. See also WN I.x.b: 118).

The consequences of the division of labor considered in terms of the specialization of the process of manufacture have an impact on the whole economy, and as Rosenberg (1965: 135) remarks, "[w]hile the structure of the social division of labour becomes more complex, the individual worker's role becomes more simple". Smith considers these phenomena, although he does not encapsulate them in a systematic theory, and the metaphor of the machine helps hold together concepts that are not always well-defined. One of them regards the relationship among the various dimensions of the economy and factory that can be interpreted in terms of "machine". The worker is like a cog-wheel in the workshop, but he is also similar to both simple and sophisticated machines, and for this reason is replaceable by them. The factory is organized like a machine whose parts are workers, and the economy is viewed as a complex machine as well, due to the social division of labor. This image of machines which in turn contain machines (worker-machines are included in the workshop-machine which is part of an economy-machine) is representative of social and economic order and seems to re-propose in different form Hume's metaphor of the world as a "great machine" composed of "an infinite number of lesser machines"

> which again admit of subdivisions, to a degree beyond what human senses and faculties can trace and explain. All these various machines, and even their most minute parts, are adjusted to each other with an accuracy, which ravishes into admiration all men, who have ever contemplated them. The curious adapting of means to ends, throughout all nature, resembles exactly, though it much exceeds, the productions of human contrivance; of human design, thought, wisdom, and intelligence. (Hume, 2007b [1779]: 19)

In this image, the beauty of order, derived from means-ends coherence, is, as in the TMS, a source of contemplation and admiration.

3.5 Further Observations on Smith's Newtonianism

Like other Scottish thinkers, Adam Smith shared the Newtonian idea that the variety of phenomena can be explained by means of basic principles. This perspective was at the same time metaphorical and methodological, in that it assumed that the methodological recommendations included in *Rules* 1 and 2, and used to investigate the physical world, could also be adopted to investigate the social and moral sphere, as a consequence of the metaphorical transfer of properties from one domain to another.

Newtonianism had a major influence on intellectual debates in Europe in the first decades of the eighteenth century. Pemberton, Algarotti and Voltaire contributed to its diffusion, and dictionaries and encyclopedias such as John Harris' *Lexicon Technicum* and Ephraim Chambers' *Cyclopædia* helped popularize the concepts illustrated in *Principia* and *Opticks*. In Scotland, the Newtonian tradition developed in the universities of Aberdeen, St. Andrews and Edinburgh, especially thanks to the works of David and James Gregory, and Colin Maclaurin, while moral Newtonianism consolidated in Hutcheson's and Turnbull's philosophical approaches. Smith's and Hume's Newtonianism took shape against this rich backdrop. Their approaches can be compared in that, while Hume showed an awareness of many developments in the science of his time, Smith showed a deep knowledge of the greatest astronomical works (Moscovici, 1956). Hume methodologically reused the *Regulae Philosophandi* in order to define his "science of man" and the limits of human knowledge (Force, 1987; Gilardi, 1988), although this did not mean that his "experimental" moral philosophy was based on experiments (Cremaschi, 2009: 81–82). Similarly, Smith dealt with Newton's teaching as a source of general orientation and methodological inspiration (Berry, 2006: 126).

Of particular importance was Smith's re-interpretation of the Newtonian analytic-synthetic method, that is, the method that Newton illustrated in "Query 31" (Newton, 1952[1704]: 404–405). In the words of Colin Maclaurin, it consisted in "analysis" and "synthesis". The former is the method which begins "with the phænomena, or effects", and proceeds "from particular causes" "to the more general ones". The latter is the method which "descend[s] in a contrary order" and from general causes, "as established principles, explain[s] all the phænomena that are their consequences, and prove[s] our explications" (Maclaurin, 1748: 8–9). The methodological role of "principles" in human inquiries resonated in Hume's words, where he pointed out that when philosophers proceed "from particular instances to general principles, they still push on their enquiries to principles more general, and rest not satisfied till they arrive at those original principles, by which, in every science, all human curiosity must be bounded" (Hume, 2007a [1748]: 3–4).

According to Freudenthal, the analytic-synthetic method in Smith can be identified in the opinion shared by Hume that the aim of science consisted in "tracing phenomena back to qualities of a single element" (Freudenthal, 1981: 137). In particular, he saw the "propensity" to barter as an essential property of human nature whereby social phenomena could be deduced (Freudenthal, 1986). In turn, Hetherington remarked that the structure of the WN and *Principia* are similar, in that they both use the "method of moving by induction from phenomena to the framing of principles, and then deducing the phenomena from the principles" (Hetherington, 1983: 504). While Newton defined the law of gravity by induction and then used deduction to demonstrate that the observed phenomena follow from it, after analyzing the phenomena, Smith in the WN delineated a general principle (the propensity to barter) by means of which they are deduced. From this perspective, propensity to barter and the resulting division of labor could be identified in both hunters' and shepherds' communities and the pin factory (ibidem: 505). In line with these views, Cremaschi points out that there are some notions, such as mechanism, force and final and efficient causes, which reveal how Newtonian physics was reused in Smith's political economy. In the WN, phenomena are linked with principles in a systematic way. And in a view in which society appears as a sum of mechanisms, that of "equilibrium or gravitation" is one of the most representative (Cremaschi, 2009: 88–90).

The gravitation metaphor was anticipated by an informal description that illustrated how self-regulation was achieved, through competition which operates on both the demand and supply sides of the market, by the equalization of market prices. This explained why "[t]he natural price [...] is, as it were, the central price, to which the prices of all commodities are continually gravitating" (WN I.vii.15: 75). However, Smith pointed out that "particular accidents", "natural causes" and "particular regulations of police" "may, in many commodities, keep up the market price, for a long time together, a good deal above the natural price" (WN i.vii.20: 77). Some forces or circumstances oppose the attractive power of the natural price, although it is powerful enough to determine a market order. As a transposition of Newtonian physics to the economic realm, the metaphor was rather imperfect because, Cohen remarks, "Smith did not take account of one of the features of Newtonian gravitation", namely, "its property of acting mutually between all pairs of gravitating bodies, so that there is always an equal and opposite force" (Cohen, 1994: 65). If Smith had considered the implications of the law of gravity, he would have had to conclude that natural prices also gravitate around market prices. However, the metaphor of gravitation was a legitimate "creative transformation" of the Newtonian approach, where the relation between economic and natural domains was established on the basis of analogy rather than on strict identity (ibidem: 68).

Cohen shows that the metaphor of gravitation, like any other metaphor, was malleable, and this led to a partial reformulation of the Newtonian relationship between principles and phenomena. An example is Smith's treatment of wages, profit and rent as components of prices. The variety of revenues was explained in reference, not to one principle (in some ways similar to the law of gravity in physics), but to "three original sources of all revenue" that cannot be further reduced. Each has a different foundation. Wages are related to the laborer's sacrifices of "ease", "liberty" and "happiness" (WN I.v.7: 50). Profits do not depend on managerial labor and "bear no proportion to the quantity, the hardship, or the ingenuity of this supposed labour of inspection and direction". In fact, they "are regulated altogether by the value of the stock employed, and are greater or smaller in proportion to the extent of this stock" (WN I.vi.6: 66). Lastly, rent is related to the formation of private property, which imposes a payment for the use of land (WN I.vi.8: 67). The "interest of money", which appears as a revenue with distinctive features, by contrast, "is always a derivative revenue, which, if it is not paid from the profit which is made by the use of the money, must be paid from some other source of revenue" (WN I.vi.18: 70). Similarly, other kinds of revenue that apparently exhibit distinctive characteristics, if carefully analyzed are found to be nothing but a combination of the original sources of revenue. In conclusion, the Newtonian idea of explaining economic order by connecting variety of phenomena to principles was preserved, although in a slightly revised form, dictated by the specific characteristics of the economic sphere. Kinds of revenue are not homogenous, and each of them is explained by its own principle.

3.6 Conclusions

Adam Ferguson (1995 [1767]: 49), a representative figure of the Scottish Enlightenment, maintained that "the materialist, by treating of man as of an engine, cannot make any change in the state of his history". A similar idea could be attributed to Adam Smith who was neither a "materialist" like La Mettrie nor a mechanistic philosopher like Descartes and used the metaphor of the machine to represent coherence, coordination and efficiency of systems of various kinds in their evolutionary dimensions.[12]

In the TMS, Smith showed how the beauty of order, a property of machines, is a feature of wealth and institutions that orients behaviors, and leads to beneficial, unintentional results. The machine does not metaphorically represent a static order, as it did in the seventeenth century, but contributes to providing some ideas on the evolution of orders which

[12] Worland (1976: 248) criticizes the view according to which "Smith's economics is a 'mechanistic analogy' borrowed from Newton, which analogy leads one to conceive of the economic system as a 'machine' the parts of which interact to produce coherence, equilibrium, and system stability" (ibidem: 248), because Smith failed "to conform with the requirements of a Newtonian, or 'mechanistic,' explanation" (ibidem: 253). But this interpretation, directed at criticizing Smith's Newtonianism, focuses on the image of market prices which gravitate around natural prices (WN, chap. VII), rather than on the metaphor of the machine.

include scientific systems, language, the factory, and economic systems. As machines, orders exhibit a harmony that it is not established once and for all, but evolves toward an increasing efficiency. The emphasis is thus on how harmonic systems acquire new features over time. It is this temporal dimension that allows us to consider the machine as a conceptual candidate for explaining the formation of order as an unintentional process that nobody plans. Philosophers, scientists and capital owners intentionally introduce specific changes in their systems, but do not plan how these systems evolve.

However, the metaphor of machine was inadequate in other respects, as the analysis on the division of labor shows. In particular, we can see the incompatibility between the division of labor in the factory and in society. In the former case, the operations of workers are geared to a specific purpose: the finished production of the good. Hence they express intentional compliance with a plan. The role of workers in a manufacturing enterprise closely reflects the hierarchy of the machine's mechanisms, in that what matters is executing what has been planned. The organization of labor in a workshop is similar to a real machine, because both are planned to produce a desired end. Consequently, the single parts can have no freedom of movement. In the social division of labor, by contrast, individuals have freedom of movement, and harmonization of their actions cannot be planned in advance. The discontinuity—not perceived by Smith—between the two aspects of the division of labor reflects the opposition between human planning and "unintended social outcomes", and prevents the image of the machine (valid, however, only as regards the workshop) from including essential aspects of market society: the independent "principle of motion" of individuals and the unintentional harmonization of their actions, on which social development depends. This principle of motion is what the "man of system" tries to suppress when he imagines "that he can arrange the different members of a great society with as much ease as the hand arranges the different pieces upon a chess-board" (TMS ii.2.17: 234). As an image describing the coherence and harmony of systems, whose beauty can engender unintended outcomes which explain the progress of society, the metaphor of the machine, however, cannot resolve the problem of the difference between the division of labor in the factory and in society. These inconsistencies call for new interpretive keys, and consequently for other sets of metaphors, both organic ones and the "invisible hand", with their greater capacity to deal with problems left unresolved by the mechanical image.

References

Anonymous. (1997). Organic and Mechanical Metaphors in Late Eighteenth-Century American Political Thought. *Harvard Law Review*, 110, 1832–1849.

Aspromourgos, T. (2009). *The Science of Wealth. Adam Smith and the Framing of Political Economy*. Routledge.

Aspromourgos, T. (2012). The Machine in Adam Smith's Economic and Wider Thought. *Journal of the History of Economic Thought, 34*(4), 475–490.

Berry, C. J. (2006). Smith and Science. In K. Haakonssen (Ed.), *The Cambridge Companion to Adam Smith* (pp. 112–135). Cambridge University Press.

Black, M. (1962). *Models and Metaphors. Studies in Language and Philosophy*. Cornell University Press.

Boyd, R. (1993). Metaphor and Theory Change: What Is "metaphor" a Metaphor For. In A. Ortony (Ed.), *Metaphor and Thought* (2nd ed., pp. 481–532). Cambridge University Press.

Boyle, R. (1772a [1666]). The Origin of Forms and Qualities, According to the Corpuscular Philosophy. In *Works* (Vol. 3). Johnston et al.

Boyle, R. (1772b [1690]). *The Christian Virtuoso, in Works* (Vol. 5). Johnston et al.

Cipolla, C. M. (1996). *Le macchine del tempo*. Il Mulino.

Clément, A. (2003). The Influence of Medicine on Political Economy in the Seventeenth Century. *History of Economics Review, 38*(1), 1–22.

Cohen, B. I. (1994). Newton and the Social Sciences, with Special Reference to Economics, or, the Case of the Missing Paradigm. In P. Mirowski (Ed.), *Natural Images in Economic Thought* (pp. 55–90). Cambridge University Press.

Condillac, E. B. (2014 [1749]).Treatise on Systems. In *Philosophical Writings of Etienne Bonnot, Abbé de Condillac* (Vol. 1). Routledge.

Cremaschi, S. (1984). *Il sistema della ricchezza. Economia politica e problema del metodo in Adam Smith*. Franco Angeli.

Cremaschi, S. (2009). Newtonian Physics, Experimental Moral Philosophy and the Shaping of Political Economy. In R. Arena, S. Dow, & M. Klaes (Eds.), *Open Economics: Economics in Relation to Other Disciplines* (pp. 73–94). Routledge.

Dascal, M. (2006). Adam Smith's Theory of Language. In K. Haakonssen (Ed.), *The Cambridge Companion to Adam Smith* (pp. 79–111). Cambridge University Press.

Davidko, N. (2013). Metaphoricity in the History of Economic Thought (on the Basis of the 17th Century Economic Discourse). *Kalbų Studijos/Studies About Languages, 22*, 86–97.

Descartes, R. (1985 [1662]). Treatise on Man. In *The Philosophical Writings of Descartes* (Vol. 1). Cambridge University Press.

Eriksen, C. B. (2017). Circulation of Blood and Money in *Leviathan*—Hobbes on the Economy of the Body. In J. Bek-Thomsen et al. (Eds.), *History of Economic Rationalities: Economic Reasoning as Knowledge and Practice Authority*. Springer.

Ferguson, A. (1995 [1767]). *An Essay on the History of Civil Society*, F. Oz-Salzberger (Ed.). Cambridge University Press.

Finkelstein, A. (2000). *Harmony and the Balance: An Intellectual History of Seventeenth-Century English Economic Thought*. University of Michigan Press.

Fiori, S. (1992). Persuasione e mercato. Note su un problema lasciato aperto da Adam Smith. *Trimestre, 25*(1–2), 41–53.

Fontenelle. (1998 [1686]). *Entretiens sur la pluralité des mondes*. Flammarion.

Force, J. E. (1987). Hume's Interest in Newton and Science. *Hume Studies, 13*(2), 166–216.

Freudenthal, G. (1981). Adam Smith's Analytic-Synthetic Method and the "System of Natural Liberty". *History of European Ideas, 2*(2), 135–154.

Freudenthal, G. (1986). *Atom and Individual in the Age of Newton. On the Genesis of the Mechanistic World View*. Reidel.

Galilei, G. (1960 [1590]). *De Motu*, EN (Vol. I, pp. 251–419); *On Motion* (I. E. Drabkin, Trans.). University of Wisconsin Press.

Gervaise, I. (1954 [1720]). *The System or Theory of Trade of the World*, with a Foreword by J. Viner, and an Introduction by J. M. Letiche. Johns Hopkins Press.

Gilardi, R. (1988). Hume e il "principio di analogia". *Rivista di Filosofia Neo-Scolastica, 80*(1), 63–104.

Harrison, J. R. (1995). Imagination and Aesthetics in Adam Smith's Epistemology and Moral Philosophy. *Contributions to Political Economy, 14*, 91–112.

Hayek, F. A. (1978). Dr Bernard Mandeville. In *New Studies in Philosophy, Politics, Economics and the History of Ideas* (pp. 249–266). Routledge and Kegan Paul.

Hetherington, N. S. (1983). Isaac Newton's Influence on Adam Smith's Natural Laws in Economics. *Journal of the History of Ideas, 44*(3), 497–505.

Hirschman, A. O. (1977). *The Passions and the Interests. Political Arguments for Capitalism Before Its Triumph*. Princeton University Press.

Hobbes, T. (1996 [1651]). *Leviathan*, J. C. A. Gaskin (Ed.). Oxford University Press.

Hobbes, T. (1998 [1642]). *On the Citizen*. Cambridge University Press.

Hooke, R. (1665). *Micrographia or Some Physiological Descriptions of Minute Bodies Made by Magnifying Glasses, with Observations and Inquiries Thereupon*. Printed by Martyn and Allestry.

Hume, D. (1985a [1777]). Of Commerce. In E. F. Miller (Ed.), *Essays Moral, Political, and Literary* (pp. 253–267). Liberty Fund.

Hume, D. (1985b [1777]). Of Refinement in the Arts. In E. F. Miller (Ed.), *Essays Moral, Political, and Literary* (pp. 268–280). Liberty Fund.

Hume, D. (1985c [1777]). Of the Balance of Trade. In E. F. Miller (Ed.), *Essays Moral, Political, and Literary* (pp. 308–326). Liberty Fund.

Hume, D. (1985d [1777]). Of the Balance of Power. In E. F. Miller (Ed.), *Essays Moral, Political, and Literary* (pp. 332–341). Liberty Fund.

Hume, D. (2007a [1748]). *An Enquiry Concerning Human Understanding*, P. Millican (Ed.). Oxford University Press.

Hume, D. (2007b [1779]). *Dialogues Concerning Natural Religion*, D. Coleman (Ed.). Cambridge University Press.

La de Mettrie, J. O. (1748). *L'homme machine*. Elie Luzac, fils.

Locke, J. (1997 [1690]). *An Essay Concerning Human Understanding*. Penguin Books.

Machamer, P. (1998). Galileo's Machines, His Mathematics, and His Experiments. In P. Machamer (Ed.), *The Cambridge Companion to Galileo* (pp. 53–79). Cambridge University Press.

Maclaurin, C. (1748). *An Account of Sir Isaac Newton's Philosophical Discoveries*. Millar and Nourse.

Magnusson, L. (2015). *The Political Economy of Mercantilism*. Routledge.

Malebranche, N. (1700 [1674–5]). *Treatise Concerning the Search After Truth*. Bowyer.

Malynes, G. (1622). *The Maintenance of Free Trade [...]*. Printed by *I. L.* for *William Sheffard*; available at: https://quod.lib.umich.edu/e/eebo/A06789.0001.001?rgn=main;view=fulltext. Accessed 14 June 2020.

Mandeville, B. (1924a [1723]). A Search into the Nature of Society. In F. B. Kaye (Ed.), *The Fable of the Bees: Or, Private Vices, Publick Benefits* (Vol. 1). Clarendon Press.

Mandeville, B. (1924b [1723]). An Essay on Charity, and Charity-Schools. In F. B. Kaye (Ed.), *The Fable of the Bees: Or, Private Vices, Publick Benefits* (Vol. 2). Clarendon Press.

Mandeville, B. (1924c [1724]). The Fable of the Bees, or Private Vices, Publick Benefits. In F. B. Kaye (Ed.), *The Fable of the Bees: Or, Private Vices, Publick Benefits* (Vol. 1). Clarendon Press.

Marx, K. (1976 [1867]).*Capital. A Critique of Political Economy* (Vol. 1), Introduced by E. Mandel. Vintage Books.

Mayr, O. (1986). *Authority, Liberty and Automatic Machinery in Early Modern Europe*. Johns Hopkins Press.

Misselden, E. (1623). *The Circle of Commerce*. Printed by J. Dawson.

Moscovici, S. (1956). A propos de quelques travaux d'Adam Smith sur l'histoire et la philosophie des sciences. *Revue d'histoire des sciences et de leur applications, 9*(1), 1–20.

Moyle, W. (1727 [1698]). An Essay on the Lacedæmonian Government. In A. Bettesworth, E. Curll, J. Pemberton, & J. Batley (Eds.), *The Whole Works of Walter Moyle*. Printed for Knapton.

Moyle, W. (1969 [ca 1699]). An Essay Upon the Constitution of the Roman Government. In C. Robbins (Ed.), *Two English Republican Tracts*. Cambridge University Press.

Newton, I. (1952 [1704]). *Opticks*. Fourth English Edition (1730). Foreword by A. Einstein, Introduction by Sir E. Whittaker, Preface by I. B. Cohen. Dover Publications.

Newton, I. (1999 [1687]). *The Principia. Mathematical Principles of Natural Philosophy*. University of California Press.

Onions, C. T. (Ed.). (1973). *The Oxford Universal Dictionary Illustrated on Historical Principles* (Vol. 1, 3rd ed.). Clarendon Press.

Pascal, B. (1995 [1670]). *Pensées and Other Writings*. Oxford University Press.

Rescher, N. (1991). *G. W. Leibniz's Monadology. An Edition for Students*. University of Pittsburgh Press.

Rosenberg, N. (1963). Mandeville and Laissez-Faire. *Journal of the History of Ideas, 24*(2), 183–196.

Rosenberg, N. (1965). Adam Smith on the Division of Labour: Two Views or One? *Economica, 32*(126), 127–139.

Rothschild, E. (2001). *Economic Sentiments: Adam Smith, Condorcet and the Enlightenment*. Harvard University Press.

Schabas, M. (2001). David Hume on Experimental Natural Philosophy, Money, and Fluids. *History of Political Economy, 33*(3), 411–435.

Shapin, S. (1996). *The Scientific Revolution*. University of Chicago Press.

Swift, J. (1701). *A Discourse of the Contents and Dissensions Between the Nobles and the Commons in Athens and Rome*. Printed for John Nutt.

Trincado, E. (2019). *The Birth of Economic Rhetoric. Communication, Arts and Economic Stimulus in David Hume and Adam Smith*. Palgrave Macmillan.

Walraevens, B. (2010). Adam Smith's Economics and the *Lectures on Rhetoric and Belles Lettres*. The Language of Commerce. *History of Economic Ideas, 18*(1), 11–32.

Wennerlind, C. (2006). David Hume as a *Political* Economist. In A. Dow & S. Dow (Eds.), *A History of Scottish Economic Thought* (pp. 46–70). Routledge.

Wight, J. B. (2014). Instincts and the Invisible Order: The Possibility of Progress. In D. F. Hardwick & L. Marsh (Eds.), *Propriety and Prosperity: New Studies on the Philosophy of Adam Smith* (pp. 223–239). Palgrave Macmillan.

Wootton, D. (2006). Liberty, Metaphor, and Mechanism: "Checks and Balances" and the Origins of Modern Constitutionalism. In D. Womersley (Ed.), *Liberty and American Experience in the Eighteenth Century* (pp. 209–274). Liberty Fund.

Worland, S. T. (1976). Mechanistic Analogy and Smith on Exchange. *Review of Social Economy, 34*(3), 245–257.

CHAPTER 4

Smith and the Organic Metaphors

Abstract Organic metaphors were used in the seventeenth century to represent the distribution of resources in the political body in terms of "nutrition" and "digestion". However, when Smith resorted to organic metaphors, he did not consider this tradition. Although he referred to a traditional image of the natural body, he used it to justify the political body's self-adjustment processes. However, the metaphor of the body was imperfect, as Tucker, Ferguson and Smith himself, in some respects, showed. Although it made it possible to ostensively identify self-regulating properties, the organic metaphor was unable to clarify the notion of the progress of society.

Keywords Nutrition • Organic metaphors • Medical metaphors • Body politick • Economic policy

4.1 Organic Metaphors in the Seventeenth Century

In the seventeenth century natural and political bodies, although conceived as hierarchical structures whose functioning is the result of the interaction among organs, were not always represented as machines. In

S. Fiori, *Machines, Bodies and Invisible Hands*,
https://doi.org/10.1007/978-3-030-85206-1_4

medical metaphors, the image of the natural body's poor health was used to illustrate the state of disequilibrium of a nation, and monarchs and legislators were viewed as physicians who fight and cure diseases. Organic metaphors often interacted with other metaphors, with the consequence that, as Lakoff and Johnson (1980, 1999) remark, different but contiguous metaphorical domains reinforced each other. This occurred, for example, with the image of the monarch as father and head of the family who rules his subjects as "children" (Finkelstein, 2000: 91). This metaphor, in which the micro-dimension of the family appears as a model for the macro-dimension of society, combined social, biological and hierarchical principles, and conveyed the idea that the household is an organic, interdependent structure.

Following Bacon, Petty's *Political Anatomy of Ireland* compared the "Body Natural, and Body Politick", and maintained that knowledge of "Anatomy" would have helped to preserve "Health and strength" of both kinds of bodies, because it would have made it possible to know their "Symmetry, Fabrick, and Proportion" (Petty, 1963b [1691]: 129).

In Malynes, human physiology, in which organs are not described in mechanical terms but appeared as interdependent, served to conceptualize economic physiology:

> the Liuer (*Money*) doth minister Spirits to the heart (*Commodities*,) and the heart to the Braine (*Exchange:*) so doth the *Brayne exchange* minister to the whole *Microcosme* or the whole Body of *Traffique*. Let the heart therfore by the liuer receiue his *Tinctured Chilus* by his owne mouth and stomacke, and the blood full of Spirits, shall fill all the Ueines, and supply the want of monyes. (Malynes, 1622: 38)

Hobbes, though resorting to mechanical images of the body in his work, also dealt with the natural and economic body in physiological terms.[1] His description of the State as a political body similar to the human body was not a simple description of features expressed in neutral language. Rather, as Eriksen (2017) maintains, it worked as a "theory-constitutive metaphor" which shaped his theory and provided content that would otherwise be inaccessible. By means of this perspective, he developed a rudimentary approach to economics, in which the metaphor

[1] Hobbes was not a Cartesian, and his approach was influenced by Galenic tradition and Harvey's discovery of the circulation of blood (Christensen, 1989). On the influence of Harvey's approach on economic thought in the seventeenth century, see Desmedt (2005).

of nourishment was the interpretative key on the basis of which economic analysis could be constructed. In his view, nutrition and digestion of food were compared to a "continual flow of materials and energetic substances extracted from the earth" (Christensen, 1989: 690). And in chapter 24 of the *Levithan*, with the vocabulary of physiology, he maintained that the "nutrition of a commonwealth consisteth, in the *plenty,* and *distribution* of *materials* conducing to life" (Hobbes, 1996 [1651]: 163, emphasis in original). He also devoted special attention to concoction, that is, digestion, a term that metaphorically meant "the reducing of all commodities, which are not presently consumed, but reserved for nourishment in time to come, to something of equal value" (ibidem: 167). Concoction, he argued, corresponds to "the sanguification of the commonwealth: for natural blood is in like manner made of the fruits of the earth; and circulating, nourisheth by the way every member of the body of man" (ibidem: 167).

Like Hobbes, who conceived of the Commonwealth as a hierarchically organized body, Mun, in *England's Treasure by Forraign Trade* (a book written circa 1630, but published posthumously in 1664) also resorted to an organic, nonmechanical metaphor to illustrate the hierarchical nature of the body politic. Princes, instead of accumulating "treasures", should invest their income, and increase the wealth of nation in many ways, for example, by building "ships of war", or buying corn to use in famine periods: "for a Prince (in this case) is like the stomach in the body, which if it cease to digest and distribute to the other members, it doth no sooner corrupt them, but it destroyes it self"(Mun, 1664: 190/70). Just as Hobbes emphasized the primary role of nutrition and circulation in a hierarchically organized political body, Mun pointed out the fundamental role of nutrition and distribution of wealth achieved by the prince-stomach's spending. By contrast, Davenant (1771 [1698]: 382), while maintaining the metaphor of digestion, reversed the image of the relationship between the prince-stomach and society, and argued that the "common people" are "the stomach of the body politic". What had to be avoided, he maintained, was what had happened in Spain in the age of Philip II, where the stomach-people ceased to perform their "due functions", with the consequence that food was not digested and the body was not nourished (ibidem: 382; see Clément, 2003). Lastly, Petty (1963a [1662]: 28) compared the circulation of blood and nourishment in the natural body to the circulation of commodities in political bodies.[2] "Retailers are needful to make

[2] The ancient idea that the circulation of blood transports nourishment dates back to Galen.

the distribution into every Village", he maintained, but some of them are like "Gamesters", who exploit the labor of the poor. As "veins and arteries" they simply "distribute forth and back the blood and nutritive juyces of the Body Politick, namely, the product of Husbandry and Manufacture".

Mandeville, who abandoned the Cartesian approach when he began to write the *Fable of the Bees* (Hundert, 1994: 39), also described society as a natural body,[3] and used the metaphor of the stomach to illustrate interdependencies and hierarchies in "Animal Oeconomy". This appears in the poem *The Hands and Feet and Belly* (De Marchi, 2001: 77), where a bodily metaphor represented the political authority (which as in Mun was the belly) as the prime mover of the mechanism of distribution.[4] This perspective was refined over time, and with it his analysis of social relationships as a system of interdependencies controlled by political power:

> by Society I understand a Body Politick, in which Man either subdued by Superior Force, or by Persuasion drawn from his Savage State, is become a Disciplin'd Creature, that can find his own Ends in Labouring for others, and where under one Head or other Form of Government each Member is render'd Subservient to the Whole, and all of them by cunning Management are made to Act as one. (Mandeville, 1924a [1723]: 347)

In this perspective, the role of government was fundamental in directing the political body by appropriate, not arbitrary, rules of the game, since it is through "the dextrous Management of a skilful Politician" that "Private Vices [...] may be turned into Publick Benefits" (ibidem: 369).[5] The body is a whole, and its coherent organization is the outcome of behavior of many individuals that "Act as one", thanks to the work of the government that favors their coordination.

Adam Smith did not employ the traditional metaphor of digestion and nutrition to conceptualize distribution, nor did he use the image of the stomach to represent economic functions performed by the prince (or, alternatively, by the people). Rather, in the TMS he dealt with the concept

[3] "Laws and government", Mandeville (1924c [1724]: 5) stated, "are the Political Bodies of Civil Societies, what the Vital Spirits and Life it self are to the Natural Bodies".

[4] "The Belly is the Government/From whence the Nourishment is sent" (quoted in De Marchi, 2001: 77).

[5] Mandeville used also mechanical metaphors. However, they were employed chiefly to denote the body's automaticity and interdependence among its parts. On this topic see Rosenberg (1963: 192–193).

of distribution by means of another metaphor: the invisible hand. This version of the metaphor, unlike the invisible hand of the WN, put forward the idea—previously developed by seventeenth-century authors, and by Cantillon and Quesnay—that there is an agent, the landlord, who determines the distribution of resources among people who work for him. In the same passage of the TMS where the invisible hand appears, Smith referred to the stomach not as a metaphorical image, but as a physical organ whose "narrow capacity" regulates the desire for food (see WN I.xi.c.7: 181), and thus prevents the landlord from fulfilling his desire to consume "the whole harvest" that grows in his land (TMS IV.I.10184). This situation, Smith maintained, is expressed by the popular proverb "the eye is larger than the belly" (ibidem: 184), but this conclusion is imprecise. The meaning of the proverb is that greed leads to indigestion because the desire for food has been satisfied by eating inordinately, but this is not the case of the landlord, who does not eat excessively but is forced to compensate the "immensity of his desires" with other kinds of consumption and consequently to distribute the "rest" among those who live from his "luxury and caprice" (see also WN I.xi.c.7: 181). In this perspective, the (limit of the) stomach triggers the mechanism of the unintentional "distribution of the necessaries of life" by the invisible hand, which in turn guides the landlord's behavior.[6]

In the seventeenth century, bodily metaphors extended to medical metaphors. They compared states of health or illness of natural and political bodies, and the statesman to a physician who helps to restore the body to health. Bacon (1625: 181) argued that natural and political bodies need exercise, and represented difficulties in business as "hasty digestion" (ibidem: 142). Chamberlayne used a similar analogy and maintained that "Manufacture is to the Body Politick, what Exercise is to the Body Natural" (Chamberlayne, 1683: 70, quoted in Besomi, 2011: 68). Misselden and Mun compared the decay of trade to illness of the natural body (Davidko, 2013: 93), and Malynes, in 1601, even in the title of a book (*A Treatise on the Canker of Englands Commonwealth, Divided into three parts; Wherein the Author, imitating the rule of good Phisitions, First, declareth the disease; Secondarily, sheweth the efficient cause thereof; Lastly, a remedy for the same*),

[6] As Ahmad (1990) maintains, it is the limit of stomach, and not human prudence or reasonableness, that circumscribes the landlord's selfishness and makes possible a distribution "which would have been made, had the earth been divided into equal portions among all its inhabitants" (TMS IV.I.10: 184–185).

resorted to the metaphor of the loss of wealth as a disease (see Harris, 1999). Disease, health, prosperity, contagion were words used by Mun, Battie and Defoe to illustrate states of the body politic (Besomi, 2011: 67–68). Petty received a medical education and used the natural body/political body analogy as a heuristic tool to discover characteristics of the social world (Sivado, 2017). Barbon, Mandeville and Quesnay were also medical men, and their education influenced their economic conceptions in different degrees. Medical and philosophical studies were contiguous in Locke (Coleman, 2001), and according to Caffentzis (2003: 220), Berkeley and Locke transferred "therapeutic methods appropriate to the diseases of the mind into cures of monetary problems". Mandeville analyzed social dynamics by employing medical metaphors. He compared avarice and prodigality as opposing "poisons" that the physician-politician should balance for therapeutic purposes (Mandeville, 1924c [1724]: 106) through the appropriate use of the "Art of Medicine" (Mandeville, 1924b [1723]: 321–322). As a consequence, Cook (1999) maintains, he viewed the physician and the skillful politician as playing a similar role (see Turner, 2016). The medical approach also influenced Quesnay's economic view (Foley, 1973, 1976, chap. 7). The model of the circulation of blood influenced the theory of production and circulation presented in the *Tableau économique* and expressed the idea of a distinct vitality of nature (Christensen, 1994). Quesnay's physiology combined neomechanistic and vitalistic perspectives (ibidem: 259; see also Groenewegen, 2001), and his view of the sexual reproduction of plants and animals, illustrated especially in the second edition of the *Essai physique sur l'oeconomie animale* (1747), had a far from marginal role in his interpretation of reproduction in agriculture and sterility in manufacturing (Fiori, 2019: 1174–1176). Also in this sense, the political body was dealt with as the "animal economy", a concept that was developed by Smith, albeit in terms that differed from those employed in that tradition of thought.

4.2 Organic and Medical Metaphors in Adam Smith

Although Smith did not consider the body as an explicit object of analysis, he referred to this concept to clarify some important parts of his theory. The body was evoked in the WN, when he referred to the laborer's "ordinary state of health, strength, and spirits" as a condition which determines the real price of commodities (WN I.v.7: 50). And, as we saw in the previous section, it was considered in the TMS, where Smith discussed how the physical limits of the stomach indirectly influence the distribution of resources. The body also played a role in other parts of the TMS, where Smith "ma[de] explicit references to the wondrous functioning of the biological organism" (Khalil, 2000: 374). In this work, Smith argued that the capacity to understand others' behavior, and to formulate moral judgments on it, depends on the capacity of our body and mind to replicate feelings experienced by our fellow men. These and other kinds of connections between the bodily and moral dimensions were debated in the eighteenth century, and probably were a source of inspiration for philosophical and medical analyses. In this respect, Forget (2003), Bourke (2012) and Packham (2012) point out that there are important analogies between the treatment of the concept of sympathy in Smith's moral theory, and in the physiological studies of the Edinburgh medical school in the late eighteenth century (see Sect. 8.2). Lastly, sight as a bodily dimension had a role in Smith's theory. In his moral philosophy, it qualifies us as "spectators" and mediates our participation in the sentiments of others.

Smith's interest in certain properties of the body went beyond occasional references. Although he was not a natural scientist, he was attentive to phenomena of life and the physiology of organisms and was aware of the debates on natural sciences of his time (see Jonsson, 2010: 1350–1351). This emerges in a letter to the *Edinburgh Review* (1755) which shows not only his knowledge of the works of Buffon and Daubenton but also his great interest in the entomological studies of Réaumur,[7] a work in which the "economy and management" of insects was accurately described (Edinburgh Review: 249).

[7] From the end of the seventeenth century, studies of microscopic life made it possible to look at the world with different eyes. Creationism, preformism and mechanism, which postulated a pre-established order, were gradually opposed by the idea that nature exhibits a vitality that cannot be reduced to the work of mechanical forces. Réaumur's entomology, and Bonnet's studies on parthenogenesis of aphides, contributed to strengthening this conviction, while Trembley's discovery that the hydra (freshwater polyp) could produce complete new animals when it was cut in half revealed unsuspected capacities of organic matter (see Magner, 2002, chap. 5). Theories of preformation and pre-existence, which maintained that the embryo pre-exists and that nature is deprived of vital powers because all organisms were originally formed at the Creation, were gradually rejected, although these approaches' persistence made the transition to vitalism extremely complex.

According to Lindgren (1973: 59), "Smith would probably have preferred the biological model to all others for representing social phenomena", and Campbell (1971: 77) remarked that he represented the relationship between human nature and society in terms of homeostatic principles similar to those that characterize "a state of equilibrium in animal organisms". More than anything else, however, it is the organic metaphors in the WN that reveal how Smith's interest in biological phenomena interacted with his theory. The idea that the body has hidden and as yet undiscovered properties—while at the same time showing a flexibility and an autonomous capacity to adapt that machines do not possess—contributed to shaping a new conception of order which influenced his economic discourse.

> The uniform, constant, and uninterrupted effort of every man to better his condition, the principle from which publick and national, as well as private opulence is originally derived, is frequently powerful enough to maintain the natural progress of things toward improvement, in spite both of the extravagance of government, and of the greatest errors of administration. Like the unknown principle of animal life, it frequently restores health and vigour to the constitution, in spite, not only of the disease, but of the absurd prescriptions of the doctor. (WN II.iii.32: 343)

The analogy between "the uniform, constant, and uninterrupted effort of every man to better his condition", whereby private and social wealth is increased, and "the unknown principle of animal life" illustrates why it is the organism and not the machine that best conveys the process of wealth formation in the presence of forces acting in the opposite direction. The production of wealth and "progress of things toward improvement" are explained by the self-regulating processes of the organism. The level and pace of development vary according to the power exerted by opposing forces, thus giving rise to different configurations of economic order. In short, the health of the body—that is, as Smith makes clear in another passage, the prevailing of parsimony over prodigality—is compared to states of economy which to varying extents approach an optimal situation. This latter is a condition in which "the extravagance of government, and of the greatest errors of administration", has been neutralized, thus removing the most significant constraint on the human propensity to improvement. However, since the erroneous behaviors of public institutions are not sufficient to stop what Smith calls "the natural progress of things", the economic order will in any case develop.

Metaphors aim at bridging conceptual gaps when analytical, causal explanations are not available. Thus, Smith provides a metaphorical argument, stating that man's efforts "to better his condition" can be interpreted as principles which regulate the life of organisms. Although many other factors could be evoked to explain the increase of welfare in society, it is the metaphorical assumption that unknown principles of "animal life" will prevail over forces which oppose them that provides a theoretical framework legitimizing the idea that the welfare of society increases over time—the latter being a theme that reappears with the invisible hand.[8] Moreover, it is the organic metaphor that makes it possible to interpret impersonal (biological) forces as factors that govern individual behaviors. In this perspective, behaviors rather than being viewed as simple consequences of intentional choices are the results of natural inclinations which precede and orient the use of reason.

We may suppose that Smith probably resorted to this metaphorical terminology because neither economic theory nor the life sciences of that time possessed well-defined conceptual categories that could give a complete causal account of the phenomena they examined. These two disciplines had not yet defined their epistemological status, and they not infrequently used figurative language to construct their theoretical principles. Phrases like "oeconomy of nature" and "animal oeconomy", increasingly used in the early decades of the eighteenth century, revealed that economics and natural sciences could have a common ground. It is thus unsurprising that the life sciences were a source of inspiration for economic thought, because they suggested ideas about the properties of organic matter that could be useful in exploring some economic phenomena. Scientific approaches which shared this perspective were chiefly antimechanistic. As the physiologist Albrecht von Haller pointed out in *Elementa physiologiae corporis humani* (1757), physiology had to handle "completely unknown causes" which seriously undermined any mechanistic paradigm (see Deleule, 1979: 264). From the mid-1750s new physiological theories were put forward and probably had an impact on Smith's

[8] As Khalil (2000: 374–375) remarks, there is a further connection between the invisible hand and "the mysteries of the living world" because the organism accomplishes great ends, for example, the propagation of species, without any awareness of how they arise from the intermediate means.

approach (Packham, 2012: 104–105). In the Edinburgh Medical School, in reaction to mechanistic models, Robert Whytt introduced a "vitalist", physiological theory to explain self-regulating and self-preserving processes of organisms. And Théophile Bordeu, who at Montpellier studied the nervous system, was a supporter of an anti-mechanistic approach (see Chap. 8).

The logic emphasized by the organic metaphor reemerges in Smith's thought even in the absence of the biological analogy. The metaphor (WN II.iii.32: 343) envisaged the prevalence of individuals' propensity to increase their wealth as a sort of biological tendency, overcoming factors (i.e., "errors of administration" conceived as erroneous "prescriptions of the doctor") which push in the opposite direction. The same logic resurfaced when Smith described frugality (or parsimony) and prodigality as opposing forces which affect the amount of private and public wealth. Frugality, the "principle which prompts to save" (WN II.iii.28: 341) and determines the increase of wealth, encapsulates the "desire of bettering our condition", is the same principle that the metaphor represents as the "unknown principle of animal life". By contrast, prodigality is the propensity to consume goods and unproductive services and dissipates wealth. Smith maintained that frugality prevails over prodigality, but he did not explain why this occurs. He simply stated that "frugality and good conduct [...] is upon most occasions, *it appears from experience*, sufficient to compensate, not only the private prodigality and misconduct of individuals, but the publick extravagance of government" (WN II.iii.31: 342–343, emphasis added). Although organism is not mentioned, the logic whereby an empirical observation (the prevalence of frugality over prodigality) is transformed into a sort of economic law follows the same logic as the organic metaphor.

Frugality, parsimony and prodigality were terms that belonged to the seventeenth century's economic vocabulary and had moral connotations. Smith employed these concepts—though only in this part of the *Wealth of Nations*—to exemplify the notion of capital: "Capitals are increased by parsimony, and diminished by prodigality and misconduct" (WN II.iii.14: 337). He also specified that "Parsimony, and not industry, is the immediate cause of the increase of capital. Industry, indeed, provides the subject which parsimony accumulates" (WN II.iii.16: 337). Although accumulated savings may not necessarily be reinvested, Smith focused on the alternative circumstance that parsimony creates the "fund" set aside for investment in productive labor (WN II.iii.17: 337). Here too, the conclusions of the organic metaphor are replicated. But the organic metaphor, in principle, added something more to the empirical observation that productive investments prevail over unproductive consumption. It provided a framework for a line of thought, not completely defined in analytical terms, which legitimized the idea that that prevalence was a sort of natural tendency.

The relationship between frugality and prodigality provided an elementary idea of social and economic order which recalls Mandeville's conception of balance between private vices and public virtues. But, while Mandeville maintained that "avarice" and "prodigality" are two connected vices which mutually support each other in equilibrium, Smith argued that "parsimony" is a more powerful inclination than prodigality (see Sect. 3.2). Like Hume, who reacted to Mandeville's conceptual metaphor of the balance, and maintained that it was preferable to favor passions that are useful to the public welfare, Smith de facto showed the inadequacy of Mandeville's view.[9] There is no balance between parsimony and prodigality: the former prevails over the other, but this disequilibrium allows social welfare to increase.

Smith also resorted to organic metaphor in his polemic against the Physiocratic system:

> Some speculative physicians seem to have imagined that the health of the human body could be preserved only by a certain precise regimen of diet and exercise, of which every, the smallest, violation necessarily occasioned some degree of disease or disorder proportioned to the degree of the violation. Experience, however, would seem to show that the human body frequently preserves, to all appearance at least, the most perfect state of health under a vast variety of different regimens; even under some which are generally believed to be very far from being perfectly wholesome. But the healthful state of the human body, it would seem, contains in itself some unknown principle of preservation, capable either of preventing or of correcting, in many respects, the bad effects even of a very faulty regimen. Mr. Quesnai, who was himself a physician, and a very speculative physician, seems to have entertained a notion of the same kind concerning the political body, and to have imagined that it would thrive and prosper only under a certain precise regimen, the exact regimen of perfect liberty and perfect justice. He seems not to have considered that in the political body, the natural effort which

[9] On Smith's and Mandeville's alternative views on frugality, see Hurtado Prieto (2004: 15–16).

> every man is continually making to better his own condition, is a principle of preservation capable of preventing and correcting, in many respects, the bad effects of a political œconomy, in some degree, both partial and oppressive. Such a political œconomy, though it no doubt retards more or less, is not always capable of stopping altogether the natural progress of a nation towards wealth and prosperity, and still less of making it go backwards. If a nation could not prosper without the enjoyment of perfect liberty and perfect justice, there is not in the world a nation which could ever have prospered. In the political body, however, the wisdom of nature has fortunately made ample provision for remedying many of the bad effects of the folly and injustice of man; in the same manner as it has done in the natural body, for remedying those of his sloth and intemperance. (WN IV.ix.28: 673–674)

"Self-preservation, and the propagation of the species", Smith maintained in the TMS, "are the great ends which Nature seems to have proposed in the formation of all animals", which are achieved through "original and immediate instincts" such as "Hunger, thirst, the passion which unites the two sexes, the love of pleasure, and the dread of pain" (TMS II.i.5.9: 77–78). In the WN, the "unknown principle of preservation", which explains the body's tendency to improve in spite of illness and of the consequences of an unhealthy "regimen", was used as metaphorical argument to reject Quesnay's doctrine. In a sense, Smith viewed the physiocratic approach as lying too close to mechanistic logic, since it conceived of only one state of equilibrium (coincidental with the optimal state, and similar in this respect to that of the machine) whose absence would lead to a state of disorder.

Smith's notion of self-interest, as a motive that guides individual behavior and promotes the increase of public welfare, can also be reconsidered in the light of the organic metaphor. In fact, what it shows is that homeostatic principles which preserve and improve the body's conditions are not an expression of individual intentionality, but precede and orient individuals' conscious and self-interested choices. There is an impersonal logic of the living—a general "principle of animal life"—which shapes individual behaviors and explains how natural and political bodies survive and develop.

Lastly, Smith's analysis of historical and social progress developed the idea that political bodies survive and gradually improve even during illness. The opinion that the political body also prospers outside the "regimen of perfect liberty" was put forward in Book III of the WN. Here, by mixing historical and conjectural analyses, Smith argued that, although some inefficient equilibria had characterized the history of Europe since the fall of the Roman Empire, the tendency of societies, as political bodies, to improve prevailed. In his view, European history was marked by the reversal of the optimal conditions for economic growth which favored the city over the countryside (WN III.i.8: 380). This process did not cause Western societies to decline; rather, it meant that the advances of market societies were "slow and uncertain" compared to the natural course of things. In particular, in pre-modern economies, guild regulations, applied in towns but not in the countryside, modified normal conditions of competition among capitals and among laborers, and increased the price of goods produced in towns, giving rise to an unequal exchange between agricultural and artisanal products. Excessive accumulation of capital in urban activities brought about a decrease in profitability, and prompted those funds to flow back into countryside, making its prosperity possible and restoring equilibrium between the agricultural and industrial sectors (see Sect. 5.3).

Like a body that survives in many "regimens of diet", modern European society was a political body that survived and gradually developed within nonoptimal regimens (the "unnatural and retrograde order"), thanks to its self-equilibrating properties. Although the adjustment mechanism determining the allocation of capital and work was less efficient than it would be if it operated in conditions of the "natural equality" of exchange, the progress of society was not stopped. Similar process also occurs, Smith points out, when the "principle of preservation" corrects a "partial and oppressive" "political œconomy", with the result that the latter can retard, but not stop, "the natural progress of a nation towards wealth and prosperity" (WN IV.ix.28: 674).

The organic metaphor was also used to clarify some unusual functions of economic policy. Smith examined the case of an excessive flow of capital toward monopolistic commerce with British colonies. Instead of being distributed regularly among the various branches of foreign commerce, this capital was concentrated in one "great channel", upsetting the "natural balance" and thus rendering "the whole state of her body politick less healthful". Therefore,

> In her present condition, Great Britain resembles one of those unwholesome bodies in which some of the vital parts are overgrown, and which, upon that account, are liable to many dangerous disorders scarce incident to

> those in which all the parts are more properly proportioned. A small stop in that great blood-vessel, which has been artificially swelled beyond its natural dimensions, and through which an unnatural proportion of the industry and commerce of the country has been forced to circulate, is very likely to bring on the most dangerous disorders upon the whole body politick. (WN IV.vii.c.43: 604–605)

The body may be subject to "dangerous disorders" which may not be resolved by the self-regenerating properties of "animal life", as is clarified by a metaphor illustrating the consequence of the violent interruption of trade with colonies:

> The blood, of which the circulation is stopt in some of the smaller vessels, easily disgorges itself into the greater, without occasioning any dangerous disorder; but, when it is stopt in any of the greater vessels, convulsions, apoplexy, or death, are the immediate and unavoidable consequences. (WN IV.vii.c.43: 604–605)

Monopolistic trade causes the disease, but this does not prevent the body from surviving, albeit in suboptimal conditions. By contrast, irreparable damage (i.e., "convulsions, apoplexy or death") can be provoked by its sudden interruption. In fact, monopolistic foreign trade, by inefficiently diverting large amounts of capital, engenders "disorders which it is often difficult to remedy, without occasioning, for a time at least, still greater disorders" (WN IV.vii.c.44: 606).

The solution that Smith suggests is that order be restored through the gradual intervention of the legislator to introduce freedom in that kind of trade.

> In what manner [...] the colony trade ought gradually to be opened; what are the restraints which ought first, and what are those which ought last to be taken away; or in what manner the natural system of perfect liberty and justice ought gradually to be restored, we must leave to the wisdom of future statesmen and legislators to determine. (WN IV.vii.c.44: 606)

While in the medical metaphor—used against Quesnay—the self-regenerating properties of bodies correct the "bad effects of a political œconomy", the metaphor of the circulation of blood in monopolistic trade points out that in some circumstances a wise statesman-physician should intervene to restore the health of the "body politick", because natural, homeostatic mechanisms are insufficient. There is no contradiction between the two metaphors, because the view of social order as an outcome of a life cycle considers that the "unknown principle of preservation" is not always sufficient to preserve the body. In both metaphors, the political authority behaves like a physician who, in one case, provides "absurd prescriptions" and in the other formulates correct strategies to restore order and health inasmuch as is possible. The conclusion is that if the body's capacities are not self-sufficient, then they should be helped and governed.

The metaphor of bodily death was certainly not new and was often used as a mere commonplace. Hume, for example, maintained that "every government must come to a period, and that death is unavoidable to the political as well as to the animal body" (Hume, 1985a [1777]: 51). However, he also was aware of the danger of applying bodily metaphors to the history of societies to deal with specific problems like, for example, those concerning the demographic comparison between populations in ancient and modern nations:

> there is no universal difference discernible in the human species; and though it were allowed, that the universe, like an animal body, had a natural progress from infancy to old age; yet as it must still be uncertain, whether, at present, it be advancing to its point of perfection, or declining from it, we cannot thence presuppose any decay in human nature. To prove, therefore, or account for that superior populousness of antiquity, which is commonly supposed, by the imaginary youth or vigour of the world, will scarcely be admitted by any just reasoner. (Hume, 1985b [1777]): 378)

The idea of attributing a life cycle to political and economic institutions caused serious perplexities. Local, although important, crises could be interpreted as a precondition for a new, alternative order, rather than as potential causes of the political body's death. Josiah Tucker, an interlocutor of Hume and Lord Kames, criticized the metaphorical overlap of organic and social domains, and considered it unacceptable that "Ideas and Terms [...] borrowed from the State of natural Bodies" be "metaphorically transferred to political Constitutions":

> It is taken for granted, that as all Animals, by having the Seeds of Decay within themselves, must die sooner or later, therefore political or commercial Institutions are subject to the like Fate, and on the same Principles. Now this remains to be proved; for the Parallel doth not hold in all Respects; and

> tho' it be true that the Body Politic *may* come to an End, as well as the Body Natural, there is no physical Necessity that it *must*. A Set of Rules and Regulations may be formed for the distributing Property, the securing and diffusing Industry, the preventing the present shocking Vices of Electioneering, and in general, for the correcting most, if not all of those Evils, which great Riches, Excess of Liberty, and Length of Time, are too apt to introduce. [...]. In one Word, the Constitution of the Body Natural is so framed, that after a certain length of Time, no Remedy in Nature can restore it to its pristine Health and Vigour; for at last old Age will necessarily destroy it, if nothing else shall put a Period to it sooner:—But the Diseases of the Body Politic are not *absolutely incurable;* because Care and Caution, and proper Remedies, judiciously and honestly applied, will produce those Effects in one Case, which it would be impossible for them to produce in the other. (Tucker, 1774: 55–56, emphasis in original)

While on the one hand, the metaphor of the life cycles of "Body Natural" could no longer be used as a model, on the other, a medical metaphor was employed to replace it. One feature of the organic metaphor could be maintained. In fact, if "Diseases of the Body Politic" are curable, then—as Tucker remarked—it makes sense to compare, as Smith did, physician and statesman, as external agents who restore the self-equilibrating properties of bodies. Such an intervention must be prudent and limited in time.

> The physician to the body politic may learn to imitate the conduct of the physician to the body natural, in removing those disorders which a bad habit, or a wrong treatment hath brought upon the constitution; and then to leave the rest to nature, who best can do her own work. For after the constitution is restored to the use and exercise of its proper faculties and natural powers, it would be wrong to multiply laws relating to commerce as it would be to be forever prescribing physic. (Tucker, *Elements of Commerce* (1755), quoted in Carey, 2017: 92)

Adam Ferguson also pointed out the danger of extending the life cycle model to the history of human societies:

> The images of youth, and of old age, are applied to nations; and communities, like single men, are supposed to have a period of life, and a length of thread [...]. The image indeed is apposite, and the history of mankind renders the application familiar. But it must be obvious, that the case of nations, and that of individuals, are very different. The human frame has a general course; it has, in every individual, a frail contexture, and limited duration; it

> is worn by exercise, and exhausted by a repetition of its functions: But in a society, whose constituent members are renewed in every generation, where the race seems to enjoy perpetuated youth, and accumulating advantages, we cannot, by any parity of reason, expect to find imbecilities connected with mere age and length of days. (Ferguson, 1995 [1767]: 198–199)

Ferguson seemed aware of the role of metaphors in constructing theories: adopting a metaphorical model means orienting inquiries, but if the analogy is wrong, the inferences which follow from it are also wrong. Tucker and Ferguson considered the image of individual body to be an erroneous model for interpreting processes of social and institutional change. And both shared the opinion that analysis of progress in society was incompatible with the life cycle metaphor of youth, maturity and old age. This kind of problem, although in some way present, remained unresolved in Smith, and perhaps this induced him to explore features of economic order with other metaphors. His organic metaphor described some concepts, like the body's tendency to prosper limitedly in spite of erroneous medical prescriptions, that were similar to those that he expressed in his interpretation of European society's slow and continuous progress over centuries. However, a political body that improves indefinitely could not be equated with any natural body. In this respect, then, Smith's opinion led to conclusions that were logically not so dissimilar from Tucker's and Ferguson's.

Despite these limits, organic metaphors had important, theoretical merits which can be appreciated if one considers the history of science from a methodological perspective. They bring to the fore features that in mechanistic models are not salient, in that—as Nicholson remarks—they point out that (1) organisms are "intrinsically purposive" whereas machines are "extrinsically purposive"; (2) organisms are self-organizing, self-regenerating, self-maintaining and self-producing, while machines are organized, assembled, maintained and repaired by external agents; (3) while the parts of a machine "retain their own distinctive properties regardless of whether or not they are integrated in the whole", the "parts in an organism are neither causally independent of, nor temporally antecedent to, the whole they constitute. Instead, they exist in a relation of collective interdependence" (Nicholson, 2014: 163). In his work, Smith dealt to some extent with the first two features, although he did not define them in theoretical terms.

Although the metaphor of the organism highlighted these properties, as we have seen, it was unable to account for how self-regulation could also result in the body's continuous improvement. The "principles of self-preservation" explained how the organism maintained balance in health, but not how the progress of society engendered a higher order equilibrium.

Moreover, the organic metaphor had further limits. The image of the body referred back to unchangeable structures and functions of organs, and this made organisms similar to machines. When "the mechanism of a plant, or animal body" is taken into consideration, Smith argued, blood circulation and digestion of food can be compared to "wheels of the watch [which] are all admirably adjusted to the end for which it was made, the pointing of the hour" (TMS II.ii.3.5: 87). While "wheels" and organs have a pre-established function, in commercial societies the functions performed by individuals and organizations are not fixed once and for all. The theoretical challenge was not to start from the body as a predefined whole (because in some respects this would have meant replicating the old image of the harmonious, well organized, static machine) but to explain order as a result of individuals' autonomous behavior. These kinds of problem were at the basis of the invisible hand, a metaphor that made it possible to interpret the order of the market as a result of a process, and not as a predetermined equilibrium from which analysis can begin.

Lastly, the difficulty of representing the dynamics of the social order can be deduced by analyzing another famous metaphor, that of society as a chessboard. This image is associated with that of the "man of system", who can operate in some respects like the doctor-statesman, both by contrasting and by favoring the order of society. The first circumstance is described in a famous passage:

> He seems to imagine that he can arrange the different members of a great society with as much ease as the hand arranges the different pieces upon a chess-board. He does not consider that the pieces upon the chess-board have no other principle of motion besides that which the hand impresses upon them; but that, in the great chess-board of human society, every single piece has a principle of motion of its own, altogether different from that which the legislature might chuse to impress upon it. (TMS VI.ii.2.17: 234)

The second circumstance is clarified a few words later. Suppressing the autonomous "principle of motion" of individuals engenders disorders. However, "If those two principles [the principle of motion impressed by the man of system, and the autonomous principle of motion of individuals] coincide and act in the same direction, the game of human society will go on easily and harmoniously, and is very likely to be happy and successful" (TMS VI.ii.2.17: 234). The man of system, therefore, can act either in accordance with individuals' behaviors, by promoting a harmonious social order, or in contrast with them.

The society-chessboard metaphor shows how difficult it is to find a model that can conceptualize order as a result of autonomous individual movements. The image of the "human society" as a "great chess-board", where "every single piece has a principle of motion of its own", is contradictory in some respects. In a game of chess, "single pieces" are always arranged by the "hand" of the player. It is unclear why this image, used metaphorically, should represent the arbitrary behavior of the man of system, given that in a game of chess pieces can never choose how to move. Moreover, even if the chess pieces could move of their own accord, their movements would be governed by precise rules. In short, the metaphor of the chessboard is insufficiently consistent in representing the idea that individuals' actions can differ from pre-established behavioral patterns. Although machines, organisms and chessboards were metaphors which helped to conceptualize order, it was the invisible hand which made it possible to think of order as a decentralized system in which individuals behave according to their plans and projects.

References

Ahmad, S. (1990). Adam Smith's Four Invisible Hands. *History of Political Economy, 22*(1), 137–144.

Bacon, F. (1625). *The Essays or Counsels, Civil and Moral.* Printed by Iohn Haviland.

Besomi, D. (2011). Crises as a Disease of the Body Politick. A Metaphor in the History of Nineteenth-century Economics. *Journal of the History of Economic Thought, 33*(1), 67–118.

Bourke, J. (2012). Pain, Sympathy and the Medical Encounter Between the Mid Eighteenth and the Mid Twentieth Centuries. *Historical Research, 85*(229), 430–452.

Caffentzis, G. C. (2003). Medical Metaphors and Monetary Strategies in the Political Economy of Locke and Berkeley. *History of Political Economy, 35*(Annual Supplement), 204–233.

Campbell, T. D. (1971). *Adam Smith's Science of Morals.* Allen & Unwin.

Carey, T. V. (2017). Adam Smith's Invisible Hand: A Brief History. In F. Forman (Ed.), *The Adam Smith Review* (Vol. 9, pp. 88–104).

Chamberlayne, E. (1683). *The Third Part of the Present State of England*. Printed for William Whitwood.

Christensen, P. P. (1989). Hobbes and the Physiological Origins of Economic Science. *History of Political Economy, 21*(44), 689–709.

Christensen, P. P. (1994). Fire, Motion, and Productivity: The Proto-Energetics of Nature and Economy in François Quesnay. In P. Mirowski (Ed.), *Natural Images in Economic Thought* (pp. 249–288). Cambridge University Press.

Clément, A. (2003). The Influence of Medicine on Political Economy in the Seventeenth Century. *History of Economics Review, 38*(1), 1–22.

Coleman, W. O. (2001). The Significance of John Locke's Medical Studies for the History of Economic Thought. In P. Groenewegen (Ed.), *Physicians and Political Economy. Six Studies of the Work of Doctor-Economists* (pp. 36–55). Routledge. https://play.google.com/books/reader?id=At15ArwgfQUC&hl=it&pg=GBS.PT71.w.6.8.0

Cook, H. J. (1999). Bernard Mandeville and the Therapy of "the clever politician". *Journal of the History of Ideas, 60*(1), 101–124.

Davenant, C. (1771 [1698]). Discourses on the Public Revenues, and on the Trade of England, Part II. In *The Political and Commercial Works* (Vol. I). Printed for R. Horsfield.

Davidko, N. (2013). Metaphoricity in the History of Economic Thought (on the Basis of the 17th Century Economic Discourse). *Kalbų Studijos/Studies About Languages, 22*, 86–97.

De Marchi, N. (2001). Exposure to Strangers and Superfluities: Mandeville's Regimen for Great Wealth and Foreign Treasure. In P. Groenewegen (Ed.), *Physicians and Political Economy. Six Studies of the Work of Doctor-Economists* (pp. 73–95). Routledge. https://play.google.com/books/reader?id=At15ArwgfQUC&hl=it&pg=GBS.PT71.w.6.8.0

Deleule, D. (1979). *Hume et la naissance du libéralisme économique*. Aubier Montaigne.

Desmedt, L. (2005). Money in the "Body Politick": The Analysis of Trade and Circulation in the Writings of Seventeenth-Century Political Arithmeticians. *History of Political Economy, 37*(1), 79–101.

Eriksen, C. B. (2017). Circulation of Blood and Money in Leviathan – Hobbes on the Economy of the Body. In J. Bek-Thomsen et al. (Eds.), *History of Economic Rationalities: Economic Reasoning as Knowledge and Practice Authority*. Springer.

Ferguson, A. (1995 [1767]). *An Essay on the History of Civil Society*, F. Oz-Salzberger (Ed.). Cambridge University Press.

Finkelstein, A. (2000). *Harmony and the Balance: An Intellectual History of Seventeenth-Century English Economic Thought*. The University of Michigan Press.

Fiori, S. (2019). Nature and Labour: Theoretical Approaches and Metaphors of Wealth Before Adam Smith. *The European Journal of the History of Economic Thought, 26*(6), 1153–1186.

Foley, V. (1973). An Origin of the Tableau Economique. *History of Political Economy, 5*(1), 121–150.

Foley, V. (1976). *The Social Physics of Adam Smith.* Purdue University Press.

Forget, E. L. (2003). Evocations of Sympathy: Sympathetic Imagery in Eighteenth-Century Social Theory and Physiology. *History of Political Economy*", Annual Supplement, *35*, 282–308.

Groenewegen, P. (2001). From Prominent Physician to Major Economist: Some Reflections on Quesnay's Switch to Economics in the 1750s. In P. Groenewegen (Ed.), *Physicians and Political Economy. Six Studies of the Work of Doctor-Economists* (pp. 96–116). Routledge. https://play.google.com/books/reader?id=At15ArwgfQUC&hl=it&pg=GBS.PT71.w.6.8.0

Harris, J. G. (1999). 'The Canker of England's Commonwealth': Gerard de Malynes and the Origins of Economic Pathology. *Textual Practice, 13*(2), 311–327.

Hobbes, T. (1996 [1651]). *Leviathan*, J. C. A. Gaskin (Ed.). Oxford University Press.

Hume, D. (1985a [1777]). *Whether the British Government Inclines More to Absolute Monarchy, or to Republic.* In E. F. Miller (Ed.), *Essays Moral, Political, and Literary* (pp. 47–53). Liberty Fund.

Hume, D. (1985b [1777]). Of the Populousness of Ancient Nations. In E. F. Miller (Ed.), *Essays Moral, Political, and Literary* (pp. 377–464). Liberty Fund.

Hundert, E. J. (1994). *The Enlightenment's Fable: Bernard Mandeville and the Discovery of Society.* Cambridge University Press.

Hurtado Prieto, J. (2004). Bernard Mandeville's Heir: Adam Smith or Jean Jacques Rousseau on the Possibility of Economic Analysis. *The European Journal of the History of Economic Thought, 11*(1), 1–31.

Jonsson, F. A. (2010). Rival Ecologies of Global Commerce: Adam Smith and the Natural Historians. *American Historical Review, 115*(5), 1342–1363.

Khalil, E. L. (2000). Beyond Natural Selection and Divine Intervention: The Lamarckian Implication of Adam Smith's Invisible Hand. *Journal of Evolutionary Economics, 10*, 373–393.

Lakoff, G. & Johnson, M. (1980). *Metaphors we live by.* The University of Chicago Press.

Lakoff, G. & Johnson, M. (1999). *The Philosophy in the Flesh. The Embodied Mind and Its Challenge to Western Thought.* Basic Books.

Lindgren, R. J. (1973). *The Social Philosophy of Adam Smith.* Martinus Nijhoff.

Magner, L. N. (2002). *A History of the Life Sciences.* Marcel Dekker.

Malynes, G. (1622). *The Maintenance of Free Trade [...]*. Printed by *I. L.* for *William Sheffard*; available at: https://quod.lib.umich.edu/e/eebo/A06789.0001.001?rgn=main;view=fulltext. Accessed 14 June 2020.

Mandeville, B. (1924a [1723]). A Search into the Nature of Society. In F. B. Kaye (Ed.), *The Fable of the Bees: Or, Private Vices, Publick Benefits* (Vol. 1). Clarendon Press.

Mandeville, B. (1924b [1723]). An Essay on Charity, and Charity-Schools. In F. B. Kaye (Ed.), *The Fable of the Bees: Or, Private Vices, Publick Benefits* (Vol. 2). Clarendon Press.

Mandeville, B. (1924c [1724]). The Fable of the Bees, or Private Vices, Publick Benefits. In F. B. Kaye (Ed.), *The Fable of the Bees: Or, Private Vices, Publick Benefits* (Vol. 1). Clarendon Press.

Mun, T. (1664). England's Treasure by Forraign Trade or the Ballance of Our Forraign Trade Is the Rule of Our Treasure. In J. R. McCulloch (Ed.) (1856), *A Select Collection of Early English Tracts on Commerce from the Originals of Mun, Roberts, North, and Others* (pp. 115–209). Printed for the Political Economy Club.

Nicholson, D. J. (2014). The Machine Conception of the Organism in Development and Evolution: A Critical Analysis. *Studies in History and Philosophy of Biological and Biomedical Sciences, 48*, 162–174.

Packham, C. (2012). *Eighteenth-Century Vitalism. Bodies, Culture, Politics.* Palgrave Macmillan.

Petty, W. (1963a [1662]). Treatise of Taxes and Contributions. In C. H. Hull (Ed.), *The Economic Writings of Sir William Petty* (Vol. 1). Augustus M. Kelley.

Petty, W. (1963b [1691]). The Political Anatomy of Ireland. In C. H. Hull (Ed.), *The Economic Writings of Sir William Petty* (Vol. 1). Augustus M. Kelley.

Rosenberg, N. (1963). Mandeville and Laissez-Faire. *Journal of the History of Ideas, 24*(2), 183–196.

Sivado, A. (2017). Resurrecting the Body Politic – Physiology's Influence on Sir William Petty's Political Arithmetick. *Early Science and Medicine, 22*, 157–182.

Tucker, J. (1774). *Four Tracts, on Political and Commercial Subjects* (2nd ed.). Printed by R. Raikes.

Turner, B. P. (2016). Mandeville Against Luxury. *Political Theory, 44*(1), 26–52.

CHAPTER 5

The Invisible Hand

Abstract Economists, philosophers and historians of economic thought have suggested many alternative interpretations of Smith's invisible hand.

The idea put forward in this chapter is that the invisible hand was a tool which helped to formulate in nondefinitional terms the conception that the order of society is (1) endogenous, beneficial, and exhibits self-organizing properties, (2) the result of movements and choices of independent individuals.

Keywords Providence • Efficient causes • Invisible hand • Unintended results • Economic system

Economists, philosophers, social scientists and historians of economic thought have suggested many alternative interpretations of Smith's invisible hand over time. Some scholars have argued that it reflects the intervention of Providence; some economists have pointed out that it intuitively anticipates the notion of economic equilibrium or, alternatively, the notion of spontaneous order. Other interpreters maintained that Smith's invisible hand was a modest product of a large movement of ideas, developed

S. Fiori, *Machines, Bodies and Invisible Hands*,
https://doi.org/10.1007/978-3-030-85206-1_5

around the 1720s, in which the concept of self-organization gradually took shape (Sheehan & Wahrman, 2015). Still others considered this metaphor as a mere rhetorical device, theoretically irrelevant, others as an important component of Smith's epistemological view, and part of them noted that it was used to investigate efficient causes of social and economic phenomena by relegating final causes to the background.

The idea put forward in this chapter is that the invisible hand was a tool which helped to formulate in nondefinitional terms the conception that the order of society is (1) endogenous, beneficial, and exhibits self-organizing properties,[1] (2) the result of movements and choices of independent individuals (who are neither cog-wheels nor organs whose functions are predetermined). In this perspective, although this metaphor helped to conceptualize order, it was not in the strict sense clearly embodied in a theoretical view.[2] Moreover, it was neither an imperfect anticipation of the theory of general equilibrium nor a periphrasis for "Providence". Especially in the TMS, Smith refers to the role of Providence in promoting harmony in the world, but this pre-analytical assumption only limitedly influenced his search for causal explanations, which was basically used to identify efficient causes of social and economic phenomena.

5.1 Interpretations of the Invisible Hand

Many scholars have pointed out that the invisible hand should be interpreted in relation to Smith's theological convictions. Macfie maintained that this metaphor in the TMS and the WN should be considered as a description "of how the natural order of 'providence' animates and directs the orderly development" of societies and the physical universe (Macfie, 1971: 596; cf. 1967: 111), although this notion, unlike Smith's "inductive theory", cannot be considered as an "original contribution" (Macfie, 1967: 125). Viner (1972) pointed out that Smith's theory is not intelligible if his providential view is disregarded. This approach has been

[1] As a search for a provisional causal explanation of order, the invisible hand was not a "theory of self-regulating markets". Rather, it "contributed two key ideas in social thought, namely the unintended-results principle and the doctrine of spontaneous emergence of order" (Cremaschi, 2017: 43; see also Kennedy, 2008: 210).

[2] By contrast, Pack (1995: 290) maintains that it was "a deliberate epistemological construct".

pursued by scholars such as D. A. Martin, C. M. A. Clark, J. Evensky, A. Denis, L. Hill and others, who in varying degrees supported the thesis of a Smithian theological approach and viewed the invisible hand as an expression of God's benevolent work. In particular, Oslington maintained that the invisible hand should be interpreted in light of "British natural theological accounts of divine action and providence, mediated through Smith's Scottish Calvinist environment". From this perspective, the famous metaphor would represent "special providence" (a term which denotes that God's interventions can be exceptional, and directed to individuals), "operating against, although ultimately supporting, general providence in the economic realm" (Oslington, 2011: 63 and 66). The arguments which support this view, however, seem more hypothetical than based on textual evidence. For example, if we consider the invisible hand of the HA, it is not clear how irregular events that polytheistic religions ascribe to the will of Jupiter are related to special providence (ibidem: 67). Moreover, as regards the invisible hand of the TMS, Oslington himself points out that "the line between special and general providence [...] is a fine one, as it would seem that the hand acting to restrain the rich acts fairly regularly" (ibidem: 68).

While Peter Harrison also supports a providentialist interpretation of the invisible hand, he provides an alternative account to Oslington's. In the modern age, two dominant conceptions of the invisible hand were applied to the realms of history and nature. The first was related to special providence, a notion derived from the Calvinist, providentialist view of history. The second was related to general providence, a notion derived from natural philosophy and natural theology, which implied that nature was a divine artifact governed by general laws. The two traditions of thought were essentially different, although they shared the idea that beneficial outcomes were not an intentional result of agents' behavior. These differences emerge in Smith's thought, where the use of the invisible hand in the TMS and WN reflects not a special but rather a general providence. In particular, the operation of the invisible hand in the realm of moral economy was considered "as directly analogous to its regular operations in the natural world" (Harrison, 2011: 47).

Although Harrison's reconstruction is very accurate, like other interpretations which point out the role of Providence in Smith's thought, it neglects the fact that the role of the invisible hand is not reducible to Divine action, and that Smith's investigation was characterized by new ways of exploring the causes of self-regulatory processes in social systems.

Some economists have criticized the interpretation according to which Smith's ideas are a manifestation of his theological convictions. The list of economists usually accused by exponents of the "new theistic view" of having secularized the notion of invisible hand includes Lionel Robbins and Mark Blaug, who reduced the invisible hand to an expression of market competition, Galbraith, who considered the invisible hand an irrelevant metaphor, and Hayek, who interpreted this metaphor as a "proto-Darwinistic" conception that can be useful in understanding the formation of spontaneous order.

However, other scholars have also contributed to secularizing Smith's thought (see Pack, 1996). Bittermann (1940a, 1940b) was one of the first scholars to introduce the idea that Smith's work can be studied without referring to theological and teleological conceptions. In his view, "There is no direct evidence to connect [the invisible hand of the WN] with the Deity [...], since the preceding and following discussions proceed in purely economic terms" (Bittermann, 1940b: 719). Haakonssen (1981: 77) maintained that in Smith "[n]othing hinges on teleological explanations", and real explanations are basically based on efficient causes. Myers (1983: 104) was of the opinion that "Smith is more interested in the operations of parts than in ultimate purposes". Flew (1987: 200) considered it "totally wrong" to interpret the invisible hand "as an instrument of supernatural direction", while Rashid (1998: 219) observed that Smith "sympathized with Hume's virulent opposition to Christianity". Fleischacker (2004: 44, emphasis in original) maintained that Smith "*uses* the existence of a providential God as a *premise* in his social scientific arguments". The latter aimed to explore efficient causes: "The 'invisible hand' thus represents social forces, not Providential ones" (ibidem: 140). Brewer (2009: 535) also pointed out the importance of efficient causes in Smith, since phenomena can be analyzed without knowing anything about the identity of the Creator. According to Herzog (2013: 24 and 33), the idea of God's existence does not influence the search for causal mechanisms that explain the world, although the deistic conception constitutes the framework of Smith's system. And in Wight's view (2014), the invisible hand basically refers to nature's powers. Smith, like deists, believed that God was the final cause of all things, but the invisible hand represents "invisible forces", namely, instincts, passions and natural appetites.

Many scholars argued that the invisible hand is an unimportant metaphor. According to Grampp, the invisible hand of the WN is related to Smith's ideas concerning the preferability of investments in the domestic economy since, by increasing the wealth of the nation, they contribute to its defense. These arguments, however, do not rest on the invisible hand, which is a "more interesting than important" rhetorical device (Grampp, 2000: 442). Grampp took into consideration, and rejected, nine explanations of this metaphor, although he considered one of them—Persky's (1989)—more interesting than others, in that Persky linked the invisible hand to individuals' preference for employing their capital in domestic sectors as a consequence of their desire for "security" and reduced risk. According to Rothschild (2001: 117), the use of the invisible hand, in the three passages in which it appears in Smith's work, reveals an ironic attitude. In the HA, he "is amused by the polytheists who believe in the invisible hand of Jupiter", and in the TMS and the WN "he is amused by the individuals who are led by the invisible hand (the hand they cannot see, or the hand behind their backs)". Rothschild's conclusion is that "the invisible hand was an unimportant constituent of Smith's thought", used for persuasive ends, not "a discovery of inherent order" (ibidem: 136–137; see Schabas, 2005: 99).

Probably the harshest criticism of the invisible hand came from Warren Samuels (2011), who analyzed this notion both in Adam Smith's thought and more generally in economics. When considering the market, the price system and competition, one has to conclude that "[t]he literature on the invisible hand as such has arguably contributed nothing to our knowledge" (Samuels, 2011: 174). We cannot say there is a "metaphoric character of the invisible hand" (ibidem: 154), because its "very existence [...] remains a matter of assertion" (ibidem: 176). Rather, this metaphor "serves the ideological and political purpose of obfuscating the power structure of society" (ibidem: 281). As for Adam Smith himself, he "would be an important economist even without his having used the term 'invisible hand'" (ibidem: 289). Kennedy (2008: 210), too, was of the opinion that the invisible hand is an insignificant metaphor that has "no role in his theory of competitive markets". What Smith said on the market mechanism did not refer to anything invisible. The invisible hand of the WN, in fact, appears after Smith explained in nonmetaphorical language why the merchant's behavior yields certain unintended results (ibidem: 220). That image described "the merchant's invisible (to others') motivations" which leads to certain beneficial consequences (Kennedy, 2017: 94), and consequently showed that the whole (the resulting order) is the sum of its parts. In short, the invisible hand was simply a "rhetorical device" (Kennedy, 2008: 213) that neither added anything to Smith's analysis nor referred to theological or mysterious contents (Kennedy, 2017: 96). This interpretation seems to be confirmed by the fact that the invisible hand was not perceived as a meaningful concept until the 1870s. Its revitalization in the twentieth century was largely due to Samuelson. After the publication of his *Economics: An Analytical Introduction* (1948), mentions of the invisible hand began to increase, especially in the mid-1970s (Kennedy, 2014). In particular, Arrow and Hanh assigned the invisible hand a special place in the history of economic thought:[3]

> Adam Smith's "invisible hand" is a poetic expression of the most fundamental of economic balance relations, the equalization of rates of return, as enforced by the tendency of factors to move from low to high returns [...] Whatever the source of the concept, [this notion] is surely the most important intellectual contribution that economic thought has made to the general understanding of social processes. [...]
>
> Thus it can be maintained that Smith was a creator of general equilibrium theory, although the coherence and consistency of his work can be questioned. (Arrow & Hahn, 1971: 1–2)

Smith's invisible hand, as "poetic expression", was the first step in a history of economic thought that gradually homed in on the concept of general equilibrium. Smith, Ricardo and John Stuart Mill contributed to refining that concept, which was further developed by Léon Walras "who stated clearly many of the leading problems, though with unsatisfactory resolutions", while "[l]ittle progress was made for many years, except for some insights of Pareto" (Arrow, 1983: 1). Only later did economic theory definitely reveal how competitive markets perform economic equilibrium. Thus, while Smith argued that the history of scientific systems should be studied without considering its "agreement or inconsistency with truth" (HA II.12: 46), Arrow seemed to suggest that the history of economic thought could be conceived as the march toward truth expressed by the notion of general equilibrium. At first only intuited, this notion was later fully understood thanks to the refinement of analytic tools. Contrary to this positivistic view, the following pages will put forward the idea that that the "poetic expression", rather than expressing a truth in embryonic

[3] Many economists praised the invisible hand. Tobin (1992: 117), for example, maintained that the "'invisible hand' [...] is Adam Smith's most important legacy to macroeconomics, as to all economics". In particular, it is "the ultimate inspiration for the New Classical Macroeconomics and for Real Business Cycle Theory".

form, was a heuristic tool used to explore the nature of partially unknown, social events. This perspective clarifies the sense in which my analysis of the invisible hand differs from other interpretations. The analyses of those who consider the invisible hand as an expression of the work of Providence, or of those economists who have reduced the invisible hand to an anticipation of economic equilibrium, and lastly of those according to whom the invisible hand is a mere "rhetorical device" have not sufficiently explored how Smith analyzed the formation of social order by resorting to many kinds of discourse. Analysis of metaphors tries to fill this gap and complements studies of those who have considered Smith's inquiry of causal mechanisms from conceptual and historical perspectives.

5.2 The Invisible Hand in the *History of Astronomy* and in the *Theory of Moral Sentiments*

The "invisible hand" appears three times in Smith's work, respectively, in the HA, in the TMS and in the WN. Although they exhibit some significant differences, they all contributed in varying degrees to form the concept of order.

The "invisible hand of Jupiter" is mentioned in the HA to denote the anthropomorphic character of polytheism, which consists in attributing irregular phenomena of nature to the changing will of "intelligent, though invisible beings" (HA III.3: 49; see Macfie, 1971: 595–599). Polytheist religions, in particular, attributed a "designing power" to gods similar to that of human beings, which manifests itself in the alteration of nature. In this context, then, the "invisible hand" is a metaphor for intentionality which reflects the deliberate behavior of "invisible beings".[4] It also shows that the polytheistic conception is flawed, inasmuch as the divine will was not viewed as a power from which uniformity of nature derives. While in those ages of humanity, nature was conceived as "inconstant in her operations", and the idea that God "governs the whole by general laws" was absent (Ancient Physics 9: 113), later religions attributed alternative features to nature and God. God was no longer represented as an intentional power which modifies nature and became the "Author of Nature" who created a world of harmony and regularity.

[4] Smith referred to the "hand" as an image of intentionality on another occasion, when he wrote of the "man of system" who with his hand tries to arrange members of a community as if they were pieces on a chessboard (TMS ii.2.17: 234).

Unlike the invisible hand of the HA, in the WN and in the TMS, this metaphor denoted something very different: the achievement of order in the economic realm which would be unattainable by means of planning. This view, however, implied a complex relationship between the image and its content, because, Iacono (1982: 11) points out, although Smith's model seeks to explain unintentional social processes, it is unable to completely free itself from the idea of intentionality associated with the presence of a "hand" that arranges and organizes. It is the metaphor that links together what theoretical explanation fails to reconcile: the local intentionality of agents and the unintentional achievement of an order which seems to conform to a plan. Moreover, the invisible hand of the WN and the TMS does not refer to someone who uses it. It is "an" and not "the" invisible hand which guides individual behaviors (Brewer, 2009: 520).

Despite their differences, there is an element of continuity between the three "invisible hands" which can be described as an attempt by Smith to understand the nature of social order. As shown in Sect. 3.4, Smith saw both language and science as systems which help to conceptualize the world as an ordered structure. Both (temporarily) organize data, giving uniformity and coherence to external reality, which thus ceases to be viewed as a "chaos" characterized by "discordant appearances" (HA II.12: 45–46). Learning about reality means constructing its internal coherence, an operation which also occurs when the order that the mind ascribes to things does not correspond to the order of the external world. This process responds to the human need to eliminate discontinuity—which prevents the imagination from moving with ease from one object to another—and to create systems whereby phenomena can be understood. Pagan cults and philosophy both endeavor to explain nature, although they do so in alternative ways: the former by erroneously resorting to the hand of Jupiter to account for unusual natural phenomena; the latter by trying to introduce order by identifying "the invisible chains" which connect apparently unrelated events and objects (HA II.12: 45). Although the concepts of nature to which these two visions of the world refer are antithetical, both deal with exceptional events as problematic elements that make our understanding of the world precarious. Pagan religions make unusual phenomena familiar by considering them as manifestations of the will of "invisible beings", while science neutralizes the uneasiness provoked by irregular events by identifying the "connecting principles" that organize nature. In short, both kinds of approaches provide "imaginary" narratives that confer order to the world, irrespective of whether they are erroneous or provisional accounts of nature.

This approach seems to outline the role of the philosopher who investigates social facts. As philosophers and scientists explain the order of nature by resorting to the "invisible chains", so the social scientist conceptualizes order in the economic realm by resorting to an "invisible hand". In both cases, the fundamental endeavor of explanations consists in conferring a known order to a complex world.

The invisible hand appears for the second time in the TMS. While in the WN the invisible hand prompts individuals to invest their capital in those sectors whose production "may be of the greatest value" (WN IV.ii.9: 456), in the TMS it intervenes in distribution. It sheds light on a specific dimension of the economy, because landlords spend their income not to buy productive labor but in unproductive consumption. Given the limitations of their stomach, they are forced to redistribute their resources

> among those, who prepare, in the nicest manner, that little which he himself makes use of, among those who fit up the palace in which this little is to be consumed, [and] among those who provide and keep in order all the different baubles and trinkets, which are employed in the oeconomy of greatness; all of whom thus derive from his luxury and caprice, that share of the necessaries of life, which they would in vain have expected from his humanity or his justice. (TMS IV.I.10: 184)

While feudal landlords exercised their power directly on man and spent their wealth to provide subsistence to the people who worked for them, the development of foreign trade enabled them to spend their income in luxury (Brewer, 2009). Foreign commerce "gradually furnished the great proprietors with something for which they could exchange the whole surplus produce of their lands, and which they could consume themselves without sharing it either with tenants or retainers" (WN III.4.10: 418). In this circumstance, thanks to their spending power, landlords

> are led by an invisible hand to make nearly the same distribution of the necessaries of life, which would have been made, had the earth been divided into equal portions among all its inhabitants, and thus without intending it, without knowing it, advance the interest of the society, and afford means to the multiplication of the species. (TMS IV.I.10: 184–185)

In this passage of the TMS, landlords appear as the engine of a complex mechanism that produces unintended results. This process reveals a tension between satiable needs and insatiable, "vain" desires. The former are imposed by the body and are bounded, while the latter, relating to landlords' "natural selfishness and rapacity", seem "to have no limit" (WN I.xi.c.7: 181).

However, landlords are only one part of society. It is noteworthy that the scenario in which the invisible hand of the WN appears is broader than that in the TMS, and the behaviors and attitudes of different social groups are examined more accurately in the WN. Unlike the corresponding metaphor in the TMS, the WN's invisible hand generalizes the mechanism of unintentional formation of order by considering the totality of individuals, and not only a social group. However, in the commercial society, great proprietors are members of a social group which is at the margin of the market processes. They tried "[t]o gratify the most childish vanity" (WN III.iv.17: 42), and "bartered their whole power and authority" for "a pair of diamond buckles" (WN III.iv.10: 418–419). By way of contrast, the "merchants and artificers" were "much less ridiculous" and conformed their behavior to their real interest (WN III.iv.17: 422). In commercial society, where "every man thus lives by exchanging, or becomes in some measure a merchant" (WN I.iv.1: 37), it is this kind of individual who characterizes the new phase of civilization.

5.3 Market Society and Unintended Order

Chapter 4 discussed how the organic metaphor represented the order of natural and political bodies as a result of opposing forces which act with different intensity. In particular, this metaphor suggested that forces which improve the body's health would prevail over forces moving in the opposite direction. Because of the latter, the body's tendency to improve its condition is slow, but not inhibited, although the logic of the metaphoric discourse implied that the death of the body was a possible outcome. The organic metaphor, in addition, introduced the rudimentary idea that bodies, given their "principles of preservation", were self-regulating systems.

In other circumstances, by mixing different types of reasoning, Smith developed the idea that order is the result of opposing forces in which self-correcting processes prevail. Rather than using the old metaphor of the balance, which was unable to illustrate the notion of self-organization, he adopted the gravitation metaphor. This image emphasized that self-equilibrating processes are at work, and that market prices tend to converge with natural prices, despite the presence of opposing forces which prevent the two kinds of price from coinciding (WN I.vii) (see Sect. 3.5).

Smith's analysis of processes which lead to the natural order also assumed that opposing forces and self-correcting processes are at work. As will be shown later, Smith identified a number of circumstances that prevent natural order from being achieved: not only the behavior of individuals or social groups that contribute to inefficiently diverting the order of society but also institutions inherited from the past that survive despite the fact that the reasons that legitimized their existence have ceased to be. Certain economic policies also contribute to inverting the "natural progress of things". All this made explaining Western societies' tendency to move toward order extremely complex. Merchants' inclination to follow their self-interest—which "is always in some respects different from, and even opposite to, that of the publick" (WNI.xi.p.10: 267)—and to obtain higher profits, thanks to monopolistic policies that distort the price mechanism, indicated a structural difficulty in achieving a state of perfect liberty. The fact that the inverted course of European societies lasted for centuries pointed to a similar difficulty.

The invisible hand emerged against this backdrop. It was part of the belief that the progress of societies takes shape despite forces which oppose it. Smith developed this perspective in two steps: (1) he examined the process that over time led to the formation of the market society, and (2) he analyzed how the market works in this kind of society, as the market is a mechanism that makes the economic order possible. The two temporal dimensions (time of the market and historical time) are mutually integrated, since the order of the market is the final part of a historical process. On the one hand, analysis of the historical process showed that the tendency toward the natural order implied the existence of self-corrective forces which worked over time and were able to correct the "unnatural and retrograde order" prevalent in pre-modern European society. On the other, analysis of the market society, as the last step in the civilization process, showed that the market was an institution capable of perpetuating itself over time, precisely because it incorporated self-correcting properties. In short, the market was conceived both as an outcome of a historical process and as a mechanism that, unlike other forms of production and exchange, directly reinforces the ability to achieve the natural order. The metaphor of the invisible hand presupposed all this and synthesized beliefs and theoretical convictions that are difficult to summarize exclusively in analytical terms.

In order to understand why Western society's progress was an unintended outcome which led to the market society, it is necessary to summarize the arguments that Smith developed in Book III of the WN, where he analyzed the history of Europe from the decline of the Roman Empire to the modern age. This history is described as a non-linear process which is not consistent with the "natural course of things". In fact, the natural course is such that "the greater part of the capital of every growing society is, first, directed to agriculture, afterwards to manufactures, and last of all to foreign commerce" (WN III.i.8: 380), and, second, that the growth of towns is made possible by the development of the country. By contrast, in European societies after the fall of the Roman Empire, the development of agriculture was not incentivized because land was used not as a productive resource, but as a means whereby a "great landlord", a "sort of petty prince", provided protection to his "tenants" (WN III.ii.3: 383). While the rural economy during the Middle Age stagnated, towns developed and increased the demand for "conveniencies and elegancies of life". Foreign trade developed in an anomalous way, inverting the "natural order of things", in which this kind of commerce would have been the last sector to increase after agriculture and manufacture, and in consequence of their exchange relations (e.g., when the domestic market was unable to absorb surplus goods). Moreover, it was not the country that favored the development of towns; on the contrary, towns were the cause of the development of the country because (a) they created a market for agricultural products, (b) the wealth of their inhabitants was used to buy and exploit lands, and (c) "commerce and manufactures gradually introduced order and good government" (WN III.iv.4: 412). Smith summarizes these important events as follows:

> this natural order of things [...] has, in all the modern states of Europe, been, in many respects, entirely inverted. The foreign commerce of some of their cities has introduced all their finer manufactures, or such as were fit for distant sale; and manufactures and foreign commerce together, have given birth to the principal improvements of agriculture. (WN III.i.9: 380)

This anomalous "course of things" lasted for many centuries. Many distortions persisted, with the consequence that the natural order was never perfectly established.

Smith explained this process by focusing on particular types of institution in the countryside during the feudal age, which opposed the general interest, and consequently "disturbed the natural course of things" (WN III.i.4: 378). They were the "law of primogeniture" and "entails", and their role consisted in maintaining land (and the power of landlords) undivided. These institutions made it possible to use land as a "means of power and protection" for people who worked for the landlord, but prevented it from being exploited as a productive resource (WN III.ii.3: 383). Initially, when entails performed the function of giving protection to individuals, they were not "unreasonable"; but they subsequently became "completely absurd" when this function came to be exerted by law. These institutions, in fact, "frequently continue in force long after the circumstances, which first gave occasion to them, and which could alone render them reasonable, are no more" (WN III.ii.4: 383). They exerted their influence on social relationships as inertial structures, in that they influenced social relationships on the basis of the anachronistic will of past generations. Although they had no rational foundation centuries after their creation, they were still operative in Smith's time (WN III.ii.6: 384). They were contrary to the interests of the "present generation" and took the form of privileges accorded to the nobility (WN, III.ii.6: 384).

In conclusion, Smith described these institutions as impersonal forces which counter human propensities that favor the betterment of society. These propensities are in a way reminiscent of the "principles of animal life" evoked in Book II of the WN. Although Smith did not mention these natural principles which orient human behavior in Book III, he remarked that the "order of things" is usually "promoted by the natural inclinations of man" (WN III.i.3: 377). He also pointed out that "If human institutions had never thwarted those natural inclinations, the towns could nowhere have increased beyond what the improvement and cultivation of the territory in which they were situated could support" (WN III.i.3: 377). While the persistence of certain institutions worked against the natural course of things, man's natural inclinations fostered it. The outcome of the interplay between these contrasting forces in European societies was the appearance of an imperfect market order that developed, despite its limits, because the tendency to betterment triumphed over the distorting effects produced by anachronistic institutions. Analysis of the emergence of the market society showed that self-correcting processes intervene in historical processes to restore the natural order. Self-equilibrating properties operate independently from the forms of society that follow each other over time. As the history of feudal society showed, they modify social formations despite their resistance to change.

The tendency to achieve the natural order up to the appearance of the market society is explained by the unorganized work of "natural inclinations", and not by a mechanism (as the market will be in commercial society) which organizes those inclinations. The turning point in the history of humanity was precisely the emergence of a new kind of society that, unlike pre-modern societies, was endowed with a structure—the market—which endogenously self-corrects and self-organizes because it coordinates human propensities. Inclinations, like self-preservation, operate in every time and place because they rely on human nature. With the advent of the modern commercial society they were embodied within a structure (the market), unknown to previous social formations.

Now, the tendency toward the natural order was due not simply to unintended consequences, whereby the correct relationship between towns and country is restored following unforeseeable circumstances which go beyond the nature of societies, and ultimately depends on human, natural propensities. It was also guaranteed by the fact that the market per se is a specific mechanism which endogenously engenders self-adjustment, promotes economic development and organizes human inclinations.

5.4 The Invisible Hand in the *Wealth of Nations*

At the end of Book II of the WN, Smith declared that Books III and IV aimed at showing "[w]hat circumstances in the policy of Europe have given the trades which are carried on in towns so great an advantage over that which is carried on in the country" (WN II.v.37: 374) and at illustrating why individuals preferred to invest in foreign commerce rather than in agriculture.

A unitary view informs the two books. The analysis in Book IV of distortions provoked by the mercantilist policies was part of the anomalous history of Europe examined in Book III. Both perspectives identify the causes that prevented the market from functioning efficiently. While Book III examines the anomalous role of foreign commerce, Book IV shows how mercantilist economic policy employed restraints on imports and encouragements to export in order to promote a favorable balance of trade.

The "monopoly of the home-market" imposed by mercantilist policies is censored because it diverts labor and capital from their natural destination to another, probably disadvantageous, one. Although these methods yield advantages for some sectors of economy, mercantilist policies do not increase the wealth of the whole nation. However, what really matters is that internal markets, by nature, spontaneously attract more investments than foreign markets, even without special protections. This occurs, if not prevented by particular circumstances, because investments should comply with a precise hierarchy (from agriculture to manufacture, and from manufacture to foreign trade) which also incorporates a sub-hierarchy in the commercial sector. In fact, commerce includes two sub-sectors—retail and wholesale—and, Smith remarks, wholesale trade "may be reduced to three different sorts. The home trade, the foreign trade of consumption, and the carrying trade" (WN II.v.24: 368), which, in this order, show a decreasing capacity to employ productive labor.

This is the framework in which the invisible hand of the WN appears. It illustrates why people, according to Smith's analysis of the "natural course", should prefer investments in domestic trade (and domestic industry), rather than riskier investments in other branches of commerce. In the pages in which Smith introduces the invisible hand, he puts forward two arguments that clarify why individuals behave in this way. Both arguments refer chiefly—but not exclusively—to domestic trade and domestic industry. The first emphasizes that individuals preferably invest their capital "as near home as [they] can" in order to reduce the "uneasiness" of being separated from it. This behavior denotes a search for "security" and a corresponding aversion to risk and uncertainty.[5] In fact, in domestic investments the capital owner's risk is reduced, because he knows both the "character and situation of the persons whom he trusts", and the legal system of his own country (WN IV.ii.6: 454; see Persky, 1989, Endres, 1996; Grampp, 2000: 447). Thus, "upon equal or nearly equal profits, every wholesale merchant naturally prefers the home-trade to the foreign trade of consumption, and the foreign trade of consumption to the carrying trade" (WN IV.ii.6: 454). This preference makes private and public welfare coherent, because public welfare is an unplanned consequence of the fact that investment in domestic trade sets more productive labor in

[5] Security, according to Smith, is a fundamental condition for civilization: "when law has established order and security, and subsistence ceases to be precarious, the curiosity of mankind is increased, and their fears are diminished" (HA III.3: 50). Security and liberty, in the modern age, are consequences of the "commerce and manufactures [that] gradually introduced order and good government" (WN III.iv.4: 412). Lastly, security is "the first and the principal object of prudence" (TMS VI.i.4: 213).

motion, activates "a greater quantity of domestic industry, and gives revenue and employment to a greater number of the inhabitants of the country" than do other branches of commerce (WN IV.ii.6: 454).

The argument for reducing risk, in this framework, is part of a more general discourse which holds that the "natural course" of investments implies a hierarchy based on security:

> In seeking for employment to a capital, manufactures are, upon equal or nearly equal profits, naturally preferred to foreign commerce, for the same reason that agriculture is naturally preferred to manufactures. As the capital of the landlord or farmer is *more secure* than that of the manufacturer, so the capital of the manufacturer, being at all times more within his view and command, is *more secure* than that of foreign merchant. (WN III.i.7:379, emphasis added)

In fact, the idea to which Smith refers is that "The capital, […] that is acquired to any country by commerce and manufactures, is all a very precarious and uncertain possession, till some part of it has been secured and realized in the cultivation and improvement of its lands" (WN III. iv.24: 426).

The second argument maintains that people tend to invest in those activities in which returns are the highest possible and which require the largest amount of productive labor. For this reason, they prefer to invest in "domestic industry" (WN IV.ii.6: 455). This perspective, in turn, refers back to the conviction that investments in domestic trade yield "a greater quantity of domestic industry" and that "[h]ome is […] the center […] round which the capitals of the inhabitants of every country are continually circulating, and towards which they are always tending" (WN IV.ii.6: 455).

This view, too, is related to the conception which holds that more profitable investments should follow their natural hierarchy, in consequence of their dissimilar capacity to set productive labor in motion in the three sectors of economy.

Lastly, the two arguments are encapsulated in the famous passage in which the invisible hand surfaces:

> By preferring the *support of domestick to that of foreign industry*, ["every individual"] intends only his own *security*; and by *directing that industry in such a manner as its produce may be of the greatest value*, he intends only his

own gain, and he is in this, as in many other cases, led by an invisible hand to promote an end which was no part of his intention. (WN IV.ii.9: 456; emphasis added)

In summary, in the part of Book IV where the invisible hand appears, Smith focuses on the commercial sector (and specifically on wholesale trade), and not on other sectors, to explain in nonmetaphorical terms why behaviors of individuals spontaneously tend to unintentionally engender general welfare. In particular, the arguments for security and for the highest returns are related to the concept of the "natural course" of investments. The latter identifies the structure of incentives which—if not diverted—favors the emergence of the natural order. The distortions generated by mercantilist policies are part of a more general history which shows that over centuries foreign commerce acquired an anomalous dimension because of unforeseeable circumstances. In particular, these monopolistic policies favored an excessive development of domestic industry. International trade should be guided by the principle "never to attempt to make at home what it will cost [...] more to make than to buy" (WN IV.ii.11: 456) to which every "prudent master of a family" refers. By contrast, restraints on imports and incentives to export did not follow this suggestion, since they were motivated by the "prejudices established by the commercial system", according to which "national wealth arises more immediately from exportation than from production" (WN IV.v.a.25: 517).

5.5 Conclusions

The "invisible hand" summarizes two explicit arguments and, Heath (2014: 178) points out, does not introduce new ones. But any metaphor is constructed on the basis of arguments usually provided by other discourses. Moreover, the invisible hand introduces the idea, not contained in the two explicit arguments, that agents' intentional behaviors engender unintentional, beneficial outcomes as if they were organized by a superior power.

A feature of metaphors is that they combine discourses that cannot be completely justified in analytical terms. The two explicit arguments of the invisible hand were unable to demonstrate that the reduction of "uneasiness" and investments in domestic industry suffice to yield an efficient use of capital. Similarly, Smith did not account in theoretical terms for the causes of the surprising divergence between the ideal "natural course" and the unnatural, real course of Western societies. Rather than explaining this divergence, he described it. He did not make clear why historical contingencies engendered by human behavior (those which led to the development of towns, and the stagnation of the country) acted against, and partially inhibited the force of natural human inclinations.[6] If human behavior did not follow its natural inclinations, what did it really follow? Contingencies ("different accidents") matter in the market, because they prevent market and natural prices from coinciding, but their role was not dealt with in theoretical terms. Individuals, in principle, strive to find the most productive investments for their capital by following their self-interest, but once again particular contingencies (e.g., "regulations of commerce"), by diverting these efforts, appear as forces that at the social level weaken natural propensities. Smith considered self-interest as the principle which universally guides economic behavior, but at the same time he showed that only one part of society ("merchants and master manufacturers") knows it: (see Chap. 9). Lastly, as Otto Mayr (1986, chap. 10) maintained, the invisible hand represents the concept of the market feedback mechanism. But it should be pointed out that this notion was illustrated only in descriptive terms and in relation to specific cases.

In short, Smith's discourse combined many elements: pre-analytical assumptions, theoretical reasoning, historical descriptions and metaphors. Although the invisible hand of the WN summarizes concepts formulated

[6] Smith, to conceptualize these events, referred to the ideal (natural) order and the real (historical) order. The ideal (natural) order, on the one hand, was used retrospectively as a speculative approach to interpret past events. It reflects Stewart's notion of conjectural history: "when we cannot trace the process by which an event *has been* produced, it is often of importance to be able to show how it *may have been* produced by natural causes" (Stewart, 1980 [1793], II.47: 293, emphasis in original). On the other hand, it was used to delineate the tendency of future events. The ideal (natural) order is also the benchmark for comparing deviations of real (historical) order. In this view, the North American colonies were closer to the natural order, while the European countries, in varying degrees, were more distant from that ideal model. In particular, the British institutional system, although it "retarded the natural progress [...] has maintained the progress of England towards opulence", because law protected the "effort to better [individual's] condition" and "allowed by liberty to exert" it (WN, II.iii.36: 345). In turn, Spain and Portugal, where "bad policy is not [...] counter-balanced by the general liberty and security", are farther from that benchmark (WN, IV.v.b.45: 541). However, the natural order was more than a neutral tool used methodologically to establish deviation from the natural course of things. Rather, it was conceived as a sort of attractor of real (historical) events.

in nonmetaphorical form, it also performs a function which goes beyond the passage in which it appears. It provides a view that Smith's theory was unable to develop in detail.

As an expression connected to the wider concept of "unintended outcomes", it had the merit of focusing attention on problems that the metaphors of the machine and body could not resolve. It was a metaphor that in some ways visualized the passage from pre-modern, hierarchical societies, to modern ones. Smith was aware that the power previously exerted directly on men is exerted in the market society on labor capacity. Power over labor capacity, or over commodities in which labor is crystallized, is now distributed among an indefinite number of individuals, and this makes the social sphere opaque. This "microphysics of power" unpredictably determines the configuration of society. The age that glorifies the individual as agent and decision-maker reveals that the individual's condition is determined by impersonal social forces which make up the network of economic relationships. The world is more segmented and, therefore, more invisible: the less direct control on the environment on which individuals act there is, the less we will be able to accurately observe behaviors that are widespread in society. The more the market system is decentralized, the less transparent it will be.

The invisible hand and the notion of unintended consequences in some ways represent a reality which is less intelligible from the individual's perspective because of its complexity and dynamism. The fact that society is populated by independent individuals means that it is difficult for the latter to correctly conceptualize the order in which they live, and to foresee future social configurations, because too many circumstances are out of their control. The conception behind the invisible hand, however, reflects the conviction that invisible forces organize and coordinate systems. Although His wisdom is mentioned in the TMS, God is not directly brought onto the scene in the WN, and economic inquiry is simply achieved by referring to principles of the market's functioning. The invisibility of forces which give shape to the social order is not metaphysical, and unfolds in three dimensions:

1. Spatial: the extent and complexity of the market relationships make individuals more and more limited in their knowledge and information. In a (metaphorical) sense, they see less.

2. Organizational: the order of society must be explained by referring to (invisible) forces that determine the physiology of the political body. The anatomy of society is no longer sufficient to explain the nature of social interdependencies; an analysis of its physiological dynamics is necessary.
3. Temporal: individuals' capacity to predict is limited. Human beings are increasingly less able to represent the distant future, because this future depends on many circumstances that are out of their control. Unlike the Middle Ages, in which some institutions crystallized the future, the future is open and continuously reconfigured (see Chap. 9).

The last two points will be dealt with in the following chapters. In particular, Chaps. 6, 7 and 8 will attempt to show how, by contrast with seventeenth-century approaches (which are dealt with in Chap. 6), both Smith and the life sciences of his time considered the "invisible" as a dimension that must be taken into account in explaining social and biological phenomena.

References

Arrow, K. J. (1983). *General Equilibrium*. Elsevier.

Arrow, K. J., & Hahn, F. H. (1971). *General Competitive Analysis*. Holden-Day.

Bittermann, H. J. (1940a). Adam Smith's Empiricism and the Law of Nature: I. *Journal of Political Economy, 48*(4), 487–520.

Bittermann, H. J. (1940b). Adam Smith's Empiricism and the Law of Nature: II. *Journal of Political Economy, 48*(5), 703–734.

Brewer, A. (2009). On the Other (Invisible) Hand .... *History of Political Economy, 41*(3), 519–543.

Cremaschi, S. (2017). Adam Smith's irony and the Invisible Hand. *Iberian Journal of the History of Economic Thought, 4*(1), 43–62.

Endres, A. M. (1996). "Security" and Capital Formation in *The Wealth of Nations. History of Economic Ideas, 4*(1-2), 149–173.

Fleischacker, S. (2004). *On Adam Smith's Wealth of Nations. A Philosophical Companion*. Princeton University Press.

Flew, A. (1987). Social Science: Making Visible the Invisible Hands. *The Journal of Libertarian Studies, 8*(2), 197–211.

Grampp, W. D. (2000). What Did Smith Mean by the Invisible Hand? *The Journal of Political Economy, 10*(3), 441–465.

Haakonssen, K. (1981). *The Science of a Legislator. The Natural Jurisprudence of David Hume and Adam Smith*. Cambridge University Press.

Harrison, P. (2011). Adam Smith and the History of the Invisible Hand. *Journal of the History of Ideas, 72*(1), 29–49.

Heath, E. (2014). Metaphor Made Manifest: Taking Seriously Smith's 'Invisible Hand'. In D. F. Hardwick & L. Marsh (Eds.), *Propriety and Prosperity New Studies on the Philosophy of Adam Smith* (pp. 169–197). Palgrave Macmillan.

Herzog, L. (2013). *Inventing the Market: Smith, Hegel and Political Theory*. Oxford University Press.

Iacono, M. (1982). *Il borghese e il selvaggio. L'immagine dell'uomo isolato nei paradigmi di Defoe, Turgot e Adam Smith*. Franco Angeli.

Kennedy, G. (2008). *Adam Smith. A Moral Philosopher and His Political Economy*. Palgrave Macmillan.

Kennedy, G. (2014). The 'Invisible Hand' Phenomenon in Economics. In D. F. Hardwick & L. Marsh (Eds.), *Propriety and Prosperity New Studies on the Philosophy of Adam Smith* (pp. 198–222). Palgrave Macmillan.

Kennedy, G. (2017). *An Authentic Account of Adam Smith*. Palgrave Macmillan.

Macfie, A. L. (1967). *The Individual in Society*. Allen & Unwin.

Macfie, A. L. (1971). The Invisible Hand of Jupiter. *Journal of the History of Ideas, 32*(4), 595–599.

Mayr, O. (1986). *Authority, Liberty and Automatic Machinery in Early Modern Europe*. Johns Hopkins Press.

Myers, M. L. (1983). *The Soul of Modern Economic Man. Ideas of Self-Interest, Thomas Hobbes to Adam Smith*. University of Chicago Press.

Oslington, P. (2011). Divine Action, Providence and Adam Smith's Invisible Hand. In P. Oslington (Ed.), *Adam Smith as Theologian* (pp. 61–76). Routledge.

Pack, S. J. (1995). Theological (and Hence Economic) Implications of Adam Smith's "Principles which Lead and Direct Philosophical Enquiries". *History of Political Economy, 27*(2), 289–307.

Pack, S. J. (1996). Adam Smith's Invisible/Visible Hand/Chain/Chaos. In L. S. Moss (Ed.), *Joseph A. Schumpeter, Historian of Economics. Perspectives on the History of Economic Thought* (pp. 181–195). Routledge.

Persky, J. (1989). Adam Smith's Invisible Hands. *Journal of Economic Perspectives, 3*(4), 195–201.

Rashid, S. (1998). *The Myth of Adam Smith*. Edward Elgar.

Rothschild, E. (2001). *Economic Sentiments: Adam Smith, Condorcet and the Enlightenment*. Harvard University Press.

Samuels, W. J. (2011). *Erasing the Invisible Hand: Essays on an Elusive and Misused Concept in Economics*. Cambridge University Press.

Schabas, M. (2005). *The Natural Origins of Economics*. University Chicago Press.

Sheehan, J., & Wahrman, D. (2015). *Invisible Hands. Self-Organization and the Eighteenth Century*. University of Chicago Press.

Stewart, D. (1980 [1793]). *Account of the Life and Writings of Adam Smith*. In A. Smith (Ed.), *Essays on Philosophical Subjects* (pp. 269–332). In W. P. D. Wightman & J. C. Bryce (Eds.), *The Glasgow Edition of the Works and Correspondence of Adam Smith*. Oxford University Press.

Tobin, J. (1992). The Invisible Hand in Modern Macroeconomics. In M. Fry (Ed.), *Adam Smith's Legacy. His Place in the Development of Modern Economics* (pp. 117–129). Routledge.

Viner, J. (1972). *The Role of Providence in the Social Order*. Princeton University Press.

Waterman, A. M. C. (2002). Economics as Theology: Adam Smith's Wealth of Nations. *Southern Economic Journal, 68*(4), 907–921.

Wight, J. B. (2014). Instincts and the Invisible Order: The Possibility of Progress. In D. F. Hardwick & L. Marsh (Eds.), *Propriety and Prosperity: New Studies on the Philosophy of Adam Smith* (pp. 223–239). Palgrave Macmillan.

PART II

Visible and Invisible Orders: The Secrets of Organization

CHAPTER 6

Paradigms of Order in the Seventeenth Century: Intelligibility as Visibility

Abstract Smith's concept of order and the notion of organization developed in the life sciences of his time differed from those philosophical and scientific conceptions that in the seventeenth century interpreted the intelligibility of natural and social phenomena in terms of visibility. These conceptions shared the idea that understanding complex phenomena depended on their visibility. The idea of intelligibility as visibility—examined in this chapter—was not a naïve conception. This idea emerged not as the immediate result of human observational capacities but as an effect of practical and theoretical approaches that could provide access to natural and social events. Technical, experimental and mathematical tools served this purpose. The more phenomena were correctly represented, the more they could be explained. Several metaphors provided arguments that strengthened this perspective.

Keywords Scientific Revolution • Book of nature • Art • Petty, Cantillon • Quesnay

S. Fiori, *Machines, Bodies and Invisible Hands*,
https://doi.org/10.1007/978-3-030-85206-1_6

6.1 Visibility and Philosophies of Nature in the Scientific Revolution

The concept of the intelligibility of nature in seventeenth-century natural philosophies was particularly important (Shapin, 1996; Dear, 2006: chap. 1). Bacon, as an advocate of inductive analysis, was of the opinion that nature becomes more intelligible thanks to experimental results. Experiments perform this function because they physically and conceptually show processes otherwise inaccessible to reason. Through them, both eyes and mind see more, so to speak. Intelligibility, in this perspective, is a special form of visibility. Nothing can be accepted in natural history except what comes from the "evidence of our eyes", he maintained (Bacon, 2000 [1620]: 21). But this evidence is not immediate. It must be acquired by eliminating deception of the senses, especially that of sight. Although "there are many things which escape the senses" because of their "rarity", small size, "distance", "slowness or speed", these perceptual "defects" can be overcome by means of "instruments", "experiments" and appropriate methods (Bacon, 2000 [1620]: 17–18). But if the limits of human perception are corrected, then knowledge can expand, and discover nature as it really is.

Other approaches in the seventeenth century legitimized the idea of intelligibility as visibility. Mechanical metaphors, and the metaphor of the clock in particular (see Sect. 2.1), were used in this sense. As products of human ingenuity, machines are wholly intelligible because, Descartes maintained, there is no

> difference between artefacts and natural bodies except that the operations of artefacts are for the most part performed by mechanisms which are large enough to be easily perceivable by the senses [...] The effects produced in nature, by contrast, almost always depend on structures which are so minute that they completely elude our senses. (Descartes, 1985a [1647]: 288; see Clericuzio, 2015: 84)

In this passage, Descartes pointed out that limits of human perception make understanding nature difficult. While components of machines are "large enough to be easily perceivable by the senses", natural objects "are so minute that they completely elude our senses". However, since natural objects and artifacts differ in size, but not in mechanical properties, it is possible to project features of machines onto nature, by exploiting the technical knowledge of artisans:

> Men who are experienced in dealing with machinery can take a particular machine whose function they know and, by looking at some of its parts, easily form a conjecture about the design of the other parts, which they *cannot see*. In the same way I have attempted to consider the *observable* effects and parts of natural bodies and track down the *imperceptible* causes and particles which produce them. (Ibidem: 288–289, emphasis added)

Scientific explanation is based on projecting visible phenomena onto non-perceptible ones. The problem of visibility (or perceptibility) is, at the same time, real (natural objects and natural effects are not readily observable) and methodological-metaphorical (the analogies drawn from the functioning of machines make natural processes intelligible).

Given the similarity between natural and mechanical objects, the visible and tangible parts of a machine built by an artisan allow us to imagine the "structure" of the small and invisible parts of natural bodies. But the analogy is not limited to this similarity. Access to artificial processes also authorizes access to natural processes. The knowledge of how components of the machine are combined makes it possible to deductively interpret how the less visible objects of nature yield certain effects. This is possible because, for Descartes, the "machine is visible, transparently articulated in a way that forms and faculties are not. It can be *shown*" (Des Chene, 2001: 73, emphasis in original). Albeit with a method which differs from Bacon's, Descartes also holds that science's task consists in increasing nature's visibility by circumventing perceptual limits not through experiments or tools, but with appropriate conjectures.

Descartes' method was intrinsically metaphorical. However, he did not perceive the heuristic function of metaphors as re-description of the *explanandum*, but considered similarities between machine and nature as the basis for an effective scientific procedure aimed at discovering real features of the world. As Lakoff and Johnson (1999: 393) argue, his theoretical approach was expressed by the idea that "Knowing Is Seeing", the "fundamental metaphor" which is the basis for the thesis that it is possible to provide foundations for a certain and indubitable knowledge based on clear and distinct perceptions. In particular, the concept of clarity from which the concept of distinctness derives was expressed in visual terms.

> I call a perception "clear" when it is present and accessible to the attentive mind—just as we say that we see something clearly when it is present to the

> eye's gaze and stimulates it with a sufficient degree of strength and accessibility. (Descartes, 1985b [1662]: 207)

Other expressions also emphasize that Descartes tacitly adopted an ocular view of knowledge. Evidence, for example, is enabled by "the natural light of reason" (Lakoff and Johnson: 395). This, in turn, implies that ideas, once removed from obscurity, are dealt with as objects accessible to vision, and which consequently produce knowledge. But if ideas and thought processes are accessible, also the "structure of the mind is directly accessible to itself" (ibidem: 396).

Hobbes, too, used mechanical analogies and argued that nature was intelligible, at least hypothetically, by means of appropriate methods,[1] and Gassendi, like Descartes, was of the opinion that "[c]oncerning natural things, we investigate in the same way as we investigate things of which we ourselves are the authors" (quoted in Shapin, 1996: 31–32). Hooke, in turn, argued that the secret "Operations of Nature" are subject to

> Demonstration and Reduction to a certain Rule, as the Operations of Mechanicks or Art. And from those, which are yet somewhat more speculative, [the natural historian] ought to proceed to acquaint himself with others more complicated Mechanical Operations: Such as Chymical, and the Physical, yea even divers Mechanical Operations in many other Trades: For by these Ways, he will be better acquainted and enabled how to deal with Nature, for the procuring and getting more hidden Jewels and greatest Mysteries. (Hooke, 1705: 20)

In this way, it was no longer necessary to refer to occult qualities, because the "small Machines of Nature" that cause phenomena could be brought to light (Hooke, 1665, in *Preface*, unnumbered page [but 25]).

Boyle, too, was convinced—although more prudently than Descartes—that fundamental properties of bodies were captured by mechanical explanations (Anstey, 2000: 53–54; see Sawday, 2007, chap. 6). In his view, universal matter was composed of corpuscles, of several sizes and shapes, joined in masses and clusters, but differentiated in their "textures"

[1] "[S]ince the causes of natural things are not in our power, but in the divine will, and since the greatest part of them, namely the ether, is invisible; we, that do not see them, cannot deduce their qualities from their causes. Of course, we can, by deducing as far as possible the consequences of those qualities that we do see, demonstrate that such and such *could* have been their causes" (Hobbes, 1991 [1658]: 42, emphasis in original).

(Shapin, 1996: 49). Although these particles were not perceptible, nature was intelligible because "one might model the invisible world of corpuscles on the visible and tangible phenomena presented by the behavior of medium-sized objects in the world of everyday experience" (Shapin, 1996: 50).[2] The invisible world interpreted on the basis of the visible one in this way ceased to be inscrutable.

The discoveries of Antoni van Leeuwenhoek strengthened the conviction that the microscope would soon make the small particles which make up bodies visible. Similarly, Hooke and Boyle expressed the hope that the microscope would reveal the structure of the corpuscles of matter (ibidem: 50). Boyle, in particular, was even more precise in defining the criterion of visibility. Besides the spiritual world (the first world) populated by angels and devils, whose nature can be interpreted from the Holy Scriptures, other two worlds exist:

> The second, is the visible world, in the usual sense of the term, consisting of all the bodies, great and little, that are objects proportioned to our unassisted sight. And the third, which for want of a fitter name, I venture to call the dioptrical world, which consists of all those creatures, that lay concealed, in former ages, from mortal eyes, and are not now discovered without dioptrical glasses, and this itself, if one please, one may, for distinction sake, distribute into telescopical and microscopical. The first whereof, comprehends the numerous fixed stars [...], and the latter [...] comprises those numerous sets of different creatures, mineral, vegetable, and animal, which, by reason of their wonderful minuteness, remain invisible to our eyes, unless they be assisted by good microscopes. (Boyle, 1772b [1690]: 773–774)

Although the "dioptrical world" cannot be seen with the naked eye, it can be investigated, as Galileo had previously shown. Only by using microscopes and telescopes, as tools which expand the natural sight, is it possible to construct a unitary image which coherently connects micro and macro aspects of the universe.

The problem of the intelligibility of nature stimulated reflections that went beyond the empirical fact that microscopes and telescopes could contribute to making nature visible. In *The Christian Virtuoso*, Boyle defended analogies as both pedagogical tools that could easily

[2] Peter Dear (2006: 24–25) points out that, for Huygens and Boyle, mechanical explanations were not necessarily true. However, their main virtue was that they were particularly "intelligible", and for this reason preferable to alternative explanations.

communicate concepts and heuristic tools which shed light on features of nature. He maintained that he had made "frequent use of Similitudes, or Comparisons", not to embellish his prose, but because he was firmly convinced that:

> 1. [...] comparisons fitly chosen, and well applied, may, on many occasions, usefully serve to illustrate the notions, for whose sake they are brought, and, by placing them in a true light, help men to conceive them far better than otherwise they would do. And 2. apposite comparisons do not only give light, but strength, to the passages they belong to, since they are not always bare pictures and resemblances, but a kind of arguments; being oftentimes, if I may so call them, analogous instances, which do declare the nature, or way of operating, of the thing they relate to, and by that means do in a sort prove, that, as it is possible, so it is not improbable, that the thing may be such as it is represented. (Boyle, 1772a [1690]: 511)

Appropriate analogies are not "bare Pictures and Resemblances", but "Arguments" by means of which parts and properties of nature that are otherwise inaccessible can be discovered. They perform a heuristic function because, by showing the "way of operating" of nature, they make it intelligible. As "analogous instances", analogies are a sort of mental visual representation of phenomena that can legitimately be conceived as real reconstructions of nature. Boyle maintained that he followed the examples of Bacon and Descartes, who used comparisons in a similar way, because:

> proper Comparisons do the Imagination almost as much service, as microscopes do the eye; for, as this instrument gives us a distinct view of divers minute things, which our naked eyes cannot well discern; because these glasses represent them far more large, than by the bare eye we judge them; so a skilfully chosen, and well applied comparison much helps the imagination, by illustrating things scarce discernible, so as to represent them by things much more familiar and easy to be apprehended. (Ibidem: 512)

As in Descartes, these statements described a sort of ocular model of science: knowing nature meant increasing its visibility. This could be accomplished by using not only technical tools such as dioptrical glasses but also analogies that, not by chance, were considered metaphorical microscopes. Analogies and metaphors were part of the scientific method, helping to investigate unknown domains and to advance plausible explanations.

The idea that nature could be understood in detail was also summed up in a famous metaphor, used by Galileo, Bacon, Campanella, Descartes, Boyle, Harvey, Malpighi, Linnaeus and others: the "book of nature". Boyle assumed the nexus between nature and book as a visual metaphor. He strengthened this meaning by pointing out that observation of that magnificent book implies an act of visual contemplation. And he expressed his confidence in the progressive visualization of nature by adding metaphor to metaphor: nature—he argued—is metaphorically a book, and this book, in turn, is a wonderful tapestry:

> The book of nature, is a fine and large piece of tapestry rolled up, which we are not able to see all at once, but must be content to wait for the discovery of its beauty, and symmetry, little by little, as it gradually comes to be more and more unfolded, or displayed. (Boyle, 1772b [1690]: 796)

As a book, nature can be correctly read or contemplated, if some conditions are satisfied. It is intelligible when its grammar is known (Galilei), deception of the senses is avoided (Bacon, Descartes, Hooke), and probabilistic limitations of knowledge are accepted (Hobbes). For Galileo, as is well known, the book of nature was "written in the language of mathematics", but he used not only mathematics but also mechanical models to re-describe nature (see Sect. 2.2). Machines were of particular importance, in that they constructed experiences by duplicating natural phenomena. "These devices or analogic phenomena—Machamer (1998: 69–70) remarks—literally demonstrate how the phenomena occur. One sees the machine or phenomenon as an instance of mathematics in the world. In this way one can know that they are real and not imaginary". Galilei, like other writers, pointed out that natural phenomena in many circumstances are simply unperceived. This is apparent in the *Dialogo*, where Salviati adopted this argument against Simplicio, the Aristotelian, who supported a naïve conception of knowledge that holds that nothing exists except what the eyes see. By contrast, certain phenomena are real, although they are not captured by the senses or subject to direct experience. The paradigm of the naïve visibility of nature, therefore, had to be rejected and replaced by an alternative conception which considers that new observations continuously redefine the horizon of visibility, expand the boundaries of "sensible experience" ("sensata esperienza") and modify the criteria by means of which the world is decoded (Galilei, 1967 [1632]: 50–51).

Lastly, embryological theories in the eighteenth century also mirrored the century-old effort to overcame the "invisible", and to dominate the secrets of the formation of life with the power of the mind (Bernardi, 1995: 65). Two systems in that period provided alternative interpretations of experimental data: epigenesis and preformism. The epigenetic theory, by assuming the criterion of "strong visibility", supposed that the observable succession of parts of the embryo corresponded to the real, progressive formation of the living being. Since phenomena of morphogenesis fall under the dominion of the naked eye, pre-existence could be not considered as a necessary requisite for the development of life. By contrast, the preformist model assumed that parts of the embryo were formed simultaneously from the beginning and that the largest parts appeared first, followed by the smallest and transparent ones. This implied a rejection of epigenesis, and the adoption of the criterion of "weak visibility", a principle which revised the direct relationship between the eyes and phenomena, because it assumed that structures existed, although they were invisible (ibidem: 66).

Unlike Aristotelian physics, Aristotelian biology, of which epigenesis was a part, survived until the middle of the seventeenth century, but subsequently declined. In particular, it was with Malpighi that preformism and the criterion of weak visibility prevailed. Malpighi did not make exceptional discoveries. Like other experimentalists, he observed how organs of chickens developed as eggs were incubated, but unlike his predecessors he interpreted morphogenesis not as the successive formation of visible parts of the new beings, but as the development of pre-existing parts. What had changed, with respect to epigenesis, was the way of looking at reality, because the microscope, by showing the limits of ocular perception, had modified how visible phenomena were to be interpreted (ibidem: 67). Only in the late eighteenth century, with Vitalism, was this paradigm definitively marginalized. Life phenomena would no longer be explained by resorting to either mechanical principles or criteria of visibility, however weak.

6.2 Art and (the Intelligibility of) Nature

During the Scientific Revolution, one of the topics that characterized the relationship between art and nature was the idea that nature reveals itself not directly but by means of arts, techniques and experiments of various kinds. In this sense, too, the criterion of "weak visibility", which presupposes that the relation between man and nature is mediated by the use of tools and methods, appeared preferable to the criterion of "strong visibility", as a principle which denotes a direct relationship between eyes and occurrences.

Like Descartes, who had maintained that the machine's intelligibility is a precondition for the intelligibility of nature, Hooke put forward the idea that studying the products of human ingenuity was fundamental to discover natural processes:

> Another way of discovering the Methods of Nature's working is, *by observing and comparing the Productions of Art with those of Nature*. And for this purpose it would be very requisite to have a perfect Account of all the Productions of Art, such as are dispers'd up and down in several Trades and Occupations of Men, whether for Profit or Pleasure; and especially all those excellent ways of working on Bodies by Chymical Operations. (Hooke, 1705: 57, emphasis in original)

"Productions of Art" reveal nature not only when they reproduce it but also when they alter it.

> Another way of Discovery is, *by observing where and by what means Art causes Nature to deviate or alter its usual Course, where it assists, promotes and perfects, and where it impedes, diverts, or destroys*. Of this there are Multitudes of Instances in all things, about which Art has been used, and therefore needs not exemplifying; but certain it is, that this Method affords extraordinary Help for Discovery of the true Nature of the efficient and material Causes of things. (Ibidem: 58, emphasis in original)

Such propositions were not new. A few decades earlier Francis Bacon had argued that "the secrets of nature reveal themselves better through harassments applied by the arts than when they go on in their own way" (Bacon, 2000 [1620]: 81). And in the *New Atlantis*, he had illustrated in literary style that art obliges natural forces to achieve ends that they do not accomplish spontaneously. These statements relied on the conviction that nature and art were not separate domains.[3] While Descartes maintained

[3] As regards the weakening and revision of the Aristotelian distinction between art and nature during the Scientific Revolution, see Dear (1995: 151); Shapin (1996: 30–32); Wootton (2015: 322–323).

that machine and nature exhibit a similar structure, Bacon argued that "artificial things differ not from natural in form or essence, but only in the efficient" (Bacon, 1868 [1623]: 79). Products of art and nature are similar in some essential traits but differ as to the material causes of the processes through which they are produced and transformed (see Newman, 2004: 259–260).[4]

Although art and nature were considered similar in some respects, many arguments were put forward in support of the thesis that art prevails over nature. The origin of this belief traces back to Aristotle, who in *Physics* maintained that "[a]rt partly completes and partly imitates the work of nature" (Aristotle, 1936, II 8199a, 15: 357; see Close, 1969). The idea that art is the imitation of nature suggested that, on the one hand, nature was a model for art and, on the other, art could reproduce nature. But the capacity to reproduce nature and use it to satisfy human needs implied a representation of art as a completion of nature, in that it prompts nature to achieve ends that it would not have accomplished by itself (Newman, 2004: 17).

This conception, developed over centuries, was reused to maintain that if art completes nature, then it also improves it. Although he was not an Aristotelian, Bacon in the *New Atlantis* gave many examples of how imitation involves harnessing and reorienting natural forces. In the utopian world described in that work, this perspective emerges from the words of the Father of Salomon's House, who illustrates the wonders of the mythical isle of Bensalem, where "caves" are used "likewise for the imitation of natural mines; and the producing also of new artificial metals", "a number of artificial wells and fountains, [are] made in imitation of the natural sources and baths", and in orchards trees and flowers are obliged "by art" "to come earlier or later than their seasons" (Bacon, 1999 [1627]: 177–179).

Many others shared the idea the art is "perfective". Daniel Sennert argued that the principle of perfective art was applied in laboratory experiments (Newman, 2004: 250–255). Alchemy, chemistry and agriculture were also considered arts that improve nature by altering it (Rossi, 1968,

[4] The same Aristotelian lexicon used by Bacon—the reference to matter/form dualism—was used by Misselden (1623: 7–9): natural and artificial things do not differ, in the sense that both result from processes which change the form of matter.

chap. 1). Thomas Browne maintained that, although art and nature shape the world in alternative ways, art is "perfection of nature" (quoted in Johnson, 1960 [1937]: 260). Moreover, since art gives form to matter, Misselden and Malynes could claim that "the forme giveth to the thing, the perfection of being" (Misselden, 1623: 10; see also Malynes, 1622: 500).

The perspective that art perfects nature was tacitly assumed in economic analyses. According to Botero (1606: 50–51), wealth derives from "art and industry". "Industrie and Art exceedeth Nature" because art improves "Materia prima" provided by the earth (Keller, 2012: 198 and 211). Hobbes (1996 [1651]: 7), in his *Introduction* to the *Leviathan*, maintained that Nature is imitated by art but also showed that nature has limited resources that only labor and industry can exploit and multiply.[5] Nature ("earth") was not so unknown if "the arts of husbandry" could force it to produce "ten times more food than it can naturally", Barbon (1859 [1685]: 11) argued. Art modifies nature not only in quantitative but also in qualitative terms because natural products "by Art are Changed into another Form than Nature gave them" (Barbon, 1905 [1690]: 10). Nature is also weak for Locke (1980 [1690], § 27: 19). Labor multiplies its products and improves their quality by changing their characteristics (ibid., § 39: 25). Similarly, Petty maintained that art, by means of "Inventions", multiplies the productive capacity of labor, which in turn increases land's productivity (Petty, 1963b [1691]: 182). In this way, art and inventions contribute to the formation of surplus.

In conclusion, the idea—originally proposed in classical antiquity, and in particular by Aristotle—that art is the completion and perfection of nature was reconsidered during the Scientific Revolution. Laboratory experiments and new techniques applied in agriculture and in craftsmen's workshops showed that it was possible to duplicate natural processes artificially and to compel nature to develop its potential. For its ability to reuse and alter the course of natural forces, art was seen as an extension of nature and, at the same time, as a tool capable of penetrating its secrets.

[5] "[P]lenty dependeth (next to God's favour) merely on the labour and industry of men" (Hobbes 1996 [1651]: 163).

6.3 Visibility and the "Chain of Being"

The idea of the "Great Chain of Being", namely, that the natural world is gradated, continuous and hierarchical, was another argument in favor of nature's intelligibility.[6] The general program of the Royal Society, as Thomas Sprat, its first historian, wrote in 1667, reflected this view. On the basis of the idea that natural and artificial things shed light on each other (see Sect. 6.1), it called on scientists to search "the secrets" of the "chain" of beings, in order "truly to command the world". The "orders of creatures", Sprat assumed, included natural and artificial beings, and this meant that "the apprehension of one of them, is a good step towards the understanding of the rest" (Sprat, *The History of the Royal Society*: 110, quoted in Lovejoy, 1936: 232). These conceptions were developed in the late seventeenth century and were reused to delineate the features of the "Great Chain of Being", which gained its greatest currency during the first decades of the eighteenth century, presumably through Leibniz's and Locke's works (Lovejoy, 1936).

Leibniz, in particular, argued that creatures that "might pass equally well for animals or for plants" exist, and trusted that "natural history will perhaps some day become acquainted with them, when it has further studied that infinity of living things whose small size conceals them from ordinary observation and which are hidden in the bowels of the earth and the depths of the sea" (quoted in Lovejoy, 1936: 145). This implied that limited access to visible aspects of nature was not insurmountable in that it depended on the combination of two easily solvable problems: the littleness of certain creatures, and the fact that they probably live in places which escape observation.

The conception of living nature's continuity was equally clear in Locke, who maintained: "In all the visible corporeal world we see no chasms or gaps" (Locke, 1997 [1690]: 399). Continuity, however, posed a problem of representation of the scale of being, because human perception is unable to grasp the imperceptible passages from one living form to another. It is thus unsurprising that in the early decades of the eighteenth century, naturalists tried to discover the "missing links" in the chain of nature. The

[6] A similar image, of "two Scales of animate beings", was used by William Petty to illustrate the connection between the visible world and God. The "two Scales of animate beings", he maintained, are organized as follows: "The one whose top is Man, and whose bottom is the smallest and the simplest animall that man can discern; and of the other scale, the maker of the aforementioned visible world is the top and Man the bottome" (Petty, 1967 [1928]: 23).

extraordinary findings of microscopic investigations, such as Trembley's discovery of the freshwater polyp (hydra) in 1739, however, were welcomed as an important step toward an ever more accurate representation of nature.

The belief in the plenitude, gradation and continuity of the scale of being coincided with the need for an inventory of nature. These ideas informed Linnaeus' classification (E. Mayr, 1982: 174). His taxonomy, based on the division in classes, orders, genera and species, and applied to the three natural kingdoms, reflected Leibniz's conviction that "Natura non facit saltus" (nature makes no leaps). An old argument was encapsulated in a new framework: the more the knowledge of nature advances, "the more gaps between the higher taxa will be filled until the boundaries between orders and classes may finally disappear" (ibidem: 175). This "geography of nature" (Koerner, 1999, chap. 1) was consistent with Linnaeus' creationism. If nature was a stable order, where evolutionary processes do not occur, then the task of the taxonomist consisted in filling gaps in the knowledge of a world characterized simply by continuous cycles of creation and destruction. Systems of classification made the harmonious order of the world accessible by visualizing nature as if it were a puzzle to be gradually completed with additional pieces. Natural science, Linnaeus argued in *Curiositas naturalis* (Linnæi, 1748: 445), provided the knowledge needed to understand the book of nature ("librum Naturae"). But this book was written neither with letters nor with mathematical symbols, but in taxonomic characters. By knowing these grammatical units, it could finally be decoded.

6.4 Visibility in Economic Thought

William Petty extended the visual model of intelligibility from natural to social sciences. In line with the cultural climate of the Scientific Revolution, he declared in *Political Arithmetick* that he aimed "to express [him]self in Terms of *Number*, *Weight*, or *Measure*", by considering "only such Causes, as have visible Foundations in Nature" (Petty, 1963a [1690]: 244, emphasis in original). These words (Number, Weight and Measure), used in the Bible (in the *Wisdom of Solomon*) to describe how God created an ordered world (Letwin, 1975: 130), were reinterpreted in the seventeenth century. They became part of Bacon's scientific program, which established a clear connection between "observation" and accurate measurements in natural history.[7] Calculating, weighing, measuring referred to operations whereby the order of the world could be made visible, and even tangible.

Petty's plan to develop a "political anatomy" also reflected the idea that hidden parts of the social body, so to speak, could be plainly brought to the surface, shedding light on the real structure of society. His training as a physician influenced his conviction that anatomy was a suitable tool for science. In medicine, anatomy is an indispensable discipline because—he argued—"minute Disections" make it possible to "find out curious and usefull engins" of animal bodies (Petty, 1967 [1928]: 172 and 173). By analogy, the art of dissection could be also used to anatomize the political body. Petty made this view explicit in *The Political Anatomy of Ireland*, where he credited this intuition to Bacon:

> Francis Bacon, *in his* Advancement of Learning, *hath made a judicious* Parallel *in many particulars, between* the Body Natural, *and* Body Politick, *and between the Arts of preserving both in Health and Strength: And it is as reasonable, that as* Anatomy *is the best foundation of one, so also of the other.* (Petty, 1963b [1691]: 129, emphasis in original)

Aware of the limits of the "first Essay of Political Anatomy", he argued that instrumentation used for his "Dissections" was metaphorically sufficient "*to find whereabout the Liver and Spleen, and Lungs lye, tho' not to discern the Lymphatick Vessels, the* Plexus, Choroidus, *the* Volvuli *of vessels within the Testicles*" (ibidem: 129).

In summary, Petty's analogies and metaphors were based on two convictions:

1. It is possible to make nature intelligible by making it visible with appropriate methods. Science proceeds not by "promiscuous Demonstrations" and wordy "tumultory discourses" (Petty, 1967 [1928]: 173) but by showing the structure of the phenomena under analysis through empirical method. God created and ordered an atomistic universe that can be explored by considering numbers, weights and measures (Sivado, 2019: 15).

[7] "Natural history contains nothing that has been researched in the proper ways, nothing verified, nothing counted, nothing weighed, nothing measured. But what is indefinite and vague in observation is deceiving and unreliable as information" (Bacon 2000 [1620]: 80).

2. Human societies are part of the knowable universe and can be studied by applying the same methods applied to the study of natural bodies. In particular, political anatomy and political arithmetic are instruments whereby the political body can be analyzed in its parts.[8] In other words, the social and economic sphere, as *explanandum*, can be interpreted through the frame and implications of the natural sphere.

Another strategy for making the political body intelligible consisted in ideally calculating the contribution of nature and labor to the production of commodities. This perspective was put forward by seventeenth-century authors and by physiocrats, although the former assigned labor a greater role in producing wealth than land (see Perrotta, 2004: 166–167), while the latter assigned the predominant role to land. Despite these differences, these approaches shared a view that was similar in some respects and had in common the idea that the structure of economic phenomena, as part of a natural world, could ultimately be delineated by means of calculations.

In the spirit of political arithmetic, Petty proposed to calculate "a Par and Equation between Art and Simple Labour", because art thanks to inventions doubles labor productivity (Petty, 1963b [1691]: 182). Thus, the natural forces employed by art not only ceased to be obscure but, thanks to calculations, could be further conceptualized in a more precise framework. Calculations were on the basis of "the most important Considerations in Political Oeconomy". They made it possible "to make a *Par* and *Equation* between Lands and Labour", in order "to express the Value of any thing by either alone" (Petty, 1963b [1691]: 181). This approach was inseparable from the language of visualization, which illustrated economic concepts in terms of physical quantities and physical differences. Rent could be measured in terms of flesh of calf; "overplus", engendered by man's labor applied to land, could be expressed in terms of "days food" (ibidem: 181), or alternatively as "the remainder of Corn",

[8] Like Petty, Davenant considered anatomy to be a useful tool for economic studies. In order to show "how the wealth and strength of England is to be secured and improved", he maintained: "It shall not be here argued, whether the skill of physic be now brought to perfection, or whether it is yet capable of further improvements; but this may be safely pronounced, that the knowledge of the sinews, muscles, arteries and veins, with the late discovery of the circulation of the blood and all the parts of anatomy, conduce very much to render this dark science more plain and certain" (Davenant, 1771b [1699]: 169). Moreover, following Petty, he considered political arithmetic as the tool needed to provide a "true account of the balance of trade" (Davenant, 1771a [1698]: 146).

once the laborer had "subducted his seed out of the proceed of his Harvest" (Petty 1963c [1662]: 43).

In the *Essai sur la nature du commerce en general*, a book written in the early 1730s, but not published until 1755, Cantillon developed the concept of proportion between land and labor more analytically (see Brewer, 1992; Aspromourgos, 1996, chap. 6). He calculated the "intrinsic value" of commodities by reducing labor employed in cultivation to a certain amount of land. This operation was possible—he wrote—because the value of labor corresponds to the subsistence produced by the land needed to maintain a man and his son, that is, twice the amount of land needed to maintain one laborer. The problem of the different quality of land and labor was not a problem for this calculation, in that it was sufficient to consider the "ordinary goodness" of land in a country (Cantillon, 2015: H88), and the ordinary subsistence of laborers, that is, subsistence resulting from social and geographical conditions.[9] Lastly, Locke (1980 [1690], § 40) also focused on the problem of "rightly estimat[ing] things", in order to evaluate "what in them is purely owing to *nature* and what to *labour*", and concluded that "we shall find, that in most of them ninety-nine hundredths are wholly to be put on the account of *labour*".

The hierarchical model of society based on expenditure by the prince and landowners that Cantillon illustrated in his *Essai* is generally considered as an anticipation of the physiocratic theory. Mirabeau, who had had the opportunity to read that book before it was published, was influenced by Cantillon's ideas.[10] However, when he later became a follower of Quesnay, he understood Cantillon's mistakes. In particular, as he wrote to Rousseau, he understood that Cantillon had done nothing but "to perfect" the error, widespread in the seventeenth century, that trade is the "principle of wealth" (Rousseau, 1932: 176). Despite this ungenerous criticism, like Cantillon, he preserved the idea that calculations show the structure of economic relationships without residues. In the *Préface* to *Philosophie Rurale* (1763), a book written in collaboration with Quesnay (Théré & Charles, 2008), he illustrated this point of view (see Steiner, 1998: 17–21). The *Tableau économique*—he remarked—is the first "arithmetic rule" which reduces economic science to exact calculation. An organic metaphor showed the fundamental function exercised by calculations:

[9] This subsistence ultimately could be calculated in terms of land needed to produce it.
[10] It is probable that he intended to plagiarize the *Essai* (see Sabbagh, 2016: 95, note 20).

> Calculations are for science what bones are for the human body. Nerves, vessels, muscles enliven it, and give it movement. The bones defend, and support them. [...] [W]ithout calculation, [economic science] would always be an indeterminate science, confused and confounded everywhere by error and prejudices. (Mirabeau, 1763: xlv–xlvi, my translation)

Quesnay's *Tableau* was the best illustration of this view. It was a model in which calculations, by clarifying the nature of economic relationships, furnished a sort of anatomical table of economic order, where the "produit net", as the physical surplus cyclically reproduced by nature, was at the basis of the surplus generated by the market as the observable difference between costs and revenues (Banzhaf, 2000: 518–523).[11] If calculations can be compared to bones which give structure to the body, it is unsurprising that, as for Petty, economic science could be described as an anatomical science which reveals the secrets of the economic system:

> we only aim at the simplest truth, through the elementary exposition of all the parts involved in the construction of the economic machine [...] It is a question here of *dissecting* it and discovering its organization by the *anatomical demonstration* of all its parts, and by tracing their intertwining, their connection and how they contribute to their mutual action. (Quesnay, 1958b [1763]: 688, emphasis in original, my translation)

These statements mirrored Quesnay's medical convictions. Commenting on the function of surgery, he had argued that "Nature only shows itself obscurely to our eyes; [...] But in observation, the mind is only a simple spectator, it sees only the outside; it is necessary, with the help of physical experience, to seek to penetrate to the sensitive principles of nature, that is to say, to prevent it, to question it, to force it to uncover itself" (Quesnay, 1888 [1743]: 724, my translation). Direct observation is unable to discover the nature of the human body without the help of physical experience which unveils structure, composition and properties of bodies. Surgery and dissection produce physical experience, and without experience, observation, although indispensable, can be subject to error and

[11] Vaggi (1987: 34–40) pointed out that wealth was not defined in simple naturalistic terms; it depended on the market; it was not reducible to material goods, and it regarded commodities exchanged at the market prices. However, he also maintained that in "Quesnay's work there is nothing like an invisible hand [...] the rulers and the sovereign [...] are in some way the 'visible hands' of the natural order" (Vaggi, 1995: 73).

prejudice. The naïve ocular model of knowledge, therefore, is rejected, but not the idea that nature (whether human or physical) can be "forc[ed] to uncover itself", nor that this revelation can acquire the character of visible "evidence". The theory which stems from practices such as anatomy and surgery, however, required further development. Quesnay saw "conjecture and analogy" as the theoretical tools whereby this task could be accomplished. Analogy and conjecture are "sources of light", since "comparison of objects that resemble each other, leads to research; and research sometimes brings a knowledge of truth" (ibidem: 735, my translation). These beliefs were not confined to the medical sphere. As an economist-anatomist, Quesnay was convinced that the aim of economic science was to unveil secrets and interdependences of the economic system which—as Smith remarked in his criticism of this approach—was viewed as a body, rather than as a mechanical device.

From this perspective, Quesnay established a symmetry between the visibility of organisms and the visibility of economic relationships. Both organisms and the body politic are orders subject to natural laws established by the Author of nature (Hoselitz, 1968). If "natural order" is "the necessary foundation of the political order" (Mirabeau, 2003 [1763]: 60), it makes sense to maintain that the "natural laws of the order of societies are the same physical laws of the perpetual reproduction of the goods needed for the subsistence, conservation and convenience of men" (Quesnay, 1958c [1767]: 921, my translation). Physical laws must be known, because wealth increases only by exploiting nature. They "constitute the natural order" of societies, and appear "with a precision that is demonstrated geometrically and arithmetically in the details" (Quesnay, 1958c [1767]: 924).

This leads to the concept of evidence. This notion, which Quesnay dealt with in an article written for the *Encyclopédie*, clarified the sense in which the world is intelligible: "There are two kinds of certainty: faith and *evidence*. Faith teaches us truths which cannot be known by the lights of reason. *Evidence* is limited to natural knowledge" (Quesnay, 1958a [1756]: 397, emphasis in original, my translation). Quesnay here replicated an approach that was widespread in his time. On the one hand, there are truths of faith. On the other, there is evidence that can be discovered and analyzed as such. There is, he maintained, an unambiguous "correspondence" between bodies and the "sensations" that they provoke, "which yields an evidence or certainty of knowledge that we cannot refute" (ibidem: 405, my translation). "Real truth", therefore, consists of "exact and evident" relationships that real objects establish with the sensations that they arouse.

6.5 Conclusions

Despite their differences, the approaches of the seventeenth century and of the first decades of the eighteenth century shared the idea that nature is intelligible, and that its hidden structure becomes visible by observation through correct procedures.

This belief, held by Bacon, Descartes, Boyle, Hooke and others, emerged from the interaction of theoretical analyses and metaphorical reasoning in explicit and implicit form. Bacon adopted a new ocular model of knowledge, where evidence of nature was established on the basis of experiments and methods that could overcome the limits of human perception. Descartes, taking a different perspective, pointed out that nature is intelligible, when it is re-described in light of the mechanical model. His idea of explicitly using one domain to explain another was part of the tacit methodological assumption that "Knowing Is Seeing". Bacon's and Descartes' views can hardly be separated from other empirical arguments. In some cases, the argument for visibility was related to the evidence that nature could be observed in greater detail thanks to the use of microscopes and telescopes. The animate world, viewed as a chain that unites all living beings, was considered as a field that could be made progressively intelligible by means of increasingly accurate classificatory systems. In other cases, the argument for visibility was related to the fact that new techniques made it possible to force nature to accomplish goals that it does not achieve spontaneously. If nature could be dominated, then its forces were neither mysterious nor occult. Lastly, the metaphor of the book of nature conveyed the idea that intelligibility and visibility are closely connected terms. Nature in principle was interpretable because it could be "read" provided that one possessed the grammar for deciphering it.

These intellectual perspectives influenced social and economic inquiries because, as Schabas (2005: 5) remarks, "until the mid-nineteenth century, economic theorists regarded the phenomena of their discourse as part of the same natural world studied by natural philosophers". This explains why confidence in the intelligibility/visibility of social and economic phenomena was expressed through theoretical and metaphorical arguments similar to those expressed by scientists and natural philosophers. The trust that calculations would make the magnitudes and interdependencies of economic systems transparent was shared to some extent by Petty and Cantillon. Quesnay even illustrated them in the *Tableau*, a term that literally means "picture", as if he wanted to evoke the visual aspect of those calculations. Some metaphors helped to clarify this perspective. One such metaphor, recurrent from Petty to Quesnay, was that economic science is comparable to anatomy, the art which brings the most hidden parts of bodies to light.

The paradigm of intelligibility as visibility was seriously called into question in the last decades of the eighteenth century, but some first signs of its decline were already apparent in the beginning of the century. In *An Essay Towards a New Theory of Vision*, whose four editions were published between 1709 and 1732, Berkeley argued that the enhancement of visibility produced by the microscope makes our perception of the world, and interaction with it, problematic because the latter is based on the relationship between sight and touch. This relationship is interrupted by the use of microscope, because the newly observed (small) objects are not tangible.

> A microscope brings us, as it were, into a new world: It presents us with a new scene of visible objects quite different from what we behold with the naked eye. But herein consists the most remarkable difference, to wit, that whereas the objects perceived by the eye alone have a certain connexion with tangible objects, whereby we are taught to foresee what will ensue upon the approach or application of distant objects to the parts of our own body [...] there is not the like connexion between things tangible and those visible objects that are perceived by help of fine microscope. (Berkeley, 2017 [1732]: 122)

The microscope is not simply an instrument which makes the world more intelligible, because its relation with sight is dual and conflictual. On the one hand, it contributes to the growth of knowledge by increasing the powers of natural sight. On the other, it inhibits a useful function exercised by the naked eye, the function which makes an interaction with the world possible, thanks to the cooperation of the senses.

However, the real change in the paradigm of intelligibility as visibility occurred in the life sciences and Scottish culture of Smith's time. Accurate descriptions, although not rejected, seemed insufficient to account for natural and economic phenomena. By contrast, what characterized the new approaches was the conviction that visible interdependencies must be related to those invisible forces that accounted for the emergence of order both in the market and in the living world. The term "invisible", far from being an empty expression, became a notion that was useful in reformulating crucial problems.

References

Anstey, P. R. (2000). *The Philosophy of Robert Boyle*. Routledge.

Aristotle. (1936). *Physics*, a Revised Text with Introduction and Commentary by W. D. Ross. Clarendon Press.

Aspromourgos, T. (1996). *On the Origins of Classical Economics: Distribution and Value from William Petty to Adam Smith*. Routledge.

Bacon, F. (1868 [1623]). *On the Dignity and Advancement of Learning*. In J. Devey (Ed.), *The Physical and Metaphysical Works of Lord Bacon*. Bell and Daldy.

Bacon, F. (1999 [1627]). New Atlantis. In S. Bryce (Ed.), *Three Early Modern Utopias. Utopia, New Atlantis, The Isle of Pines* (pp. 149–186). Oxford University Press.

Bacon, F. (2000 [1620]). *The New Organon*, L. Jardine & M. Silverthorne (Eds.). Cambridge University Press.

Banzhaf, S. H. (2000). Productive Nature and the Net Product: Quesnay's Economies Animal and Political. *History of Political Economy, 32*(3), 517–551.

Barbon, N. (1859 [1685]). An Apology for the Builder. In J. R. McCulloch (Ed.), *A Select Collection of Scarce and Valuable Economical Tracts* (pp. 3–26). Printed for the Political Economy Club.

Barbon, N. (1905 [1690]). A Discourse of Trade. In J. H. Hollander (Ed.), *A Reprint of Economic Tracts* (pp. 9–43). John Hopkins Press.

Berkeley, G. (2017 [1732]). An Essay Towards A New Theory of Vision. In *Saggio su una nuova teoria della visione. Trattato sui principi della conoscenza umana*, facing English text. Bompiani.

Bernardi, W. (1995). La conquista del mondo invisibile: modelli epistemologici e teorie della vita nella rivoluzione scientifica. In *Storia della filosofia, storia della scienza. Saggi in onore di Paolo Rossi* (pp. 59–75). La Nuova Italia.

Botero, G. (1606). *A Treatise, Concerning the Causes of the Magnificencie and Greatnes of Cities*. Richard Ockould and Henry Tomes.

Boyle, R. (1772a [1690]). The Christian Virtuoso. In *Works* (Vol. 5). Johnston et al.

Boyle, R. (1772b [1690]). The Christian Virtuoso. The Second Part. In *Works* (Vol. 6). Johnston et al.

Brewer, A. (1992). Petty and Cantillon. *History of Political Economy, 24*(3), 711–728.

Cantillon, R. (2015). *Richard Cantillon's Essay on the Nature of Trade in General. A Variorum Edition* (R. van den Berg, Trans. & Ed.). Routledge.

Clericuzio, A. (2015). Le forme e i moti della materia. Trasformazioni del meccanicismo nel Seicento. In P. Pecere (Ed.), *Il libro della natura* (Vol. I, pp. 67–107). Carocci.

Close, A. J. (1969). Commonplace Theories of Art and Nature in Classical Antiquity and in the Renaissance. *Journal of the History of Ideas, 30*(4), 467–486.

Davenant, C. (1771a [1698]). Discourses on the Public Revenues, and on the Trade of England. In *The Political and Commercial Works* (Vol. I). Printed for R. Horsfield.

Davenant, C. (1771b [1699]). An Essay Upon the Probable Methods of Making a People Gainers in the Balance of Trade. In *The Political and Commercial Works* (Vol. 2). Printed for R. Horsfield.

Dear, P. (1995). *Discipline and Experience. The Mathematical Way in the Scientific Revolution.* University of Chicago Press.

Dear, P. (2006). *The Intelligibility of Nature. How Science Makes Sense of the World.* University of Chicago Press.

Des Chene, D. (2001). *Spirits and Clocks. Machine and Organism in Descartes.* Cornell University Press.

Descartes, R. (1985a [1647]). Principles of Philosophy. In *The Philosophical Writings of Descartes* (Vol. 1). Cambridge University Press.

Descartes, R. (1985b [1662]). Treatise on Man. In *The Philosophical Writings of Descartes* (Vol. 1). Cambridge University Press.

Galilei, G. (1967 [1632]). *Dialogue Concerning the Two Chief World Systems—Ptolemaic & Copernican* (2nd ed.). University of California Press.

Hobbes, T. (1991 [1658]). On Man. In B. Gert (Ed.), *Man and Citizen.* Anchor Books.

Hobbes, T. (1996 [1651]). *Leviathan*, J. C. A. Gaskin (Ed.). Oxford University Press.

Hooke, R. (1665). *Micrographia or Some Physiological Descriptions of Minute Bodies Made by Magnifying Glasses, with Observations and Inquiries Thereupon.* Printed by Martyn and Allestry.

Hooke, R. (1705). *The Posthumous Works of Robert Hooke,* published by R. Waller. Printed by S. Smith and B. Walford.

Hoselitz, B. F. (1968). Agrarian Capitalism, the Natural Order of Things: François Quesnay. *Kyklos, 21*(4), 637–664.

Johnson, E. A. J. (1960 [1937]). *Predecessors of Adam Smith.* Augustus M. Kelley.

Keller, V. (2012). Mining Tacitus: Secrets of Empire, Nature and Art in the Reason of State. *The British Journal for the History of Science, 45*(2), 189–212.

Koerner, L. (1999). *Linnaeus: Nature and Nation.* Harvard University Press.

Lakoff, G., & Johnson, M. (1999). *Philosophy in the Flesh. The Embodied Mind and Its Challenge to Western Thought.* Basic Books.

Letwin, W. (1975). *The Origins of Scientific Economics.* Greenwood Press.
Linnæi, C. (1748). *Amoenitates Academicae.* Cornelium Haak.
Locke, J. (1980 [1690]). *Second Treatise of Government* (C. B. Macpherson, Trans. & Ed.). Hackett Publishing Company.
Locke, J. (1997 [1690]). *An Essay Concerning Human Understanding.* Penguin Books.
Lovejoy, A. O. (1936). *The Great Chain of Being.* Harvard University Press.
Machamer, P. (1998). Galileo's Machines, His Mathematics, and His Experiments. In P. Machamer (Ed.), *The Cambridge Companion to Galileo* (pp. 53–79). Cambridge University Press.
Malynes, G. (1622). *Consuetudo, Vel Lex Mercatoria.* Adam Islip.
Mayr, E. (1982), *The Growth of Biological Thought. Diversity, Evolution, and Inheritance.* The Belknap Press of Harvard University Press.
Mirabeau, (V. Riqueti, marquis de). (1763). *Philosophie Rurale.* Libraires Associés.
Mirabeau, (V. Riqueti, marquis de). (2003 [1763]). Extract from 'Rural Philosophy'. In R. L. Meek (Ed.), *The Economics of Physiocracy. Essays and Translations* (pp. 57–64). Routledge.
Misselden, E. (1623). *The Circle of Commerce.* Printed by J. Dawson.
Newman, W. R. (2004). *Promethean Ambitions. Alchemy and the Quest to Perfect Nature.* University of Chicago Press.
Perrotta, C. (2004). *Consumption as an Investment: I. The Fear of Goods from Hesiod to Adam Smith.* Routledge.
Petty, W. (1963a [1690]). Political Arithmetick. In C. H. Hull (Ed.), *The Economic Writings of Sir William Petty* (Vol. 1). Augustus M. Kelley.
Petty, W. (1963b [1691]). The Political Anatomy of Ireland. In C. H. Hull (Ed.), *The Economic Writings of Sir William Petty* (Vol. 1). Augustus M. Kelley.
Petty, W. (1963c [1662]). Treatise of Taxes and Contributions. In C. H. Hull (Ed.), *The Economic Writings of Sir William Petty* (Vol. 1). Augustus M. Kelley.
Petty, W. (1967 [1928]). *The Petty Papers. Some Unpublished Writings of Sir William Petty* (Vol. II). Marquis of Lansdowne (Ed.), reprint. Augustus M. Kelley.
Quesnay, F. (1888 [1743]). Mémoires de l'Académie Royale de Chirurgie – Préface. In A. Oncken (Ed.), *Œuvres économiques et philosophiques.* J. Baer & C., Libraires Éditeurs.
Quesnay, F. (1958a [1756]). Évidence. In *François Quesnay et la physiocratie* (Vol. II). I.N.E.D.
Quesnay, F. (1958b [1763]). Chapitre VII de la "Philosophie Rurale". In *François Quesnay et la physiocratie* (Vol. II). I.N.E.D.
Quesnay, F. (1958c [1767]). Despotisme de la Chine. In *François Quesnay et la physiocratie* (Vol. II). I.N.E.D.
Rossi, P. (1968). *Francis Bacon: From Magic to Science* (S. Rabinovich, Trans. & Ed.). Routledge and Kegan Paul.

Rousseau, J.-J. (1932). *Correspondance Générale de J.-J. Rousseau*, T. Dufour (Ed.), Tome 17. Librairie Armand Colin.

Sabbagh, G. (2016). Cantillon in French and English. Two Editions by Richard van den Berg and Antoin E. Murphy: New Facts and Hypotheses. *Contributions to Political Economy, 35*(1), 91–125.

Sawday, J. (2007). *Engines of the Imagination. Renaissance Culture and the Rise of the Machine*. Routledge.

Schabas, M. (2005). *The Natural Origins of Economics*. University of Chicago Press.

Shapin, S. (1996). *The Scientific Revolution*. University of Chicago Press.

Sivado, A. (2019). The Ontology of Sir William Petty's Political Arithmetic. *The European Journal of the History of Economic Thought, 25*(5), 1003–1026.

Steiner, P. (1998). *La "science nouvelle" de l'économie politique*. Presses Universitaires de France.

Théré, C., & Charles, L. (2008). The Writing Workshop of François Quesnay and the Making of Physiocracy. *History of Political Economy, 40*(1), 1–42.

Vaggi, G. (1987). *The Economics of François Quesnay*. Macmillan.

Vaggi, G. (1995). The Limits of Physiocracy and Smith's Fortune. In *Economies et Sociétés*, Série Œconomia, Histoire de la Pensée économique, P.E., *22–23*(1–2), 59–77.

Wootton, D. (2015). *The Invention of Science: A New History of the Scientific Revolution*. Harper.

CHAPTER 7

The Invisible Order: Imagination, Nature and the Economic Sphere

Abstract Some signs that Smith had revised models of knowledge based on the principle of visibility can be found in the *History of Astronomy* and the *Theory of Moral Sentiments*. The visible order is not simply an order that finally, without residues, becomes observable as a result of applying correct techniques and methods, but is the outcome of invisible forces that organize it.

These topics are examined in this chapter, which explains how (1) the notion of scientific and moral imagination involves a cluster of conceptual metaphors, and how this leads to a revision of seventeenth-century ocular metaphor; and (2) visible and invisible dimensions interact in Smith's economic analysis.

Keywords Scientific imagination • Moral imagination • Division of labor • Prices • Productive labor

S. Fiori, *Machines, Bodies and Invisible Hands*,
https://doi.org/10.1007/978-3-030-85206-1_7

7.1 Scientific Imagination as a Conceptual Metaphor

According to Mark Johnson (2008: 44), "our abstract concepts are defined by conceptual metaphor and metonymy". This is especially true for the idea of imagination, a notion that was central in Hume's and Smith's theories. It was developed in the HA and in the TMS, where Smith, rather than theoretically defining what imagination is, metaphorically showed how imagination works. In particular, in the HA, (scientific) imagination was a concept sketched by means of metaphors that sought to illustrate a fundamental role of science: connecting apparently unrelated events.

Hume's argument on the association of ideas as a consequence of the "resemblance" among things or phenomena was developed in the second section of the HA, where Smith pointed out that it is aesthetically gratifying to observe "resemblances" (HA II.1: 37). However, resemblance entails something more than this, in that it is at the basis of a specific form of knowledge, as is evident in naturalists' taxonomies, where natural objects are ordered according to their similarities. Although the work of naturalists consists in placing natural objects in increasingly detailed classes, Smith did not conclude that classifications necessarily provide an increasingly—and objectively—accurate representation of nature, as seventeenth-century scientists and philosophers would have pointed out. Rather, he noted that observing resemblances sometimes produces an illusory knowledge, because our ability to reorganize taxonomies on the basis of similarities neither derives from nor necessarily produces a knowledge of the objects under examination.

> Whatever, in short, occurs to us we are fond of referring to some species or class of things, with all of which it has a nearly exact resemblance; *and though we often know no more about them than about it*, yet we are apt to fancy that by being able to do so, we show ourselves to be better acquainted with it, and to have a more thorough insight into its nature. (HA II.3: 38–39, emphasis added)

Classifications have a psychological impact, in that they convince us that we have a deep knowledge of nature. But this belief falters when scientists discover an unusual object that defies classification. This engenders "wonder", an unpleasant "sentiment" associated with the awareness that a certain classificatory system is inadequate, and that nature consequently appears less familiar. Our need to confer order to nature by means of classifications is deeply rooted, and cannot coexist with the discontinuity introduced by objects which do not fit our criteria for representing the world. It is imagination aided by memory that seeks to restore confidence in our knowledge of nature. This operation is illustrated by means of the figurative, rather than theoretical, language of personification. Like a person, Smith maintains, imagination "in vain look[s] around all [its] classes of ideas in order to find one under which it may be arranged", and "fluctuate[s] to no purpose from thought to thought" (HA II.4: 39).

There is another kind of wonder that, unlike the previous instance, arises not from the difficulty of finding a suitable place for a natural object but from an "unusual succession of things" (HA II.9: 42). In this case, imagination is not only personified but also described by means of metaphorical expressions relating to the idea of movement. Usually, Smith maintains, when we see objects "to follow" each other, imagination "passes" "from the conception of the one to that of the other" (HA II.7: 40–41). "As its ideas *move* more rapidly than external objects, [imagination] is *continually running* before them, and therefore anticipates, before it happens, every event which falls out according to this ordinary course of things". Phenomena appear closely and reciprocally connected, "[w]hen objects *succeed* each other in the same train in which the ideas of the imagination have thus been accustomed *to move*". In this circumstance, objects are adapted to the natural path (the "natural career") of imagination. When ideas are coherently connected, they "*float* through the mind of their own accord, without obliging it to exert itself, or to make any effort in order to *pass* from one of them to another" (HA II.7: 41, emphasis added).

Imagination is metaphorically represented as a person that "passes", "runs", "moves" from one point to another, and the ideas that it forms are viewed as something that "float[s] through the mind", carried by the current, as it were. In accordance with this view, scientific systems are conceptualized as "imaginary machine[s]" which "connect together in the fancy those different *movements* and effects which are already in reality performed" (HA IV.19: 66, emphasis added).

In that it reproduces external movements, this representation of imagination is also a spatial metaphor. Smith uses the spatial vocabulary to show how imagination works. When imagination passes easily from one object to another, Smith represents this operation by resorting to the image of a path which must be traversed, where there is "no *break*, no stop, no *gap*, no *interval*" (HA II.7: 41). By contrast, when the succession of objects is unusual, imagination "endeavours to find out something which may fill up the *gap*, which, like a *bridge*, may so far at least unite those seemingly *distant* objects, as to render the passage of the thought betwixt them smooth, and natural, and easy" (HA II.8: 41–42, emphasis added). The work of imagination consists in metaphorically creating "bridges" and building paths that link phenomena. These latter, in turn, are dealt with as points in space which can be physically connected. In this perspective, the image of the "invisible chains" whereby philosophers link apparently distant phenomena is also a conceptual, spatial metaphor which belongs to the same cluster of metaphors which includes the images of the bridge and the path.

Scientific systems reproduce real movements in the mind. They are imaginary, but not arbitrary devices. While on the one hand, they construct possible connections, on the other, they try in some way to follow real movements of natural events. Imagination creates paths, bridges and chains that connect two natural events by providing hypothetical causal relations, and at the same time it tries to adhere to the real paths, chains and movements of nature. Both real objects and imagination "move". What changes in the course of time is how scientific imagination accounts for movement of the world out there. The first step is observation, and the second is the attempt—achieved in various ways by alternative scientific approaches—to relate visible phenomena to their causes.

Imagination is the faculty which produces and visualizes images. Unsurprisingly, then, visual metaphors illustrate how imagination works. Evoking the ancient argument of the *theatrum mundi*, Smith maintains that nature is a "spectacle" to contemplate and admire. But the spectacle that we see is the result of a complex, hidden mechanism which brings it before us. When "a connecting chain of intermediate events" is discovered, although "it rarely happens that we can discover so clearly this connecting chain", we are "admitted behind the scenes", where the "machinery of the opera-house" stands (HA II.9: 42–43). The theatrical metaphor not only is connected to other metaphors which illustrate how scientific imagination works but also conceptualizes the relationship between visible effects (the spectacle) and the invisible structure (the machinery of the opera house) which makes the theatrical performance possible. In this perspective, the problem is not only to further expand nature's visibility but to produce by means of imagination a (provisional) knowledge of causal relations that remain behind phenomena.

Philosophical systems "sooth the imagination" and "render the *theatre of nature* a more coherent, and therefore a more *magnificent spectacle*, than otherwise it would have appeared to be" (HA II.12: 46, emphasis added). These visual metaphors are connected to the fact that nature must be coherently narrated in order to be appreciated as a theatrical performance. Since the "imagination is fundamentally creative and story-telling" (Griswold, 1999: 337), scientific systems can be viewed as theatrical narrations of nature that have followed each other over time. Philosophy, explained through its history, "is the most sublime of all the agreeable arts, and its revolutions have been […] the most distinguished of all those that have happened in the *literary world*" (HA II.12: 46, emphasis added). If scientific systems are narrations, it makes sense to examine them by regarding not "their absurdity or probability" but their narrative consistency.

In conclusion, metaphors of movement, spatial and theatrical metaphors, metaphors of narration and the metaphor of systems as machines are all instruments which identify in conceptual, although not in definitional terms, the notion of the scientific imagination.

7.2 Moral Imagination as a Conceptual Metaphor

The TMS also does not provide a definition of imagination. Rather, with the help of a set of metaphors, Smith describes how imagination works, revises the old model of knowledge based on the principle of visibility and establishes a relation between the visible dimension of phenomena and the less visible forces which lead to the formation of moral (and social) order.

Imagination is vividly described in the opening pages of the TMS. Our senses do not inform us about our fellows' pains and suffering. They "never did, and never can, carry us beyond our own person, and it is by the imagination only that we can form any conception of what are [another individual's] sensations", by placing "ourselves in his situation" (TMS I.i.I.2: 9–10). We cannot identify ourselves with "others", since we have not "immediate experience of what other men feel" (TMS I.i.I.2: 9), but we can be "spectators" of their behavior. If scientific imagination is a "bridge" that joins "distant objects", moral imagination is a bridge that joins the observer and the observed person. This occurs thanks to sympathy, the faculty which essentially arises from "the situation which excites it" (TMS I.i.I.10: 12), and allows us to participate in others' emotional experiences. This concept has a significant role in explaining the moral order, because it represents the invisible force that organizes moral, empirical relationships widespread in society. It leads to the formulation judgments approving or disapproving individuals' behaviors and ultimately to the formation of shared moral rules.

The observer-observed model is replicated in the process of self-evaluation. In this process, we see ourselves with the eyes of an "impartial spectator", and observe our behaviors "by placing ourselves before a looking-glass", because we can thus "view ourselves at the distance and with the eyes of other people" (TMS III.I.4: 112). The model of conscience can be (metaphorically) viewed as a dialogue with oneself that is directly related to the "metaphor of vision": "In TMS the activities of watching, seeing and observing all constitute forms of moral judgment, and the impartial spectator is simply the proper and most objective moral judge" (V. Brown, 1994: 60).[1]

By means of imagination we "suppose ourselves the spectators of our own behaviour", and this "is the only looking-glass by which we can, in some measure, with the eyes of other people, scrutinize the propriety of our own conduct" (TMS III.I.5: 112). The fact that the impartial spectator represents the gaze of society reflects the idea that morality is basically a social phenomenon. A man who lives without contacts with other human beings has no idea "of his own character, of the propriety or demerit of his own sentiments and conduct", but "Bring him into society, and he is immediately provided with the mirror which he wanted before" (TMS III.I.3: 110).

The figure of the looking-glass is interesting because, unlike a real mirror, the moral mirror does not reproduce an image identical to the original, such that the individual perfectly recognizes herself. Its function consists precisely in projecting an image of ourselves that differs from the one we perceive in its absence. In short, the gaze of the self which takes the point of view of the impartial spectator differs from the gaze of the self which does not observe itself with the "eyes of other people". This puts a distance between the two selves of the agent, namely, the self that observes and the observed self (TMS III.I.6: 113). As Forman-Barzilai (2010: 156) remarks, the "impartial spectator imposes a sort of affective distance on us and prompts us to reflect, to be less partial, more objective, judges". The work of imagination, so well described through visual metaphors ("looking-glasses", "mirrors", "impartial spectators", "eyes" that

[1] On the image of two selves in Shaftesbury, see V. Brown (1994, chap. 3).

"scrutinize", etc.), unveils a "spatial texture of sympathetic activity" (ibidem: 20) and emphasizes a distance that is instrumental in formulating correct judgments.

The right distance between spectator and observed person can be viewed as a "cognitive distance" which meets the methodological criterion for self-evaluating with the eyes of the impartial spectator. But there is also another aspect of the distance that must be taken into consideration. If individuals' judgments tend to converge, because people comply with the principle of the right distance, then the "moral distance" among individuals is reduced. Therefore, the right cognitive distance creates conditions to reduce the "moral distance". In this regard, Smith points out that individuals should constantly try to reduce the distance between the image from the mirror of the impartial spectator and the one they perceive when they do not see themselves through the spectator's gaze. Similarly, when we evaluate the behavior of others, we should try to decrease the distance between us and them. This distance can never be completely eliminated, because we do not identify with others, and as "spectators" we are necessarily distant from them. Nevertheless, a "perfect harmony of sentiments" (TMS I.i.1: 19) can be achieved thanks to a sort of cooperation between the observed person and spectator. This sympathetic relationship involves two procedures. First, the spectator must "strive to render as perfect as possible, that imaginary change of situation upon which his sympathy is founded" (TMS I.i.4.6: 21). Second, "the person principally concerned" must take the spectator's point of view (TMS I.i.4.8: 22). The consequence is that the observed person to some extent becomes spectator, and in turn the spectator becomes the observed person. In particular, the individual whose behavior and feelings are under observation "is as constantly led to imagine in what manner he would be affected if he was only one of the spectators of his own situation" (TMS I.i.4.8: 22). This results in harmony between the "sentiments" of individuals who have established a moral relationship, although this outcome is more a balance than a coincidence due to an absolute reduction of the distance between individuals' feelings.[2]

[2] These processes are facilitated by self-control, a virtue learned with sociality. A child soon learns how to moderate his passions, whose excessive expression is not appreciated by his peers (TMS, III.3.20: 145). Self-control, therefore, favors the convergence of sentiments, and behaviors that are compatible with each other.

These processes entail revising the model of knowledge based on immediate visibility and accepting the Baconian idea that deception of the senses must be avoided:

> As to the eye of the body, objects appear great or small, not so much according to their real dimensions, as according to the nearness or distance of their situation; so do they likewise to what may be called the natural eye of the mind: and we remedy the defects of both these organs pretty much in the same manner. (TMS III.3.2: 134–135)

Since "nearness or distance" can be misleading, we must avoid distortions produced by the "eye of the body" and by the "eye of the mind". Here again, Smith invokes the search for a right distance. It is this appropriate distance that allows us to correctly compare our interests and the interests of others, and to reject the view induced by selfish passions that prompts us to consider pursuing a small advantage as much more important than the great disadvantage that we can cause to a stranger (TMS III.3.3: 135, see also III.3.4: 137). Visual images illustrate how balance is achieved among opposite or divergent interests. The cognitive distance adopted by the impartial spectator allows this to be accomplished:

> We must view [our interests and those of another individual], neither from our own place nor yet from his, neither with our own eyes nor yet with his, but from the place and with the eyes of a third person, who has no particular connexion with either, and who judges with impartiality between us. (TMS III.3.3: 135)

These operations lead to the formation and internalization of "general rules of morality" (TMS III.4). Norms are socialized in a network of human relationships in which spectators and observed persons continually change their positions. This is reminiscent of the condition described by the "invisible hand" of the market. Decentralized processes for which individuals establish moral relationships lead to a beneficial, moral order that no one has either planned or foreseen. This order is engendered and explained by an invisible moral force, sympathy, which governs human relationships, silently induces the formation of shared social norms and unintentionally makes the convergence of behaviors possible.[3] In this

[3] See Haakonssen (1996: 131), Griswold (1999: 342) and Forman-Barzilai (2010, chap. 3).

perspective, mutual sympathy acts as an invisible organizing principle that accounts for the variety of observed ethical phenomena (Lecaldano, 1995: 25. See also Haakonssen, 1981: 58–59).

Visual metaphors, by representing sympathetic imagination as a principle which is operational in the "society of spectacle", give shape to these concepts (de Bolla, 1996: 74). If the scientific imagination constructed the coherence of the "theatre of nature", the moral imagination, according to Marshall (1984), can be interpreted as a theatrical construction, where "the self personates two different persons who try to play each other's part, change positions, and identify with each other" (ibidem: 599). But social relationships are also structured as theatrical relationships between agents, in which two individuals try to interpret each other's feelings. In the spectacle of human life, spectators and actors alternate, and "the phenomenology of the [TMS] is oriented around a spectator-actor dichotomy" (Griswold, 1999: 65).[4]

Although scientific and moral imaginations are similar in their capacity to establish relations, respectively, among objects and among individuals, they differ in some important respects. Scientists and philosophers are spectators, who observe natural phenomena from outside. They are able to connect distant objects by developing hypotheses about the causal structure of the world. By contrast, the spectator of the TMS is not a subject who analyzes moral phenomena from outside. Rather, s/he is part of the social sphere that s/he observes and participates in its construction along with many other spectators. In short, while the scientific imagination is a theoretical activity which constructs causal hypotheses, moral imagination is an activity related to practices of individuals which involve the unintentional construction of reality.

Analysis of practices, as Foucault has shown, reveals that subtle and pervasive forms of power characterize social relationships and institutions. Forman-Barzilai (2010: 64), referring to *Discipline and Punish*, has suggested that, although "the Foucauldian or Benthamite architect is absent in Smith's account", for Smith the individual is "subjected 'to a field of visibility' and is thus transformed into a 'principle of his own subjection'",

[4] Some themes, later developed by Smith, were anticipated in the famous periodical *The Spectator*, founded by Joseph Addison and Richard Steele in 1711. Its aim was to create a public consisting of "every one that considers the World as a Theatre, and desires to form a right Judgement of those who are actors in it" (*Spectator*, n. 370, quoted in Hundert, 1994: 149).

with the consequence that "we become on Smith's account unwitting organs of panoptic coercion against ourselves and others". While it is true that the "field of visibility" performs an important role in Smith's approach, the idea that sympathetic relationships develop a form of power in some way similar to "panoptic coercion" is more problematic, although intriguing. The prison designed by Bentham, according to Foucault, was a general model for the exercise of power in society in the last decades of the eighteenth century. In this model, power took the form of a "permanent, exhaustive, omnipresent surveillance capable of making all visible, as long as it could itself remain invisible" (Foucault 1995 [1975]: 214). Ideally in the penitentiary, a prisoner—and in principle, a madman, a patient, a worker and a schoolboy, respectively, in an asylum, a hospital, a factory and a school—confined in his/her cell was constantly seen, but could not see the supervisor placed in a central tower (ibidem: 200–202). The effect of visibility was entirely organized around surveillance as a condition that assured the automatic functioning of a widespread power in which many intermediate levels of control ensured that everyone mutually surveils (conversation with Foucault, in Bentham, 1983: 21). What is surprising—as Foucault remarks—is that such institutions, organized hierarchically, gave rise to relationships of power, where many individuals surveilled and at the same time were surveilled (Bentham, 1791: 29).

For Bentham, as for Smith, the visible refers to an invisible structure, but, unlike Smith, he conceived the relation between visible and invisible dimensions as a result of a planned, hierarchically structured system of surveillance. In Smith the gaze of the impartial spectator favors a (moral) discipline which the agent internalizes as a norm. In this sense, it is a tacitly exerted disciplinary power, but it is not an act of surveillance. Since everyone is at the same time spectator and observed, the system based on the relationship between these figures is the outcome of a decentralized process which leads to the formation of a moral order which is neither planned nor mediated by coercive institutions. Thus, the decentralization of the relationships between spectators and observed gives rise to a "microphysics of power" which does not take an institutional form. Individuals are at the same time subject and object: subject, in that they create and continually modify norms from which social order ensues, and object, in that the social order and the "general rules of morality" appear to them as external conditions with which they comply.

Lastly, there is another realm in which Bentham's and Smith's views are contiguous, although they differ. In Bentham's project, the penitentiary was a place in which prisoners' work would preferably be organized and exploited. It was a model for the perfect factory, where a "manufacturer" could start a business in conditions that for him were ideal. Bentham illustrated this point of view to a hypothetical interlocutor:

> You, who have been so much of an English traveller, cannot but have met with instances in plenty, if you have happened to note them down. Many are the instances you must have found in which the part taken by each workman is reduced to some one single operation of such perfect simplicity, that one might defy the aukwardest and most helpless idler than ever existed to avoid succeeding in it. Among the eighteen or twenty operations into which the process of pin-making has been divided, I question whether there is any one that is not reduced to such a state. In this point then he is upon at least as good a footing as other manufacturers: but in all other points he is upon a better. What hold can any other manufacturer have upon his workmen, equal to what my manufacturer would have upon his? What other master is there that can reduce his workmen, if idle, to a situation next to starving, without suffering them to go elsewhere? What other master is there, whose men can never get drunk unless he chooses they should do so? (Bentham, 1791: 87–88)

The technical division of labor in Smith's pin factory, to which Bentham refers, was not conceived as a mechanism of social control, but it had a feature—its visible organization—that Bentham believed was useful for his project. The visibility of the work processes in the penitentiary-workshop made it possible to transform the pin factory into a perfect, disciplinary mechanism under the manufacturer's watchful eye:

> And to crown the whole by the great advantage which is the peculiar fruit of this new principle, what other master or manufacturer, is there, who to appearance constantly, and in reality as much as he thinks proper, has every look and motion of each workman under his eye? (Bentham, 1791: 89)

7.3 The Two Levels of Natural Order

The relationship between visible and invisible appears in Smith's analysis of the natural order.

Man establishes two kinds of relationship with nature, which correspond to two related but alternative ways of representing its order. On the one hand, "artizans" establish a pragmatic relationship with natural forces, and on the other, "philosophers" reconceptualize nature.

An artisan does not perceive the need to discover connections among phenomena that he observes in his work. He

> has been for many years familiar with the consequences of all the operations of his art [...]. They fall in with what custom has made the natural movement of his imagination: they no longer excite his Wonder. (HA II.11: 44)

Nature is simply used by artisans. They pragmatically perceive a visible order of things, on whose basis they develop a knowledge whereby they control natural forces and transform natural objects. As for Hume, this is a knowledge based on habit and custom.

By contrast, philosophers "look for a chain of invisible objects to join together two events that occur in an order familiar to all the world" (HA II.11: 45). The "unusual succession of things" (HA II.9: 42) that philosophers, unlike artisans, perceive as an anomaly, gives rise to the second type of wonder. Philosophers look for "intermediate events" that restore continuity and make nature intelligible again. When this operation has been accomplished, nature appears in a new light, and its new features can consequently be narrated. The visible order to which this new image of nature corresponds does not end with itself but is related to invisible chains which organize it. The visible order that we saw earlier is not the same visible order observed in light of the new connecting principles, because these principles have introduced new criteria of visibility. Although Smith at the end of his digression seems to have found in the law of gravity a real explanation of physical phenomena, the logic of his analysis is that new anomalies observed in the future could make it necessary to revise Newton's theory, and stimulate the identification of new invisible chains whereby the order of nature can be reconceptualized.[5]

While conceptions of the seventeenth century and the early decades of the eighteenth suggested that the "Chain of Being" could adequately represent (living) nature through increasingly detailed classifications, Smith seems to suggest that if the "connecting principles of nature" change, the

[5] See Raphael and Skinner (1980: 21), Cremaschi (1984: 45) and Raphael (1985: 110–111).

classificatory systems also change, and this leads to the redefinition of the image of nature. If so, then understanding of nature consists not only in extending but also in reconfiguring its field of visibility. To make the "Chain of Being" visible through an appropriate taxonomy is the correct strategy for responding to the first kind of wonder, because it reduces the unease provoked by the perception of new elements which introduce uncertainty and disorder in our world. But this strategy is ineffective when the second type of wonder appears. In the first circumstance, the incompleteness of the picture of nature is overcome by perfecting the representation provided by classification, whereas in the second the visibility of nature must be reconsidered, because the succession of phenomena we observe is incomprehensible without a new interpretative paradigm.

The identification of a "great connecting principle" (HA IV.19: 66) is what irreversibly modifies the image of nature. The metaphor of the machine-system shows that at the beginning theoretical systems try to incorporate observed anomalies in the existing paradigm, but new "connecting principles" later replace the old ones. While, according to Smith, models of nature change over time, the Chain of Being, as "a perfect example of an absolutely rigid and static scheme of things" (Lovejoy, 1936: 242), implicitly assumed that that change was inessential. Improving the representation did not change the interpretation of nature.

Visible and invisible orders have a circular relation. While on the one hand, the field of visibility is continuously redefined in accordance with how science explains the invisible order, on the other, the visibility of phenomena influences how the invisible order is conceptualized. Scientists and artisans perceive the same visible order, and in many cases they share the same "prejudices of sense". For both, although to differing extents, the visible order is the first step in identifying the forces which govern it. It is the empirical premise for selecting explanations familiar to the imagination and rejecting representations that contradict the perception of the senses. Only later, the invisible order, in some way explained by science, allows us to see nature with different eyes.

Another circumstance shows that visible order influences the identification of the invisible chains:

> we observe that, in general, that no system, how well soever in other respects supported, has ever been able to gain any general credit on the world, whose connecting principles were not such as were familiar to all mankind. (HA II.12: 46)

This is confirmed by the history of chemistry, whose principles, being unknown to most men, did not establish a connection among phenomena in the popular imagination. The statements of chemistry can be extremely convincing, but the fact that they were unfamiliar hampered the development of this science, which remained in obscurity for centuries. Science and common sense share the same need to create a narrative that allows the imagination to connect phenomena with ease. But if these two forms of knowledge do not interact because they are too distant, new interpretations of the world do not "gain any general credit on the world", and science does not advance.

The view that holds that the relationship between visible and invisible order is circular was not circumscribed to the analysis of nature. It was also at the basis of Smith's economic theory. The visible phenomena influence the direction of any inquiry, because they provide the material for explanations. However, it is precisely the search for explanations that allows us to reconceptualize external reality. This circular relation also has some implications for the relationship between common sense and science, as illustrated by the history of chemistry and astronomy. Science can remain in obscurity if its "connecting principles" are not familiar "to all mankind", but at the same time it can gradually change the way common sense perceives explanations as familiar, as when the heliocentric view put forward by modern astronomers was finally accepted, although it described a universe that is not perceived by the senses.

7.4 The Two Forms of Knowledge

Artisans and philosophers develop two different conceptions of natural order. One is pragmatic and elementary; the other is conceptually complex. They correspond to two distinct forms of knowledge that, to use Haakonssen's words, can be defined as "concrete knowledge" and "system knowledge". "Concrete knowledge" is empirical knowledge based on the visible image of natural phenomena, while "system knowledge" is the abstract knowledge that identifies "invisible chains" which explain the structure of nature (Haakonssen, 1981: 79).

The dual character of the knowledge of nature is replicated in man's relationship with natural forces:

> To apply in the most advantagious manner those powers which are allready known and which have already been applyed to a particular purpose, does

> not exceed the capacity of an ingenious artist. But to think of the application of new powers, which are altogether unknown and which have never before been applied to any similar purpose, belongs to those only who have a greater range of thought and more extensive views of things than naturally fall to the share of a meer artist. When an artist makes any such discovery he showes himself to be not a meer artist but a real philosopher, whatever may be his nominal profession. (ED: 570)

On the one hand, artisans, as stated in the HA, usefully combine natural forces, although they do not know what they really are. Most of the time they limit themselves to replicating the same practices in their workshops. Some of them, however, may introduce simple modifications in the machines they use to employ in "the most advantagious manner" natural forces which are "allready known" (ED: 570). Similar innovations are also introduced in the factory, where it may be that a young worker modifies the "fire-engine" with a string to save labor. Though he does not know the force embodied in the machine, his "concrete knowledge" allows him to subdue it, and for this reason he may considered more than a "meer artist".

On the other hand, scientists discover "new powers" and make them available for use. Unlike the young workman, who invented a new way to exploit the force incorporated in the machine,

> [i]t was a real philosopher only who could invent the fire engine, and first form the idea of producing so great an effect, by a power in nature which had never before been thought of. (ED: 570)

Accordingly, man can relate to nature in three ways. The first two pertain to "concrete knowledge". In one case, the use of the forces of nature is replicated in the same way indefinitely in factories and workshops, while in the other these forces are exploited in an innovative fashion. Neither case requires that nature be known intrinsically. It is sufficient to know how to use and divert its energy. The third way, which pertains to "system knowledge", requires a greater knowledge of nature. Moreover, the three forms of exploitation of nature have in common the same instrumental character and share the same pragmatic origin. However, it was with the development of civilization that innovations, especially if technical in nature, "became the business of a peculiar trade" introduced by "philosophers or men of speculation" (WN I.i.9: 21).[6] The knowledge that made it possible to understand natural forces was thus institutionalized.

Nature is a field characterized by forces which invisibly are at work, and produce phenomena, as the experiences of artisans, innovators and philosophers show. This aspect also emerges in the essay on *Imitative Arts*, where Smith compares products of human art and nature:

> The nobler works of Statuary and Painting appear to us a sort of wonderful phænomena, differing in this respect from the wonderful phænomena of Nature, that they carry, as it were, their own explication along with them, and demonstrate, even to the eye, the way and manner in which they are produced. (IA I.16: 185)

In the seventeenth century, from Descartes to Hobbes, the imitative capacity of art was assumed as a criterion for the intelligibility of nature. If nature is a machine, then—Descartes, Boyle and others argued—studying the machine sheds light on natural mechanisms. Art and new techniques, Bacon and Hooke maintained, reveal the "secrets" of nature (see Chap. 6). By way of contrast, according to Smith, at least as regards artistic products, (imitative) art is not an extension of nature, because there is no transitive property that makes it possible to project intelligibility of art over nature. Only art can immediately reveal the processes whereby its own objects are produced. It belongs to the sphere of the visible, because understanding an artistic product does not require the search for invisible chains which explain the process which has led to its production. There is no gap between the visible dimension and the procedure that yielded the artistic object. While the latter is visible to "the eye, even of an unskillful spectator" (IA I.16: 185), the processes which engender natural phenomena can remain invisible to the eye of the observer. Smith points out:

> The works of the great masters in Statuary and Painting, it is to be observed, never produce their effects by deception. They never are, and it never is intended that they should be mistaken for the real objects which they represent. (IA I.15: 184)

[6] The philosophers described in the HA and in the WN, however, differ in some respects. In the HA, philosophers elaborate general scientific theories which explain the nature of the universe, while the philosophers described in the WN elaborate theories that involve a technical level of abstraction.

Unlike (imitative) art, where procedures followed by artists are observable and "never produce their effects by deception", nature deceives when it influences the human world. Nature achieves its ends by means of complex processes that are neither visible nor predictable. The process of forming an artistic product is similar to the productive process in a workshop. It requires an intentional activity addressed to the production of an object, in which each phase of the work is planned to achieve a certain result. By way of contrast, Smith points out in the TMS, where he deals with the argument of nature's deception, nature does not induce the production of wealth by relying on human intentionality. Wealth is appreciated not because it is useful, but because we are fascinated by the "beauty of order" that strikes us when we observe the means-ends coherence of the machine of wealth (see Sect. 3.3). Only apparently is the desire to satisfy our material needs the motive which prompts us to obtain wealth. But, by contrast, it is the beauty of order that unknowingly guides our behavior.

This explains nature's deception as a gap between what we intentionally do and what we achieve without planning:

> It is this deception which rouses and keeps in continual motion the industry of mankind. It is this which first prompted them to cultivate the ground, to build houses, to found cities and commonwealths, and to invent and improve all the sciences and arts, which ennoble and embellish human life; which have entirely changed the whole face of the globe, have turned the rude forests of nature into agreeable and fertile plains, and made the trackless and barren ocean a new fund of subsistence, and the great high road of communication to the different nations of the earth. The earth by these labours of mankind has been obliged to redouble her natural fertility, and to maintain a greater multitude of inhabitants. (TMS IV.I.10: 183)

7.5 The Two Dimensions of the Division of Labor

Like nature, the sphere of economic relations also exhibits two dimensions. The first concerns the visibility of the technical division of labor in the workshop, as a planned activity which corresponds to behaviors aimed at achieving specific ends. The second dimension is related to the social division of labor in society, a sphere which cannot be planned. If the metaphor of the machine seems to describe the workshop as a system intentionally modified and made more efficient by reducing its "principles of movement", it cannot be used to describe the division of labor in society, because machines do not produce effects other than those for which they are designed (see Sect. 3.4).

Smith declares that the best way to appreciate the division of labor is to observe it where it is most visible, that is, in the production of pins in a workshop. This visibility is lost, however, when one passes to large-scale manufactures, where it is impossible to aggregate a large number of workers into the same place.

In fact:

> In those trifling manufactures which are destined to supply the small wants of but a small number of people, the whole number of workmen must necessarily be small; and those employed in every different branch of the work can often be collected into the same workhouse, and placed at once under *the view of the spectator*. In those great manufactures, on the contrary, which are destined to supply the great wants of the great body of the people, every different branch of the work employs so great a number of workmen, that it is impossible to collect them all into the same workhouse [so that] the division [of labor] has accordingly been *much less observed*. (WN I.i: 14, emphasis added)

Thus, the size of the manufacture determines what the eyes of the observer perceive. In the "great manufactures", the part of the process that does not fall under the gaze of the "spectator" is invisible only because of the eye's limited capabilities. But this limit can easily be overcome. The technical division of labor is observable in principle even though workers are not collected in the same "workhouse". Consequently, small and large manufactures do not differ in substance.

By contrast, the social division of labor shows a type of invisibility which does not depend only on the observer's limited capacity to perceive the organization of labor dispersed over large spaces. The analysis of the division of labor developed in Chap. 1 of the WN describes the visible advantages of labor productivity. They derive from the fact that workers increase their "dexterity", save time "lost in passing from one species of work to another" and contribute to inventing machines that make labor more productive (WN I.i.5–8: 17–20). It would be hard to maintain that these events from which tangible advantages derive are not intentional. By contrast, the description of the origin of the division of labor set forth in Chap. 2 refers to social advantages which are not achieved intentionally.

While in principle labor productivity can increase without exchange relationships, since even an isolated individual can improve her "dexterity", and invent simple machines or techniques which allow her to be more productive, a human inclination at the basis of the (social) division of labor requires, and at the same time creates, market relationships. Smith defines this human predisposition as "the propensity to truck, barter, and exchange one thing for another". While the increase in a factory's labor productivity depends on human wisdom and capacity to foresee future advantages that derive from it, the social division of labor "is not originally the effect of any human wisdom, which foresees and intends that general opulence to which it gives occasion" (WN I.ii.1: 25). In this case, the (social) division of labor loses its visibility not because of its spatial fragmentation, but because the advantages that it produces depend on an organization of the market which develops independently of any form of planning. Coordination among different branches of activity takes shape irrespective of the will of agents and develops in a way that they do not control. Through the social division of labor, the visible surface of the planned organization of manufactures—to which the technical division of labor specifically refers—is related to the less observable system of economic relations.

The connection between the social and technical division of labor leads Smith to think that the passage from one to the other is only a matter of scale, since the small scale of the workshop is not qualitatively different from the large scale which characterizes the division of labor in the "great society" (WN I.viii. 57: 104). The source of this conviction is that the division of labor entails a specialization that increases productivity both in a pin factory, where labor is divided into "eighteen distinct operations", and in society, where labor is divided among different professions. But the visible effects of the social division of labor cannot be separated from the invisible process which unintentionally shapes the market society, determines collective advantages and induces new specializations of employment.

In conclusion, the technical and social division of labor revealed a circular relationship between visible and invisible orders. The organization achieved by the technical division of labor in small "manufactures" is immediately visible, while it is less perceptible in "great manufactures". This perceptual limit, however, can be easily overcome. Smith does not capture the difference between the technical and social division of labor. The division of labor among professions gives rise to the economic organization of society, which is invisible not only because the gaze cannot observe it in its entirety. This organization is an order that produces beneficial effects that no one has planned and that cannot be reduced to the immediate advantages consequent on increasing labor productivity. While any workshop can organize labor more efficiently, no one can plan a more efficient organization of society.

7.6 The Two Dimensions of Prices: Nominal and Real Prices, and Market and Natural Prices

The relation between visibility and invisibility also features in Smith's analysis of nominal and real prices, and market and natural prices.

Smith distinguishes value in use and value in exchange. Value in use pertains to the level of visibility because as a result of concrete labor, it refers to the tangible utility of things. The nature of value in exchange is perhaps less evident. However, since it involves the familiar practice of transactions, value in exchange can similarly be considered as a notion which refers to observable phenomena that occur in the market. While the nature of value in use is self-evident, that of value in exchange requires an additional explanation because, in order to have an empirical understanding of the proportions and prices at which commodities are exchanged, it is necessary to develop a more abstract notion of value. For this reason Smith states that his aim is "to investigate the principles which regulate the exchangeable value of commodities" and "what is the real measure of this exchangeable value" (WN I.iv.14–15: 46). If individuals use "concrete knowledge" to evaluate value in use and value in exchange, the analysis of what really determines the value of commodities beneath the surface of market relationships calls for a "system knowledge" that can identify the less evident cause of this phenomenon. The hidden cause which acts as a "connecting principle", and explains how transactions occur, is labor.

Here again, Smith puts forward a dualistic view, as the title of Chap. 5 of the WN suggests: "Of the real and nominal Price of Commodities, or of their Price in Labor, and their Price in Money". The real (but invisible) price is the "toil and trouble" generated by the labor needed to produce commodities, when it is performed by the worker in "his ordinary state of health, strength and spirits [and] in the ordinary degree of his skill and dexterity", in that "he must always lay down the same portion of his ease, his liberty, and his happiness" (WN I.v.7: 50). The body, therefore, is dealt with as unity of measure of labor. In fact, "Equal quantities of labour, at all times and places, may be said to be of equal value to the labourer" (WN I.v.7: 50).

The nominal (and visible) price, by contrast, is related to the relative price. Initially, in fact, the value of a good is measured in terms of a certain amount of other goods, and subsequently by money. But, as mentioned earlier, the invisible measure (invisible to common sense) is labor. Thus, Smith maintains:

> Every commodity besides, is more frequently exchanged for, and thereby compared with, other commodities than with labour [...] The greater part of people too understand better what is meant by a quantity of a particular commodity, than by a quantity of labour. The one is a *plain palpable object*; the other an *abstract notion*, which, though it can be made sufficiently intelligible, is not altogether so natural and obvious. (WN I.v.5: 49, emphasis added)

As philosophical knowledge of nature unveils invisible chains that are not captured by common sense, so theoretical knowledge finds relations that are not immediately perceived in normal transactions. Since the exchange relationship is normally conceptualized as an exchange of "plain" and "palpable" commodities, common sense stops at the threshold of the visible in understanding the transaction. Only the use of an "abstract notion", such as the notion of labor, can go beyond this limit, permitting access to the hidden dimension of exchange to which real prices refer.

One might ask what the reasons are which prevent labor from being used as a pragmatic measure of value in the market, given that labor is "the only accurate measure of value [...] at all times and places" (WN I.v.17: 54). This question is justified by the fact that, in the opening of Chap. 6 of the WN, Smith maintains that in an "early and rude state of society", beavers and deer were bartered by calculating the exchange value in terms of "quantities of labor" (WN I.vi. 1–2: 65). But he also specifies that it became impossible to calculate the exchange value in this way, when in advanced societies profit and rent were included as parts of the price of commodities. However, there is another reason which explains why the value of transactions is calculated pragmatically by comparing quantities of commodities and not quantities of labor:

> But though labour be the real measure of the exchangeable value of all commodities, it is not that by which their value is commonly estimated. It is often difficult to ascertain the proportion between two different quantities of labour. *The time spent in two different sorts of work will not always alone determine this proportion.* The different degrees of hardship endured, and of ingenuity exercised, must likewise be taken into account [...] *But it is not easy to find any accurate measure either of hardship or ingenuity.* In exchanging indeed the different productions of different sorts of labour for one another, some allowance is commonly made for both. *It is adjusted, however, not by any accurate measure, but by the higgling and bargaining of the market, according to that sort of rough equality which, though not exact, is sufficient for carrying on the business of common life.* (WNI.v: 48–49, emphasis added)

The difficulty of ascertaining "the proportion between two different quantities of labour" (a topic developed in Chap. 10 of the WN) depends on the fact that "it is not easy to find any accurate measure either of hardship or ingenuity" of labor. Labor as "measure of value" cannot be dealt with in precise terms because it includes variables that are not readily treated in arithmetical terms. The consequence is that values are equalized pragmatically by the market, although this entails a certain degree of uncertainty and indeterminateness. Nominal prices act as simple indicators of real values, but despite the limits of this tool, Smith does not think that quantities of labor could be used as a substitute for the nominal price. Rather than look for a method for pragmatically replacing nominal with real prices, he prefers to investigate how corn and silver approximate the "universal measure of value" (WN I.v.17: 54). This engenders a peculiar relation between nominal and real prices. The nominal prices are not replaced by the real prices, in that they continue to be the reference point in exchanges, while the less visible real prices account for the level of nominal prices, although they cannot be used empirically.[7]

The relationship between market and natural prices also involves a dual dimension. The process of the adjustment of market prices is due to the fact that individuals, by striving to achieve the highest returns, activate a mechanism which allows the market to self-regulate. In fact, market prices are leveled by competition, which operates on both the demand and supply sides of the market, and this produces a tendential convergence toward

[7] By contrast Schumpeter maintained that, according to Smith, the quantity of labor exchanged with commodities in the market is a useful substitute for monetary prices (Schumpeter, 1997 [1954]: 307–310).

the natural price, that is, that price which includes the "natural rates of wages, profit, and rent" prevailing "at the time and place" (WN I.vii.3: 72), and varies according to "riches or poverty", and "advancing, stationary, or declining state of the society" (WN I.vii.34: 80). The natural price may diverge from the market price in that market prices are determined by the quantity supplied and the "effectual demand", and this means that "[d]ifferent accidents may sometimes keep them suspended a good deal above [the natural price], and sometimes force them down even somewhat below it". However, the natural price is "the central price" toward which the market price is "continually gravitating" (WN I.vi.15: 75).

Natural price in Smith, as in other classical economists, Caravale (1992: 19) maintains, acts as the center of gravity, is thus "more hidden" and "less observable" than the market price, and in no case is directly perceived. Similarly, Harcourt and Kriesler (2012: 5) remark, "Ever since the Physiocrats and Adam Smith, political economists have wrestled with the relationship between observable market prices, underlying natural prices [...] and the tendency to establish the equality of sectoral rates of profit with the overall macroeconomic economy-wide rate of profits in competitive conditions". This helps clarify the sense in which Smith adopts a dualistic logic. The natural price is invisible; it is at the basis of normal transactions and explains the nature of the market price, which, in its turn, is the visible signal which induces individuals to react to the excess of supply or demand. This behavior is consistent with the pursuit of self-interest. But perception of our own self-interest depends on our limited horizon of visibility. Although our decisions as economic agents are not influenced by the natural price, it confers order on the movements of market prices, and this entails a circular relationship between the two kinds of price. The invisible explains the visible; yet the latter is not a mere, superficial phenomenon, because it determines the choices made by agents, who, in this way, contribute to modifying the structure of natural prices over time.

7.7 The Two Dimensions of Productive Labor

The logical duality of Smithian theory also emerges in his treatment of productive labor, a topic dealt with in Book II of the WN, but directly connected to arguments in Book I.

Productive labor is that kind of labor which "adds to the value of the subject upon which it is bestowed" (WN II.iii.1: 330), while unproductive labor does not add value, because it produces services, but not commodities. But in what does the value-added consist? It is not visible as such, while its existence is deduced from the fact that labor transforms matter. What we can observe is only the performance of the work, and the consequent metamorphosis of the matter to which it is applied. This process can be interpreted as an invisible transfer of value, not by the evidence of things, but by a theoretical vision. It is not by chance that metaphorical language expresses this idea. By means of such language, labor is dealt with as a tangible thing: it is "stocked and stored" in commodities, and it is "fixed" when it "realizes itself in some particular subject or vendible commodity" (WN I.iii.1: 330). It follows that to define the capacity of labor to add value, it is necessary to visualize this concept in physical terms. In this way, what is unobservable—the addition of value—becomes, so to speak, "plain and palpable". The tangible result of applying work becomes the indisputable sign that new value has been brought forth.

From Barbon to Locke, and Quesnay (see Sects. 6.2 and 6.4), labor was conceived as the capacity to modify nature both in qualitative terms—because it changes the form of natural matter—and in quantitative terms, because it multiplies products provided by nature. Labor, therefore, does not "add value", but simply transforms, and according to Quesnay, it does not create (or add) value, because it is sterile. In these authors, the interpretation of economic phenomena was based on the description of the visible order. This perspective influenced not only Barbon, Petty and Locke, but also Quesnay, who considered the analysis of nature as a condition for exploring exchange relationships which occur in the market. By contrast, introducing "value" brought the invisible as well as the visible dimension of productive labor into the picture.

Unproductive labor, however, seems to differ in character. It is visible, but since it is not materialized in any commodity, it does not possess other invisible qualities. Like productive labor, it is useful and requires "toil and trouble". But, Smith states, it does not produce value.

7.8 Visibility and Invisibility in Historical Perspective

In Book V of the WN, in the part devoted to the "Expence of Justice", where Smith alludes to the stadial development of society (hunting, pasturage, agriculture and commerce), he analyzes the notion of authority in relation to the transformation of the forms of property. He argues that four causes legitimize authority "antecedent to any civil institution": (1) "superiority of personal qualifications, of strength, beauty, and agility of body; of wisdom, and virtue, of prudence, justice, fortitude, and moderation of mind", (2) "superiority of age", (3) "superiority of fortune" and (4) "superiority of birth". The latter, however, is not an autonomous source of authority. It depends on the third type of cause, because it presupposes an "antient superiority of fortune in the family of the person who claims it" (WN V.i.b. 5–8: 711–713).

The causes which give an individual a particular power over his fellow men should be visible and indisputable. In this perspective, the first source of authority ("superiority of personal qualifications") is precarious or provisional. Physical strength, although it is visible, is temporary, and without "qualifications of the mind" is unlikely to be a source of authority on its own. Qualifications of the mind, in turn, are "invisible qualities", and this makes them "always disputable, and generally disputed". For this reason, barbarous and civilized societies tried to find a "more plain and palpable" source of authority (WN V.i.b. 5: 711).

The second source of authority ("superiority of age") is generally accepted in different kinds of society. It is "a plain and palpable quality which admits of no dispute", and in the feudal age was at the basis of the rule whereby all landed property was transferred to the eldest son on his father's death (WN V.i.b. 6: 711).

The third source of authority ("superiority of fortune") was the most effective in creating relations of subordination. It is tangible in that, if consisting in "herds and flocks", it enabled the "Tartar chief" to maintain "a thousand men". Its distinctive feature is that it does not depend on personal qualities, which by definition persist only for a limited time. For this reason, property, "even in an opulent and civilized society" (WN V.i.b. 7: 712), was considered the measure of power. This perspective also emerges in Book III of the WN, where the tangible source of power that Smith discusses is the ownership not of cattle but of land. Feudal lords used it as a "means, not of subsistence merely, but of power" (WN III.ii.3: 383), to exert their authority over people who lived under their protection.

In short, in the ages preceding the advent of the commercial society, with the exception of the ancient societies based on hunting, the source of authority took the "plain and palpable" form of property. As a result, relations of subordination were established among mankind, social hierarchies were formed, and power was exercised as direct command over other men. The transition to the market society changed the way power was exerted.

In consequence of "the silent and insensible operation of foreign commerce and manufactures" (WN III.iv.10: 418), the great landed proprietor, the figure who historically replaced the feudal lord, was able to spend his excess revenue to buy commodities. This gradually led to the end of power exercised directly over other men, and the emergence of a new form of power: the "command over all the labour" (WN I.v.3: 48).

This command, exercised as the capacity to buy either labor time or commodities, is widespread in a commercial society, where "[e]very man [...] lives by exchanging" (WN I.iv.1: 37). It is pervasive, in that it is exercised to some extent by every individual, and shapes society differently than in the past. It is invisible, in the sense that no one can control how other members of society use share of their power, and in doing so engender the economic order. While in the past "plain and palpable" sources of authority served to establish hierarchies in society, now a more subtle power invisibly shapes the structure of society.

7.9 Conclusions

Some conclusions can be drawn from the topics discussed in this chapter:

1. Scientific and moral imaginations are concepts that can be clarified through a system of metaphors. These metaphors explain the relationship between visible and invisible phenomena which occur in moral and natural realms. In the moral sphere, in particular, visual metaphors explain how the individual horizon of visibility should be redefined. The "eye of the mind" should correct the distortions produced by an incorrect perspective. Rather than extending the ocular capacities, the relationship between the observer and the observed person should be reorganized. Spectators and mirrors are pressed into service to explain how people should regard their own and others' behavior. Society as a whole is organized as a decentralized system of relationships among individuals, who are at the same time spectators and observed persons, where sympathy is the organizing principle whereby the rules of morality are formed (see Schabas, 2005: 88–89).
2. The knowledge of nature also involves a relation between visible and invisible phenomena. In particular, scientists and natural philosophers provide narratives about the nature of the "invisible chains" that determine visible phenomena. The latter are the starting point of their

analyses. But the new formulation of the principles which connect natural objects yields a redefinition of the visible world.

3. Two forms of knowledge deal with visible and invisible events in the natural and economic realms.
4. Visible and invisible orders characterize commercial societies. They are circularly linked, as shown by Smith's analysis of the division of labor, real and nominal price, natural and market prices, and the notion of productive labor.
5. In the market society, the principles which legitimize authority, from which the form of social subordination derives, differ from those applied in past societies. Property is still the visible source of power in the market society, as it was in the past. But this power is no longer exercised directly on men. The power of commanding labor capacity, or buying labor crystallized in commodities, is decentralized. However, this decentralization engenders not chaos, but a form of coordination that no one has planned.

References

Bentham, J. (1791). *Panopticon or, the Inspection-House*. T. Payne.

Bentham, J. (1983). *Panopticon*, M. Foucault & M. Perrot (Eds.). Venezia.

Brown, V. (1994). *Adam Smith's Discourse. Canonicity, Commerce and Conscience*. Routledge.

Caravale, G. (1992). Alcune considerazioni sulla nozione di equilibrio nella teoria economica. *Studi economici, 47*(2), 5–44.

Cremaschi, S. (1984). *Il sistema della ricchezza. Economia politica e problema del metodo in Adam Smith*. Franco Angeli.

de Bolla, P. (1996). The Visibility of Visuality. In T. Brennan & M. Jay (Eds.), *Vision in Context: Historical and Contemporary Perspectives on Sight* (pp. 65–81). Routledge.

Forman-Barzilai, F. (2010). *Adam Smith and the Circles of Sympathy. Cosmopolitanism and Moral Theory*. Cambridge University Press.

Foucault, M. (1995 [1975]). *Discipline and Punish: The Birth of the Prison* (Alan Sheridan, Trans.). Vintage Books.

Griswold, C. L., Jr. (1999). *Adam Smith and the Virtues of Enlightenment*. Cambridge University Press.

Haakonssen, K. (1981). *The Science of a Legislator. The Natural Jurisprudence of David Hume and Adam Smith*. Cambridge University Press.

Haakonssen, K. (1996). *Natural Law and Moral Philosophy: From Grotius to the Scottish Enlightenment*. Cambridge University Press.
Harcourt, G. C., & Kriesler, P. (2012). *Introduction* (To Handbook of Post-Keynesian Economics: Oxford University Press: USA), Australian School of Business Research, Paper No. 2012 ECON 33: 1–70.
Hundert, E. J. (1994). *The Enlightenment's Fable: Bernard Mandeville and the Discovery of Society*. Cambridge University Press.
Johnson, M. (2008). Philosophy's Debt to Metaphor. In R. W. Gibbs Jr. (Ed.), *The Cambridge Handbook of Metaphor and Thought* (pp. 39–52). Cambridge University Press.
Lecaldano, E. (1995). Introduzione. In A. Smith (Ed.), *Teoria dei sentimenti morali*. Rizzoli.
Lovejoy, A. O. (1936). *The Great Chain of Being*. Harvard University Press.
Marshall, D. (1984). Adam Smith and the Theatricality of Moral Sentiments. *Critical Inquiry, 10*, 592–613.
Raphael, D. D. (1985). *Adam Smith*. Oxford University Press.
Raphael, D. D., & Skinner, A. S. (1980). General Introduction. In Adam Smith, *Essays on Philosophical Subjects*, W. P .D. Wightman & J. C. Bryce (Eds.). In *The Glasgow Edition of the Works and Correspondence of Adam Smith*. Oxford University Press.
Schabas, M. (2005). *The Natural Origins of Economics*. The University Chicago Press.
Schumpeter, J. A. (1997 [1954]). *History of Economic Analysis*. Routledge.

CHAPTER 8

Organization and Invisible Forces in the Life Sciences of the Late Eighteenth Century

Abstract Some features of Smith's theory can be better appreciated if compared with the theoretical developments that took place in the life sciences of his time. What Smith's economic theory and coeval biological knowledge had in common was the shift from the analysis of observable interdependencies to the analysis of the order (or organization) engendered by invisible forces which account for social and economic coordination.

In some respects, the invisible hand was similar to the image adopted by Théophile Bordeu, who described the natural body as a "swarm of bees" which behaves as a unitary system, although it is formed by distinct insects. Buffon, Maupertuis, Diderot and scholars of the Medical School of Montpellier also maintained that life cannot be explained in mechanical terms, and the visible dimensions of biological phenomena must necessarily refer to unknown forces which fix the organization of living beings.

Smith's notion of order had some elements in common with these medical and physiological conceptions, although economic theory and the sciences of life essentially revisited their analytical tools independently. This chapter discusses how these approaches changed the foundations of the two disciplines.

Keywords Organization • Life sciences • Buffon • Vitalism

S. Fiori, *Machines, Bodies and Invisible Hands*,
https://doi.org/10.1007/978-3-030-85206-1_8

8.1 Invisible Principles of Organization of Living Beings

Although the term "organization" became popular in the second half of the eighteenth century, it was not absent in the works of philosophers of the late seventeenth century.

In his *Essay Concerning Human Understanding*, Locke introduced the notion of organization as a criterion for defining the identity of vegetables, animals and human bodies. Bodies, he maintained, are not simple aggregates of matter. An oak differs from a "mass of matter" because it exhibits an "organization" which allows it "to receive and distribute nourishment, so as to continue and frame the wood, bark, and leaves, etc." (Locke, 1997 [1690]: 298). A plant is an organized system whose parts interact and partake "of the same life". This condition confers identity to plants, but it is not an exclusive trait of the living world:

> Something we have like this in machines, and may serve to illustrate it. For example, what is a watch? 'Tis plain 'tis nothing but a fit organization, or construction of parts, to a certain end, which, when a sufficient force is added to it, it is capable to attain. If we would suppose this machine one continued body, all whose organized parts were repaired, increased or diminished, by a constant addition or separation of insensible parts, with one common life, we should have something very much like the body of an animal. (Ibidem: 299)

The essential difference that Locke notes between machines and living beings, including human beings, is that

> in an animal the fitness of the organization, and the motion wherein life consists, begin together, the motion coming from within; but in machines, the force coming sensibly from without, is often away when the organ is in order, and well fitted to receive it. (Ibidem: 299)

What Locke sees as a negligible difference between living beings and machines is, on the contrary, a feature that invalidates the comparison and prevents bodies from being reduced to machines. As Nicholson (2014) maintains, organisms differ from machines precisely because organisms are "intrinsically purposive", whereas machines are "extrinsically purposive".

Organisms are not built by an external agent, and their parts, unlike those of a machine, exist only in relation to a collective interdependence, and not in isolation.

In the life sciences of the second half of the eighteenth century, living beings were not compared to machines. They exhibited an organization, and this was interpreted as a manifestation of the fact that life is irreducible to mechanical laws. François Jacob has shown that the concept of "organization", as described by Buffon and Maupertuis, implied the notion of a superior structure to which the perceptible properties of living beings were related.[1] Thus, with the end of the eighteenth century and the beginning of the nineteenth, "a new science was to appear. Its aim was no longer to classify organisms, but to study the processes of life; its object of investigation was no longer visible structure, but organization" (Jacob, 1973: 74). Initially, around the mid-eighteenth century, the hidden structure of nature was conceptualized in relation to Newtonian mechanics, where "secret combinations of particles underlay visible combinations of surfaces and volumes" (ibidem: 75). The properties of bodies were explained not only in relation to the nature of the atoms that compose matter "but also by the relations of attraction or affinity between these atoms" (ibidem: 75). However, as Diderot later argued, this was not sufficient to explain life. Rational mechanics' claim that nature is nothing but inert mass and motion was opposed by the idea of an active matter, capable of organizing itself and of producing living beings (Prigogine & Stengers, 1984: 82–83).

The concept of organization gradually replaced that of "visible structure" and provided "a hidden foundation for the bare data of description, for the being as a whole and for its functioning" (Jacob, 1973: 83). Living beings ceased to be represented as a simple association of organs, and

> anatomists no longer limited their work to describing independently each organ of a living being. They attempted to relate organ to performance and to compare the same organ in different animals or the different kinds of organs in the same animal. (Ibidem: 83)

[1] This was related to the decline of preformation theory: "As long as living organisms were perceived as combinations of visible structures, preformation provided the simplest explanation for the persistence of those structures through succeeding generations. The linear continuity of the living world in space and time required a continuity of form through the actual process of generation" (Jacob, 1973: 74).

As Ernst Mayr (1982: 183) points out,

> Taxonomists prior to Cuvier had acted on the whole as if each character was independent of every other character, and as if an organism with a different character had a different essence. Buffon had been the first to disagree with this atomistic approach. An organism was not an arbitrary jumble of characters, as it appeared from the writings of the Linnaeans; rather the composition of the characters was dictated by their "correlation."

A good vantage point for observing the changes that occurred in the life sciences is the late eighteenth-century history of embryology, where epigenetic theories reappeared after a long period dominated by preformation theory. In a context influenced by Newtonian and Leibnizian approaches, Maupertuis proposed an epigenetic theory focused on the idea of "attraction" as an active force in the organic and inorganic worlds (Solinas, 1967: 70–80; Casini, 1980: 389–395; Roe, 1981: 13–15). Why, he asked, should the same disposition of matter to form aggregates, observed in astronomy and chemistry, not operate in animal bodies (Maupertuis, 1965a [1745]: 88–89)? Some conjectures could be made on the basis of the invisible principle that accounted for the formation and organization of bodies. The seminal fluid in both male and female—he argued—contained particles which produced the organs, so that the embryo resulted from the mix of these two fluids. However, since attraction cannot explain why infinitesimal parts of matter join to form one organ instead of another, he maintained that the smallest particles of a living organism had capacity for "desire, aversion, memory" (Maupertuis, 1965b [1754]: 147; Roe, 1981: 13–15).

In his *Histoire naturelle*, Buffon argued that bodies form because "penetrating forces", that is, forces similar to those that govern gravity, magnetic attraction and chemical affinity, join and organize organic particles into "internal molds". Internal molds give external and internal shape to bodies, and in animal bodies in particular, they organize the matter received from nutrition. Human senses (especially sight) can only represent what happens outside, but cannot perceive and represent the internal structure of matter on which the "penetrating forces" act. In fact, penetrating force is an "active power" which does not depend on the "external qualities" of things. To perceive this force, it would be necessary that "eyes", instead of representing "surfaces", be able "to penetrate [...] the inner ["intime"] composition of matter". Since this is beyond our sensory system's abilities, we do not have a precise idea about this power, although it clearly exists. It is as substantial as gravity ("force de la pesanteur") and manifests itself by attracting "organic parts of nourishment" and penetrating bodies (Buffon, 1750: 17).

As Reill (2005: 43) remarks, Buffon's "goal was to relate the visible outer form to its invisible, deeper, and more important foundation". The invisibility of penetrating forces was not due to limits of ocular perception that could be resolved by enhancing sight with appropriate instruments. Senses simply are not able to capture what happens in the inner structure of organic and inorganic matter. This view opposed the one suggested by preformation theory, which held that the invisibility of living particles, due to microscopic dimensions of embryo, was a temporary condition, resolved by the body's development process. The mechanist approach, which considered the body as an aggregate of inert, elementary particles, was also untenable: "Life was not a 'metaphysical principle' as the Cartesians and Leibnizians maintained, 'but is a physical property of matter'" (ibidem: 43). Buffon remarked that mechanical principles consider extension, impenetrability, divisibility, motion, "external figure", "impulse" (engendered "by the action of springs") of matter. These properties are perceived by the senses, but "If the conformation of our senses were different, we would recognize qualities in matter that are very different from those enumerated above" (Buffon, 1750: 19, my translation). The senses give access to only one dimension of phenomena, but in principle many others are beyond their control. Therefore, "Only wanting to admit to matter the qualities that we know it to have seems to me a vain and unfounded pretension" (ibidem: 19, quoted in Reill, 2005: 43).

Penetrating forces were not occult forces in the traditional sense. They were not a metaphysical notion, but a plausible conjecture which arose from experience. Lastly, although the relation between visible phenomena and invisible forces remained indeterminate, Buffon believed that his system was the more comprehensive because it included other approaches:

> In my explanation of development and reproduction, I first admitted the mechanical principles, then the penetrating force of gravity ["force pénétrante de la pesanteur"], and, from analogy and experience, I have concluded that there are other penetrating forces which work on organized bodies. (Ibidem: 20, my translation)

Buffon proposed an image of living nature in which forces that govern organisms yield a permanent equilibrium similar to the equilibrium of the solar system. This conception "was also the model adopted by Adam

Smith in political economy: the fluctuations in prices oscillate constantly around a perfect equilibrium as if maintained by an 'invisible hand'" (Roger, 1997: 230). Buffon's and Smith's ideas are similar, Roger argues, because "nature", like the market, is a self-regulating system which corrects itself by means of its fluctuations (ibidem: 231).

Buffon harshly criticized the Linnaean assumption that living systems are hierarchical, and also denied the idea associated with the Great Chain of Being of the continuity of nature (Reill, 2005: 48–49).[2] Classificatory systems are necessarily incomplete because they arbitrarily establish univocal criteria that do not fully consider the complexity of nature. Living nature proceeds by "unknown gradations", it passes from one species to the other, and from one genus to another one, in "imperceptible shades" (Buffon, 1749: 18). Moreover, there are innumerable relations among species that are continuously discovered (see Roger, 1997, chap. 18). Given the multidimensional structure of nature, any attempt to produce a complete picture of nature is vain.

This explains why, according to Buffon, the Great Chain of Being could not be interpreted in terms of the "book of nature". The meaning of this famous image, used in the seventeenth century and by Linnaeus, was that nature could be interpreted by knowing its grammar. For Linnaeus in particular, this "book" was written not in letters, but in taxonomic characters (see Sect. 6.3). By examining the methods of previous studies in natural history, Buffon proposed an alternative interpretation: nature is not a book. The book of nature is not written by God, but by naturalists, who used a "dictionary" whose entries, placed in a "relative order", are "as arbitrary as the alphabetical order" (Buffon, 1749: 34). His conclusion was that attempting to systemize visible characters, without referring to the invisible organization of organisms, is misleading in understanding how nature works. However, classifications provided by naturalists over time, although arbitrary, are not useless. They have to be taken into consideration because a more precise picture of nature can emerge from comparing them.

With Diderot, the debate on organization shifted further on philosophical terrain. Influenced by the vitalist physician Théophile Bordeu, Diderot, like Buffon, reversed the traditional idea that the book of nature is fully intelligible in principle:

[2] More precisely, Buffon denied the idea of continuity among species, although he believed that there is a continuity within species (Reill, 2005: 49–50).

> And if, as an even clearer sign of his omnipotence than the wonders of nature, the Almighty had deigned to sketch out the mechanism of the universe on sheets inscribed in his own hand, is this great tome likely to be more intelligible to us than the universe itself? [...] For us, these pages would represent a fairly good yardstick of our breadth of mind, but an even better satire of our vanity. We could say: Fermat reached this page or that, and Archimedes went a few pages further. (Diderot, 1999 [1753]: 38)

No hypothetical book on nature written directly by God could be fully understood by man. Only a few pages of such a book could be read, but not the whole. Such a text would be endless; there could be no last page because nature has many dimensions and changes continuously. Nature "has chosen to use the same mechanism in an infinite number of different ways" (ibidem: 40) which become observable only over time. Nature's visibility is related to time because "beings change in gradual stages by passing through the most imperceptible of nuances", and this creates "the greatest possible difference between forms which existed in the remote past, those existing today, and those which will exist in the distant future". The erroneous view that nature lacks dynamism is due to conditions which prevent evolutionary processes from being perceived, namely, "the inadequacy of our organs, the imperfections of our instruments, and the brevity of our lives" (ibidem: 73). Therefore, the claim that a fully intelligible image of living nature can be attained is unfounded:

> if each living being is in a perpetual state of change [...] All our natural sciences become as transitory as the words we utter. What we take for natural history is merely the far-from-complete history of a single instant. (Ibidem: 75)

No increase in visibility can fully reveal how living beings change their observable traits over time, because our knowledge of nature is limited to "a single instant". An open world in perpetual evolution is opposed to the closed world of a Linnaeus, but also of preformists and creationists. Nature is characterized by invisible processes due to its temporalization, and this entails the need to abandon the "preconception"

> that nothing takes place takes beyond the realms of the senses, and that everything beyond our view ceases to exist. But one of the main differences between the *observer* and the *interpreter* of nature is that the latter begins at

the point where the former ceases to use his senses and his instruments. (Ibidem: 71; emphasis in original)

8.2 The Vitalist Approach and the Sciences of Life

Buffon's and Diderot's works helped to demolish old paradigms, and this favored the emergence of vitalism, the approach developed in the late eighteenth century in the Faculty of Medicine at Montpellier, which holds that life must be explained not in mechanical terms, but as a pervasive force, located in living organisms and capable of coordinating biological functions which determine the body's self-preservation.

With some variants, these ideas spread not only in France but also in other European countries.[3] In Scotland, physiologists investigated the role of the nervous system in organizing and directing animal economy. Whytt at Edinburgh put forward the thesis that a "sentient principle", located in the nervous system, was responsible for bodily sensitivity, the faculty through which the body responds to external stimuli. Since nerves "are endued with feeling", he inferred that "as there is a general sympathy which prevails through the whole system, so there is a particular and very remarkable *consent* between various parts of the body" (Whytt, *Observations on the Nature*..., quoted in Bourke, 2012: 436, emphasis in original).

According to some scholars, the idea developed by physiologists that the organic world is ruled by sympathetic forces can be linked to some aspects of Smith's approach. Lawrence (1979: 32) remarks that Smith's description of sympathy, as a "feeling" related to the nervous system, "might equally well be found in contemporary medical texts". Although the process that explains the work of sympathy in the moral sphere does not reflect in detail the one identified by physiologists like Cullen and Whytt, Forget argues that we can see

[3] In the late eighteenth and early nineteenth centuries, J. F. Blumenbach (1752–1840) dealt with vital forces as a concept close to a Newtonian type of force. Haller (1708–1777) assumed that the physiology of fibers depends on irreducible vital forces such as irritability. In turn, Needham (1713–1781) suggested the existence of a "vegetative force", as a principle of generation and development of living beings; Wolff (1733–1794) identified a "vis essentialis" as a vital principle that works on organic matter by coordinating simple parts into more complex structures. Prochaska (1749–1820) introduced the Newtonian method in the life sciences and compared attractive and nervous forces.

> a logical continuity between physiological and sociological investigations. The same physiological communication that was imagined to account for somatic sympathy was used to explain the effects of the "passions of the mind" on the sensations and impressions of the body. (Forget, 2003: 283)

The idea that bodily organs interact by establishing relations by means of yet unknown processes based on sympathy was extended to human relationships, and this brought about an "epistemological continuity between the physiological theories of the Edinburgh medical school and the social theories of Smith and Hume" (ibidem: 292). This continuity was more the result of a shared cultural climate than a systematic work of identifying analogies in the two fields of inquiry.[4] It was also because the circulation of ideas was favored by the fact that philosophers and physicians like David Hume, Adam Smith and William Cullen were linked by friendship. In addition, many of them were members of the Edinburgh Philosophical Society, where issues of medicine and philosophy were debated (Bourke, 2012: 437).[5]

Sympathy, in the Smithian view, presupposed a complex conception of the body. According to Packham (2012, chap. 2), sympathy was conceived in the TMS as a sort of "near-physical function" which linked our ability to understand other people's experiences to bodily reactions.[6] Analogies would not be limited to this, in that "a distinct parallel" can be found

> in the realm of economics with […] medical and physiological theories [developed in Scotland at that time], a parallel which is underlined by Smith's periodic depiction of the economy as a "vitalist" body and which suggests that this depiction is more than simply a handy metaphor. (Packham, 2002: 470)

[4] On the nature of the reciprocal influence of the two approaches, the debate is still open. Demeter (2016, chap. 7) maintains that Hume provided a vitalistic account of human nature, and traces of a vitalistic outlook are present in Smith and Ferguson. By contrast, Wolfe (2018) criticizes the connection that some scholars identify between vitalist and Smithian/Humean notions of sympathy.

[5] These debates in part reflected the need to answer the mind-body problem developed by Descartes in his mechanistic approach (Bourke, 2012: 435–436).

[6] Hume, too, emphasized the relationship between sympathy and the body and metaphorically described it as a "contagion" of passions "in which the ideas of the mind become, in some unexplained way, impressions of the body" (Packham, 2012: 64).

These perspectives were not confined to Scotland. Blumenbach resorted to "native sympathy", a sort of elective affinity, to illustrate how similar parts in nature are mutually attracted. And Barthez, a prominent member of the school of Montpellier, supposed that sympathetic reactions related to bodily sensibility depended on the mutual "affection" between organs. As in Smith, where sympathy was the organizing principle of order in the moral sphere, in Barthez, as Reill (2005: 141) points out, "sympathies acted as the hidden hand guiding the specific functions and reactions of an organized body".

Théophile Bordeu played a special role in the School of Montpellier. He was a scholar of physiology and anatomy, who spent many years studying living beings with experimental techniques. He believed that bodies had the power to pursue specific ends and to interact harmoniously in processes which engendered life. In particular, organisms possessed a sort of force ("sensitivity"), diffused by the nervous system throughout the whole body, which made these operations possible (Moravia, 1978: 54). Bordeu put forward a "republican" view of the animal economy in which human body was described as a "federation of organs" in which each part is relatively autonomous:

> In order to perceive the particular action of each part of a living body, we compare it to a swarm of bees ["essaim d'abeilles"], assembled in a cluster and hanging from a tree like a bunch of grapes. One cannot consider wrong what a celebrated ancient author said of the organs of the lower abdomen: it was an *animal in animali*. Each part is, so to speak, certainly not an animal, but a species of an independent machine, which in its own way contributes to the general life of the body. Thus, to pursue the comparison of the cluster of bees, it is a whole stuck to a tree branch by the action of many bees who must act together in order to stay fast; there are some who are attached to the first ones and so forth; all cooperate to form a solid enough body; each one, however, has, in addition, its specific action. A single one who stops or acts too vigorously, will throw the whole mass askew. At the moment when they will all conspire to embrace each other mutually, according both to the order and proportions required, they will compose a whole, which will exist until they are disturbed. The application [of the comparison] is easy; the organs of the body are linked with each other; they each have their distinct sphere and their action; the relations of these actions, the harmony that results from them, make health. (Bordeu, *Recherches anatomiques*, I, § CXXV: 187, translated in Reill, 2005: 133)

The metaphor of the "swarm of bees" showed, on the one hand, that the life of the organism had to be considered in its "psycho-physical totality and unity", on the other, that the body was made up of relatively independent parts (Moravia, 1978: 58). In this sense, the organism appeared as a decentralized system from which life issues. A living being is not a machine, but an "être sensible" with an internal vitality, and whose organs interact irrespective of external stimuli. The body, as vitalists believed, has many centers that work by means of mutual reciprocity, sympathy and consensus (Reill, 2005: 136).

Although scholars like Whytt, Haller and Bordeu provided alternative interpretations of organic processes, they shared the idea that living systems differ radically from mechanistic systems.

> They called this living system an "organization" or an "organized body", defined as driven by goal-directed active powers. Unlike the "blind" forces of mechanism, vital powers could "see", could aspire to an end, and hence were analogous to moral forces. (Reill, 2005: 134)

The sharp distinction between the "animal economy" and alternative forms of mechanical aggregation became a central assumption in Enlightenment Vitalism. And this reinforced "the manner in which 'economy' and 'economics' were radically revised in the same period" (ibidem: 135), not least because the vitalists' notion of organization suggested a rethinking of the relation between visible and invisible phenomena. In fact, it was clear that "unlike physical, mechanical, and normal chemical effects, physiological activities demonstrated no immediately visible cause" (ibidem: 135).

The image of the bee-swarm that Bordeu used to conceptualize the animal economy was not an empty metaphor but a heuristic instrument for exploring the emergent character of life (Wolfe, 2017: 239). It is not by chance that he made use of this and other similes to describe the relationships between organs and the body. It was not easy to specify in definitional terms how organs, as unities which work autonomously, were capable of giving rise to a superior form of organization: the body. Thus, organs were compared to independent "machines" and "bees who must act together", while living bodies were compared to a "swarm of bees" and a "bunch of grapes".

The force of these metaphorical descriptions contributed to the relative success of Bordeu's theory. Diderot referred to them in *Le Rêve de*

D'Alembert to illustrate the unity of the animal body as an organization: a swarm of bees, that is, "a being, an individual, a kind of living creature" (Diderot, 1996 [1769]: 68). And Ménuret used the same image to establish a "structural, relational, positional approach to what makes living bodies unique" (Wolfe, 2017: 241).

Bordeu, Diderot and Ménuret saw the notion of decentralized systems in more radical terms than Mandeville. In the *Fable of the Bees*, the organization of the society-hive was influenced by the "skillfull politician", who favored the transformation of private vices into "publick benefits". The balance between vices and virtues was not independent of this figure's role. Unlike Mandeville, Bordeu, Diderot and Ménuret did not use the conceptual metaphor of the balance (see Sect. 3.2). They introduced a new metaphor, only apparently similar to Mandeville's, to answer to a problem that had not been resolved analytically: the emergence of properties of the whole (the body) as a result of the behaviors of parts that in principle are autonomous. In Smith as well, the statesman-physician impacts on the economic order, when his "political œconomy" either provokes "bad effects" or helps restore homeostatic processes in the political body. However, his invisible hand suggested a view of the economic order that is more similar to the concept of organization encapsulated in the metaphor of the swarm of bees than the one put forward by Mandeville. In both Smith and Bordeu, the order/organization was at the same time an external condition which affects the actions of individuals and the result of their independent behaviors. Moreover, explaining order/organization called for an analysis not only of the visible sphere but also of the invisible processes which shape it, although the latter were not defined in precise terms.

8.3 An Epistemological Turn

With Buffon and Diderot, investigations on nature could no longer ignore the problem of temporalization. This issue affected not only the life sciences but also other fields of research. One of them was geology, a science which was renewed by Buffon's and Hutton's theories about the history of the Earth. Newtonianism too could be reformulated in the light of the concept of organization as evolving system. The concept's triumph, especially in chemistry, led to conceiving the organized body as a "structural emergence" of a network of invisible elementary forces, in mutual and incessant relation (Deleule, 1979: 64). Unlike Linnaeus, according to whom nature in the three kingdoms was characterized by a stationary equilibrium, the new approaches showed that nature had a history. But since evolution could not be directly observed, invisibility could be thought of as a trait of evolutionary changes in the living world (Ernst Mayr, 1982: 309). This conception was not so dissimilar from Smith's theory of historical processes. Individuals, he maintained, do not perceive social changes in their entirety and focus even less on the real causes which lead to the formation of social order over the centuries. Future configurations of social order cannot be foreseen because the future to some extent is open, although there are reasons to think that societies tend toward natural order.

The emergence of the new paradigm has been illustrated by Michel Foucault. He argued that in the second half of the eighteenth century the "order of discourse" changed in three correlated spheres of knowledge: general grammar, natural history and the analysis of wealth, giving rise to three new disciplines—philology, biology and political economy. This change involved the passage from one form of knowledge (called "classical") to another. The classical, pre-Smithian, age (from the seventeenth century to the eighteenth century) was marked by the relationship between visible phenomena and the signs that represent them. This occurred in (a) mercantilists' economic analysis, where money represented wealth; (b) natural science, where "natural being was *characterizable*, and could thereby find its place in a *taxonomy*"; and (c) language, where "any representation was *signifiable* and could find its place" (Foucault, 2005 [1966]: 190, emphasis in original). While in the age of Mercantilism, "money [...] receive[d] its value from its pure function as sign" (ibidem: 191), in Linnaean taxonomy visible traits of nature were signs, that is, taxonomic characters, and nature itself was seen at the same time as a collection of real objects and (metaphorically) as a book written by its Creator. With Smith, by contrast, economic inquiry shifted from the analysis of wealth to the consideration of "a principle of order that is irreducible to the analysis of representation", whose central concept was "labour, that is, toil and time" (ibidem: 244). In the last decades of the eighteenth century, a similar change also occurred in other fields of research. Natural history was no longer the description of visible characters, but

> a principle alien to the domain of the visible—an internal principle not reducible to the reciprocal interaction of representations. This principle

> (which corresponds to labour in the economic sphere) is *organic structure*. (Ibidem: 246, emphasis in original)

The "organization" shows itself in the "character" of beings, but this is not "established by a relation of the visible to itself; it is nothing in itself but the visible point of a complex and hierarchized organic structure in which function plays an essential governing and determining role" (ibidem: 247).

> To classify, therefore, will no longer mean to refer the visible back to itself, while allotting one of its elements the task of representing the others; it will mean, in a movement that makes analysis pivot on its axis, to relate the visible, to the invisible, to its deeper cause, as it were, then to rise upwards once more from that hidden architecture towards the more obvious signs displayed on the surfaces of bodies. (Ibidem: 249)[7]

The concept of organization developed in the sciences of nature exhibited some analogies with the notion of order developed by Smith in economic inquiry, although, according to Foucault, the shift from classical to modern "episteme" was later fully developed by Ricardo (Vigo de Lima & Guizzo, 2015).[8] If considered in relation to the division of labor, this notion explained both the dimension of factory and the market as a self-regulating system governed by an invisible hand. The process of self-regulation made it possible to consider the time of the market as a part of the historical time in which natural order takes shape. For these reasons, temporalization started to play a role, although sometimes as a tacit notion, in economic analysis. With respect to Cantillon and Quesnay, the novelty with Smith's invisible hand—viewed, as it was, in relation to the market and to historical processes—was that the latter introduced a

[7] The "element of invisibility" expressed in the "invisible hand", Foucault maintains, is rooted in the market system: "Invisibility is not just a fact arising from the imperfect nature of human intelligence which prevents people from realizing that there is a hand behind them which arranges or connects everything that each individual does on their own account. Invisibility is absolutely indispensable. It is an invisibility which means that no economic agent should or can pursue the collective good" (Foucault, 2008: 280).

[8] As Vigo de Lima and Guizzo (2015: 589–90) summarize, in "the classical episteme or 'the age of representation', the space occupied by things and their visibility (their surface) were privileged", while in the episteme of the modern age the basic trait was that "representation could no longer provide the foundation of knowledge by itself". See also Versieren (2016).

dynamic idea of order, as a spontaneous coordination which included time as an economic variable. By contrast, Cantillon's and Quesnay's views, although they identified relationships of interdependence among different economic actors and groups, mirrored a conception close to steady equilibrium.[9]

The "invisible" was a perceptible experience, related to processes which govern economic and biological realms. It could be treated in qualitative, but not in definitional terms, and embodied something unknown that undermined confidence in the possibility of tracking down an original, fully intelligible cause of phenomena. This difficulty was also apparent in Newton's approach. As Alexandre Koyré (1968: 15–6) remarked:

> In spite of the rational plausibility and mathematical simplicity of the Newtonian law […], there was in it something that baffled the mind. Bodies attract each other, act upon each other […]. But how do they manage to perform this action, to overcome the chasm of the void that so radically separates and isolates them from each other? We must confess that nobody, not even Newton could (or can) explain, or understand, this *how*.

Newton, therefore, did not exhaustively resolve the problem of how physical phenomena occurred. As he admitted in the *General Scholium*, he had not been able to assign a cause to gravity (Newton, 1999 [1687]: 589). The descriptive science that refused "hypotheses" discovered something invisible under the visible surface of phenomena. The gap between the two dimensions was further pointed out:

> We see only the shapes and colors of bodies, we hear only their sounds, we touch only their external surfaces, we smell only their odors, and we taste their flavors. But there is no direct sense and there are no indirect reflected actions by which we know innermost substances. (Ibidem: 588)

[9] Foucault argues that the differences between Quesnay and Smith can be examined by considering how they dealt with the problem of visibility. Quesnay conceived economic inquiry as an analysis which, by illustrating visible relationships, can be useful to the political authority. The *Tableau* offered "the sovereign a principle of analysis and a sort of principle of transparency in relation to the whole of the economic process" (Foucault, 2008: 285). By contrast, Smith's invisible hand showed that the legislator does not possess this knowledge, because "the world of the economy must be and can only be obscure to the sovereign" (ibidem: 280).

Thus, according to Voltaire (who was a Newtonian), Newton could have answered his critics that "attraction" is "a certain and indisputable effect of an unknown principle; a quality inherent in matter, the cause of which persons of greater abilities than I can pretend to may, if they can, find out" (Voltaire, 1951 [1733]: 87).

Despite the difficulty of fully accounting for the invisible processes that work behind phenomena (Cassirer, 1968, chap. 2, part 2; Koyré, 1968: 62; Cohen, 1980), the invisible sphere could be conceptualized as a "certain and indisputable effect". The notions of absolute (and relative) space and time reinforced this conviction:

1. Absolute, true, and mathematical time, in and of itself and of its own nature, without reference to anything external, flows uniformly and by another name is called duration. Relative, apparent, and common time is any sensible and external measure (precise or imprecise) of duration by means of motion; such a measure—for example, an hour, a day, a month, a year—is commonly used instead of true time.
2. Absolute space, of its own nature without reference to anything external, always remains homogeneous and immovable. Relative space is any movable measure or dimension of this absolute space; such a measure or dimension is determined by our senses from the situation of the space with respect to bodies and is popularly used for immovable space (Newton, 1999 [1687]: 54–55).

Absolute time and space, that is, time and space per se, are not captured by the senses; they are not visible or perceptible; nevertheless they are "true". On the contrary, senses perceive only relative times and spaces, which are "commonly used instead of true time" and are "commonly taken for immovable space". Therefore, the visible dimension of phenomena can be explained only if related to the invisible dimension, because the former can be understood only via the latter.

References

Bourke, J. (2012). Pain, Sympathy and the Medical Encounter Between the Mid Eighteenth and the Mid Twentieth Centuries. *Historical Research, 85*(229), 430–452.

Buffon, G.-L. Leclerc de. (1749). *Histoire naturelle, générale et particulière*, nouvelle édition, tome I. Imprimerie Royale.

Buffon, G.-L. Leclerc de. (1750). *Histoire naturelle, générale et particulière, avec la description du Cabinet du Roi*, tome II. Pierre le Hondt.

Casini, P. (1980). *Introduzione all'illuminismo* (2 vol.). Laterza.

Cassirer, E. (1968). *The Philosophy of Enlightenment.* Princeton University Press.

Cohen, B. I. (1980). *The Newtonian Revolution. With Illustration of the Transformation of Scientific Ideas.* Cambridge University Press.

Deleule, D. (1979). *Hume et la naissance du libéralisme économique.* Aubier Montaigne.

Demeter, T. (2016). *David Hume and the Culture of Scottish Newtonianism: Methodology and Ideology in Enlightenment Inquiry.* Brill.

Diderot, D. (1996 [1769]). *Le Rêve de D'Alembert.* In *Il sogno di D'Alembert,* facing French text. Rizzoli.

Diderot, D. (1999 [1753]). *Thoughts on the Interpretation of Nature.* Clinamen Press.

Forget, E. L. (2003). Evocations of Sympathy: Sympathetic Imagery in Eighteenth-Century Social Theory and Physiology. *History of Political Economy, Annual Supplement, 35,* 282–308.

Foucault, M. (2005 [1966]). *The Order of Things. An Archeology of the Human Sciences.* Routledge.

Foucault, M. (2008). *The Birth of Biopolitics* In M. Senellart (Ed.), *Lectures at the College de France, 1978-79.* Palgrave Macmillan.

Jacob, F. (1973). *The Logic of Life. A History of Heredity.* Pantheon Books. Trans. from the French edition: *La logique du vivant. Une histoire de l'hérédité.* Gallimard, 1970.

Koyré, A. (1968). *Newtonian Studies.* The University of Chicago Press.

Lawrence, C. (1979). The Nervous System and Society in the Scottish. In B. Barnes & S. Shapin (Eds.), *Natural Order: Historical Studies of Scientific Culture,* 19–40. Sage.

Locke, J. (1997 [1690]). *An Essay Concerning Human Understanding.* Penguin Books.

Maupertuis, P. L. Moreau de. (1965a [1745]). *Vénus physique* In *Oeuvres* (Vol. II). Georg Olms.

Maupertuis, P. L. Moreau de. (1965b [1754]). *Sistème de la Nature. Essai sur la formation des corps organisés.* In *Oeuvres* (Vol. II). Georg Olms.

Mayr, E. (1982). *The Growth of Biological Thought. Diversity, Evolution, and Inheritance.* The Belknap Press of Harvard University Press.

Moravia, S. (1978). From Homme Machine to Homme Sensible: Changing Eighteenth-Century Models of Man's Image. *Journal of the History of Ideas, 39*(1), 45–60.

Newton, I. (1999 [1687]). *The Principia. Mathematical Principles of Natural Philosophy.* University of California Press.

Nicholson, D. J. (2014). The Machine Conception of the Organism in Development and Evolution: A Critical Analysis. *Studies in History and Philosophy of Biological and Biomedical Sciences, 48,* 162–174.

Packham, C. (2002). The Physiology of Political Economy: Vitalism and Adam Smith's Wealth of Nations. *Journal of the History of Ideas, 63*(3), 465–481.
Packham, C. (2012). *Eighteenth-Century Vitalism. Bodies, Culture, Politics.* Palgrave Macmillan.
Prigogine, I., & Stengers, I. (1984). *Order Out of Chaos: Man's New Dialogue with Nature.* Bantam Books.
Reill, P. H. (2005). *Vitalizing Nature in the Enlightenment.* University of California Press.
Roe, S. A. (1981). *Matter, Life, and Generation. Eighteenth-Century Embryology and the Haller-Wolff Debate.* Cambridge University Press.
Roger, J. (1997). *Buffon: A Life in Natural History.* Cornell University Press.
Solinas, G. (1967). *Il microscopio e le metafisiche. Epigenesi e preesistenza da Cartesio a Kant.* Feltrinelli.
Versieren, J. (2016). The Moral Foundations of Adam Smith's Transitional Society: Reappraising Foucault's Representations of Wealth and Marx's Reconstruction of Value Theory. *Capital & Class, 40*(3), 1–22.
Vigo de Lima, I., & Guizzo, D. (2015). An Archaeology of Adam Smith's Epistemic Context. *Review of Political Economy, 27*(4), 585–605.
Voltaire. (1951 [1733]). *Lettres philosophiques ou lettres anglaises.* Garnier.
Wolfe, C. T. (2017). Models of Organic Organization in Montpellier Vitalism. *Early Science and Medicine, 22*, 229–252.
Wolfe, C. T. (2018). Smithian Vitalism? *Journal of Scottish Philosophy, 16*, 264–271.

PART III

Forms and Experiences of Time

CHAPTER 9

Time and Social Order

Abstract This chapter shows how the notion of order was related to the notion of time, especially in commercial societies, where individuals do not control social processes, and individual experiences are not a sufficient basis for reliable predictions.

Although the transmission of property was a bridge between past, present and future, "blindness" to the future was a trait that could not be ignored. Individuals, as Smith noted, control only a small portion of their future, and the prudent men, given the limited horizon of their decisions, formulate plans that allow them to gradually accumulate wealth.

However, although the distant future could not be planned, the rhythm of time could be governed in workshops. The reorganization of labor in society meant that the division between productive and unproductive labor ceased to be an issue relating to how individuals decide to organize their private time. In the market society, productive and unproductive labor occupy distinct social spaces, and this entails the creation of a social time.

All these events had an impact on individuals' capacity to interpret their "real" self-interest correctly. In particular, laborers and landowners showed little ability to understand how the improvement of their condition is related to the social welfare.

Keywords Time of the market • Historical time • Property • Social forms of time • Prudent man

S. Fiori, *Machines, Bodies and Invisible Hands*,
https://doi.org/10.1007/978-3-030-85206-1_9

9.1 Historical Changes, Experiences and Temporal Horizons

The difficulty of defining the evolution of societies appears in the four-stage theory. In the *Lectures on Jurisprudence*, Smith interpreted the development of societies as a succession of stages, where each stage was characterized by a distinct way of procuring subsistence (hunting, pasturage, agriculture and commerce). Although the scheme, in general, represented this succession as a linear passage, some exceptions showed that the process was not always so regular.[1] Of particular interest was the commercial stage, which was viewed as a result of the development of the agriculture stage. In fact, commercial relationships between towns and countryside, and among nations, became possible because agricultural surplus could be exchanged (LJ (A) i.31–32: 15–16). On the one hand, if the advent of the commercial stage was a consequence of the previous stage, because commerce requires a certain development of agriculture (Fiori & Pesciarelli, 1999), on the other, it was a drastic change in the history of human civilization. While in the ages preceding the commercial stage the order was hierarchical and static, in the age of commerce it was dynamic and subject to incessant changes.

This perspective can be examined by considering how the structure of social relationships in the two periods (before and during the commercial society) influenced how individuals perceived the structure of time in which they lived.

A suggestion comes from Reinhart Koselleck, a scholar who has analyzed this problem starting from the relationship between individual experiences and the perception of time. His thesis is that in the eighteenth century, as a result of the Industrial and French revolutions, the perception of historical time changed. The "space of experience", which expanded because of the proliferation of increasingly complex events experienced by individuals, came to diverge from their "horizon of expectations". The

[1] An example of this irregularity is the following: "The whole of the savage nations which subsist by flocks have no notion of cultivating the ground. The only instance that has the appearance of an objection to this rule is the state of the North American Indians. They, tho they have no conception of flocks and herds, have nevertheless some notion of agriculture" (LJ (A) i.29: 15). In this connection, see Skinner (1979: 77). On the relation between four-stage theory, mode of subsistence, and modes of production, see Pesciarelli (1977, 1988: 93–125). On the history of stadial approaches, see Meek (1976). On the interpretation of these events in Rome and ancient Greece, see Haakonssen (1981: 159–164).

future became less and less predictable, and past experience was increasingly less able to provide a guide for the future. History ceased to be *magistra vitae*, because of its "acceleration", and this meant that expectations formulated on the basis of past experience showed themselves to be wrong.

The concept of heterogenesis of ends, developed at the end of the eighteenth century, which in some respects includes the notion of the invisible hand, illustrates this point:

> The unexpected undermines the expected [...]. This historical specification of temporal sequence is based upon the given difference of experience and expectation. The one cannot be transferred into the other without interruption. Even if one could formulate this as an irrefutable experiential statement, no precise expectations could be deduced from it. (Koselleck, 2004 [1979]: 261)

To understand in which sense the distance between experience and expectations increased during the *Neuezeit*, it is sufficient to remember that only a few centuries ago 80% of Europeans lived in the rural world, and peasants' life was punctuated by the repetitive cycles of nature. In addition, technical innovations were extremely limited and "did not bring about any rupture in the pattern of life". Similar conditions characterized the "urban life of the artisan whose guild regulations, however restrictive they might have been individually, made sure that everything would remain the way it was" (ibidem: 263–264). In these circumstances, past, present and future were closely connected: the expectations of peasants and artisans were influenced by those of their predecessors and in turn influenced those of their successors. What, on the contrary, characterized the age of Enlightenment was the emergence of a "new horizon of expectation" which led to the invention of the concept of "progress", a notion that implied that the future is not only different from but better than the past.

Smith believed that the "progress of society" depended on the increasing division of labor and on the introduction of machines in manufacturing processes (ibidem: 270). He was aware of the gap which separates market and pre-modern societies and examined the concept of progress from a historical perspective. Book III of the WN, entitled "Of the Different Progress of Opulence in Different Nations", showed how the static time of feudal societies had been replaced, although irregularly, by the dynamic time of commercial society. In this new stage of human society, order continuously assumed new forms. As a consequence, it was no longer conceived as an expression of hierarchies and immutable social relationships. Whereas in the feudal age the law of primogeniture and entails had crystallized social relationships, in the market society social order was continually reconfigured. The future became open in the sense that, as the result of many decentralized behaviors, it could not be intentionally shaped by the will of individuals. The more the increasing succession of events was perceived as a flow, the more individuals abandoned the idea of controlling the future. However, although they neither intentionally governed historical processes nor were able to predict future scenarios, they could control the "rhythm" of time with the technical division of labor whereby labor time could be compressed and reorganized.

The relationship between the time of the market and historical time can be analyzed by considering in which sense the invisible hand produces unintended outcomes. Schliesser argues that "Smithian invisible hand processes", and "Smithian social explanations" exhibit dissimilar features. A "Smithian invisible hand process is a relatively short-term process in which an agent produces unintended and, to him or her, unknown consequences" (Schliesser, 2017: 235). However, these "consequences are, in principle, knowable to the right kind of observer (either theoretically informed or by accumulated common sense) at the time" (ibidem: 235). This view is explained in the famous passage of the WN in which the invisible hand appears:

> Smith does not claim that the merchant can never know that his activities may contribute to national wealth; in fact, it follows from Smith's account that once the merchant is familiar with a correct (that is, *Smith's*) political economy, he can also intend to promote national wealth just in virtue of pursing [sic] maximal profit. (Ibidem: 247)

By contrast, Smithian social explanations "involve cases where the consequences are visible or knowable only after the fact. Generally they take place over much longer amounts of time than any given invisible hand process" (ibidem: 235). It seems to me that the invisible hand of the TMS, which is related to the argument that nature's deception makes the development of civilization possible, clarifies this point, in that the unintended consequences to which Smith refers "accumulate over centuries", and are "visible" after (historical) facts occurred.

Schliesser rightly points out that the work of the invisible hand involves a short-term process, while—if I interpret his argument correctly—the course of events engendered by nature's deception involves long-term processes. Despite the differences between the two kinds of process, he remarks that "Smithian social explanations can include invisible hand processes as sub-components (or mechanisms)" (ibidem: 235). In my terms, this implies that the time of the market (and events that take shape in it) is included in historical processes which lead to the formation of the natural order. However, though consequences engendered by the invisible hand processes are "in principle, knowable" by a well-informed observer, who knows a "correct (that is, Smith's) political economy", this does not mean that this knowledge produces correct predictions, except in a very general sense. Having a theory that allows us to consider how individual behaviors promote national wealth means being aware of the mechanism by means of which private and public welfare increase, but not having the capacity to predict in analytical terms all possible, future configurations of the market. This awareness is at the basis of some general recommendations about behaviors with which individuals and legislators should comply, but it helps to formulate only an approximate view of future scenarios. Individuals possess only a local, limited knowledge about events that occur in society and behaviors of others, and this means that processes which culminate in the market equilibria remain—at least partially—unknown.

Unlike Smith, Condorcet trusted in human ability to predict the future.[2] He took a leading role in the French Revolution and, like other revolutionaries, believed that it was possible to explain "how one must create (***produire***) and direct (***diriger***) a Revolution for the benefit of liberty" (Koselleck, 2004 [1979]: 55). He expressed his trust in the predictive power of reason, and his conviction that present experiences make it possible to foresee the future, in the "tenth epoch" of his *Esquisse*:

[2] Smith and Condorcet, however, were similar in some respects (Rothschild, 2001, chap. 8). In the "ninth epoch" of the *Esquisse*, Condorcet implicitly referred to Smith's invisible hand. Despite the apparent chaos of society determined by conflict of "opposite interests", he argued, "we still perceive, by a general law of the moral world, the efforts of each individual for himself conducing to the good of the whole" (Condorcet, 1795: 236). Foucault (2008: 277) in this respect observes, "This means, on the one hand, that each is dependent on an uncontrollable, unspecified whole of the flow of things and the world. In a way, the most distant event taking place on the other side of the world may affect my interest, and there is nothing I can do about it".

> If man can predict, almost with certainty, those appearances of which he understands the laws; if, even when the laws are unknown to him, experience of the past enables him to foresee, with considerable probability, future appearances; why should we suppose it a chimerical undertaking to delineate, with some degree of truth, the picture of the future destiny of mankind from the results of its history? (Condorcet, 1795: 316)

Smith was less optimistic than Condorcet about the human capacity to know the future. Imagination constantly tries to connect present and future, but the way in which it represents this connection changes continuously. Therefore, to understand how we anticipate the future on the basis of the analysis of the present, it is necessary to understand how imagination establishes a temporal continuity between current and future events.

9.2 Conceptualizations of Time and Order

Lindgren observed that in the HA the attempt to dissipate wonder answers a precise need: "Men attempt to anticipate the future in order to prepare themselves emotionally for whatever it brings" (Lindgren, 1973: 3). When we formulate a new interpretation about causal connections of events, "wonder is diminished if not eliminated" (ibidem: 3). The world appears tractable, and this allows us to face the future with calm and tranquility. In particular, Smith points out, scientific systems, by providing possible explanations of the regular succession of phenomena, introduce "order" into "chaos" of "discordant appearances". Since the perception of changes and successions of events in the physical world determine how human beings conceptualize the flow of time, there is a close connection between time and order. Both scientists with their theories and "common artizans" in their "work-houses" anticipate how phenomena occur (HA II.11: 44). By predicting what will happen—albeit to a different extent—their imagination enables them to form plausible expectations about the future, with the result that the future appears less unknown and unstable. Scientific systems influence common sense in many respects, and their search for "some chain of intermediate events" culminates in the identification of a temporal coherence among phenomena.

In short, the perception of regularly flowing time is related to the mind's capacity to adjust our visions to what we consider the causal structures of the world. When this happens, this causal order makes it possible to define the connection among events in terms of past, present and future. Scientific systems "sooth the imagination", when they eliminate the discontinuity introduced by observed anomalies, and represent nature as a realm characterized by regular movements. Although they continuously revise their predictions, as "imaginary machines", they reduce the uncertainty associated with the future, at least in psychological terms. Newton's theory is certainly an illustration of "the most important and sublime truths", but if the history of astronomy shows that philosophical systems are "mere inventions of the imagination" (HA IV.76: 105), the issue of how we conceptualize future events remains problematic.

This topic was dealt with by Hume, whose notion of cause was an example of how trust in projecting a present condition onto the future is fallacious:

> Your appeal to past experience decides nothing in the present case; and the utmost can only prove, that that very object, which produc'd any other, was at that very instant endow'd with such power; but can never prove, that the same power must continue in the same object or collection of sensible qualities; much less, that a like power is always conjoin'd with like sensible qualities. (Hume, 1985 [1739–40]: 139)

In a skeptical perspective, temporal continuity cannot be based on the projection of past experiences onto the future. On the other hand, the origin of this psychological attitude depends not on reason but on custom and habit.

> Custom, then, is the great guide of human life. It is that principle alone, which renders our experience useful to us, and makes us expect, for the future, a similar train of events with those which have appeared in the past. (Hume, 2007 [1748]: 32)

In Hume, as in Smith in many respects, the ways ideas connect to each other (i.e., resemblance, contiguity in space or time, cause and effect) determine an order of representation from which our experience of time derives. The future seems knowable when habit establishes connections in terms of causal successions. And causal connections, in turn, depend on how a network of analogies and resemblances is perceived. Accordingly, custom acts as a mechanism which constructs temporal sequences because we assume that causes that in the past have produced certain effects will also operate in similar ways in the future. If the system of resemblances changes, the perception of causal sequences also changes.

However, causal knowledge is fundamental, especially in historical inquiries. Historians in their work basically use "cause and effect" connections, "since it is by this knowledge alone, we are enabled to controul events, and govern futurity" (ibidem: 179). On the other hand, the "chief use" of history

> is only to discover the constant and universal principles of human nature, by shewing men in all varieties of circumstances and situations, and furnishing us with materials, from which we may form our observations, and become acquainted with the regular springs of human action and behaviour. (Ibidem: 60)

Other disciplines also try to govern time in a similar way. In fact, "The only immediate utility of all sciences, is to teach us, how to control and regulate future events by their causes" (ibidem: 56). However, it would be a mistake to forget that "it is impossible to give any just definition of cause" (ibidem: 56). One can observe that an object follows another, and that "objects, similar to the first, are followed by objects similar to the second", but "We have no idea of this connexion" (ibidem: 56).

9.3 Property and Social Forms of Time

In Smith, institutions have a role in determining how individuals relate to time in terms of past, present and future. In the LJ, he examined five causes (occupation, accession, prescription or "usucapio", succession and voluntary transfer) which give rise to a particular institution: property. The premise of his analysis was that, while the origin of the greatest part of natural rights is "evident to reason", "not altogether plain, is [...] that of property" (LJ (A) i.15: 13). While for Locke the work employed in picking an apple from a tree legitimizes the property right over that object (Locke, 1980 [1690] §§ 28–29: 19–20), for Smith it is unclear why "an apple [...] should be altogether appropriated to me and all others excluded from it merely because I had pulled it of the tree" (LJ (A) i.15: 13). Property not only is based on the relationship between man and thing but is an institution that legitimizes itself through the relationship between men. It rests on the approval of the "spectator"—the figure introduced in the TMS (see Haakonssen, 1981: 104–105)—and this determines its social character.

Occupation, as an exclusive right of the possessor over a thing (the "bare possession of a subject"), is the first form of property whose foundations are analyzed. A spectator would approve of the behavior of someone who defends his possession "against any violent attack", because he believes that the possessor has "a reasonable expectation of using the fruit or whatever it is in what manner he pleases" (LJ (A) i.36: 17). Expectations prefigure a possible future, since they anticipate benefits deriving from the use of the possessed object. For this reason, Smith points out, a "reasonable expectation [...] is the ground on which the right of property is acquired by occupation" (LJ (A) i.37: 17).

Another element which legitimizes property rights is the fact that the possession of an object entails "time and pain" in procuring it. When Locke examined the origin of property, he considered labor not in relation to time but as a cause which modifies the original (natural) state of an object. By contrast, Smith relates labor to duration. Pain and sacrifice increase over time, and the present sacrifice legitimizes future enjoyment of the fruits of labor. From this perspective as well, present "time and pain" determine a "reasonable expectation" of future benefits.

Smith's analysis of the relationship between time and property also unfolds from the following question: "how long and in what circumstances property continues and at what time it is supposed to be at an end"? (LJ (A) i.40: 18). In the hunting stage, property arose and ended with possession (LJ(B) 150: 460), but later became more stable and started to be transmitted among generations. It is in these circumstances that "pain and time" in present labor became a condition which confers stability, and allows property to be transmitted over time. This problem was taken into consideration in eighteenth-century Scottish culture. It was examined in reference to agriculture by Smith's pupil, John Millar (Millar, 1803: 11), who argued that "future possession of the land" depends on "past improvements" made by labor.

Adam Ferguson also pointed out that property allows man to project himself toward the future. Property is "a matter of progress" which includes "effects of time" which have to be considered to define possession.

> The very desire of [property] proceeds from experience; and the industry by which it is gained, or improved, requires such a habit of acting with a view

to distant objects, as may overcome the present disposition either to sloth or to enjoyment. (Ferguson, 1995 [1767]: 81)

Coming back to Smith, "prescription" (i.e., the right to an object possessed for a long time, although the user is not the proprietor) involves a temporal relation between an object and its possessor from which expectations are approved by the spectator derive.

[T]he right of prescription is derived from the opinion of the spectator that the possessor of a long standing has a just expectation that he may use what has been thus possessed, and that the form(er) proprieter and has so far lost all right to it, has no expectation of using it. (LJ (A) i.76: 32)

Lastly, succession ("the transference of property from the dead to the living") is *par excellence* a way to acquire property which is related to time.

In conclusion, Smith shows that property is related to a dimension which is at the same time social and temporal. In his analysis, the more property is based on "reasonable expectations", the more the future will hold no surprises, if the rights which ensue from these expectations are warranted. Property is a bridge to the future, and if the wealth accumulated today can be transmitted to later generations, this stabilizes social relationships. This process had a particular relevance in the stage of agriculture and in the feudal age, where some institutions which governed the transmission of property, by crystallizing social order (i.e., the law of primogeniture and entails) also fixed the structure of time by giving it a social form (see Sect. 5.3). Landed property became a stable source of authority, independent of individuals' qualities, and this facilitated the formation of an equally stable social structure (see Sect. 7.8). But the transfer of inalienable and indivisible property by succession caused European societies to stagnate precisely because an inefficient system of exploitation of land bound past to present, and present to future:

There is no maxim more generally acknowledged than that the earth is the property of each generation. That the former generation should restrict them in their use of it is altogether absurd; it is theirs altogether as well as it was their predecessors in their day. It would (be) altogether absurd to suppose that our ancestors who lived 500 years (ago) should have had the power of disposing of all lands at this time [...] This right is not only absurd in the highest degree but is also extremely prejudiciall to the community, as it excludes lands intirely from commerce. The interest of the state requires

> that lands should be as much in commerce as any other goods. (LJ (A) i.164–166: 69–70)

The call to abandon old, feudal institutions was also a demand to free society from constraints whereby the past order influenced the future one. The "right of making a will", to ensure transmission of property, was the instrument through which that influence was exerted. It was based on "the reverence and respect which we feell for the commands of the dead", but "it involves in it something more than what is necessary to constitute property" (LJ (A) v.99: 309–310). The dead establish a link with the past, but—Smith implicitly suggests—a spectator cannot approve that there will be a way for mortgaging their descendants' future. The will of past generations, transmitted by means of entails and right of primogeniture, is a ballast that must be cast off, and whose influence contrasts with the needs of the nascent market economy. It is at the origin "of the almost total bad husbandry that prevails in those countrys where they are in use" (LJ (A) i.166: 70).

None of these processes, however, were the result of a plan, and even less was the "silent and insensible" transition to commercial society intentional (WN III.iv.10: 418). Adam Ferguson expressed this concept clearly in a sentence dear to F. A. Hayek:

> Every step and every movement of the multitude, even in what are termed enlightened ages, are made with equal blindness to the future; and nations stumble upon establishments, which are indeed the result of human action, but not the execution of any human design. [...] We are therefore to receive, with caution, the traditionary histories of ancient legislators, and founders of states. Their names have long been celebrated; their supposed plans have been admired; and what were probably the consequences of an early situation, is, in every instance, considered as an effect of design. [...] This is the simplest form under which we can consider the establishment of nations: and we ascribe to a previous design, what came to be known only by experience, what no human wisdom could foresee, and what, without the concurring humour and disposition of his age, no authority could enable an individual to execute. (Ferguson, 1995 [1767]: 119–120)

"Blindness to the future", irrespective of how institutions affect the perception of time, is a general condition of humankind. The belief that societies are shaped by a "human design" is an error of perspective, due to the fact that one assigns responsibility to "human wisdom" for what, by contrast, depends on the concurrence of many events which are beyond the control of those who design society. John Millar, in the third edition of the *Origin*, also expressed doubts about legislators' capacity to predict the outcomes of the political changes they introduce, and pointed out the reasons that explain the persistence of institutional orders:

> notwithstanding the concurring testimony of historians, concerning the great political changes introduced by the lawgivers of a remote age, there may be reason to doubt, whether the effect of their interpositions has ever been so extensive as is generally supposed. Before an individual can be invested with so much authority, and possessed of such reflection and foresight as would induce him to act in the capacity of a legislator, he must, probably, have been educated and brought up in the knowledge of those natural manners and customs, which, for ages perhaps, have prevailed among his countrymen. Under the influence of all the prejudices derived from ancient usage, he will commonly be disposed to prefer the system already established to any other, of which the effects have not be ascertained by experience. (Millar, 1779: 7–8)

Legislators are sons of their time, and consequently their behaviors reflect the limits of their education. They do not foresee the future and chiefly tend to reproduce the existing order. Since they act "under the influence of all the prejudices derived from ancient usage", their plans, by mirroring this situation, can reduce society's dynamism. It is thus unsurprising that the "patriotic statemen"

> instead of being actuated by a projecting spirit, or attempting, from visionary speculations of remote utility, to produce any violent reformation, they confined themselves to such moderate improvements as, by deviating little from the former usage, were in some measure supported by experience, and coincided with the prevailing opinions of the country. (Ibidem: 8)

In conclusion, while Smith described how certain institutions in the feudal age crystallized social relationships, Millar, in a more general sense, saw the persistence of prejudices, custom and traditions which affect the behavior of the "statemen" as the reasons which determine the reproduction of social order. However, he pointed out that "moderate improvements" which deviate "little from the former usage" also cause significant social and institutional changes in the long term. For both Smith and Millar, these changes are not planned, because human beings are able neither to foresee nor to plan the future consequences of their present actions. Smith, in particular, showed how the dissolution of feudal societies was brought about silently by a number of events that neither landed proprietors nor merchants had planned. The century-long process that led from the feudal economy to market society was marked by the increasing importance of towns, which acquired liberty and independence before the countryside. The "reversed" order of European societies meant that only later did the gradual development of commerce stimulated by towns lead, slowly, to the development of agriculture. This resulted in a "revolution of the greatest importance to the publick happiness" which was "brought about by two different orders of people ['great proprietors' and 'merchants and artificiers'], who had not the least intention to serve the public" (WN III.iv.17: 422). Consequently, individuals, especially in the countryside, were increasingly freed from feudal constraints, ceasing to receive subsistence from feudal lords, and becoming part of that society in which everyone was "in some measure a merchant" (WN I.iv.1: 37).

The new structure of social relationships called for a rethinking of how social order is formed. As Koselleck suggests, one can suppose that processes which led to the formation of the market society modified the perception of time. Individuals' expectations, less and less grounded on past experience, became the basis for foreseeing future equilibria because of the dynamism of commercial society. The "blindness to the future" of which Ferguson spoke, although it was a general human condition, became much more marked in the age of the market. The governance of time could no longer be accomplished by imposing institutional structures which remain unchanged for centuries. What began to be perceived was that in modern societies, social order spontaneously reproduces itself by means of impersonal, self-regulating processes which were unknown in hierarchical societies.

Not by chance, this change in social systems was reflected in the set of metaphors of order which entered philosophical and economic literature. The metaphor of the machine, used in the seventeenth century to represent hierarchical systems, was reformulated by Smith, who also employed organic metaphors and lastly introduced the invisible hand. The latter implied that individual time was determined by the time of the market. In particular, the identification of individual time was based on the idea that since individuals' predictions are limited by their local knowledge, they formulate expectations which can rarely anticipate the future correctly. The horizon of individual decisions was circumscribed, because—to use a

Hayekian concept—the knowledge possessed by individuals is fragmentary but still sufficient to orient them in the market. This general condition is shared by all individuals, including the sovereign, who likewise possesses only a limited knowledge. Neither the sovereign's knowledge nor other "human wisdom or knowledge" can organize "industry of private people", and efficiently direct it "towards the employments most suitable to the interest of the society" (WN IV.ix.51: 687). On the one hand, if the best thing is that individuals use their knowledge, on the other, individuals have limited control over the consequences of their decisions. They formulate their plans by considering only a small part of future scenarios resulting from their actions, and this determines how they relate to time. Individuals' time, therefore, takes shape from projections toward the future embodied in their plans and projects. What the invisible hand brings to the fore is that individual times integrate in a social time, which is a dimension where individual experiences are recomposed.

9.4 Expectations and Future-Oriented Behaviors: From the "Prudent Man" to the Individual as Economic Agent

Many scholars have pointed out that there is no contradiction between the TMS and the WN. Although the two books deal with different topics, they have many points of contact. One of them is the concept of prudence.

The virtue of prudence consists of two useful qualities approved by the spectator. They are

> first of all, superior reason and understanding, by which we are capable of discerning the remote consequences of all our actions, and of foreseeing the advantage or detriment which is likely to result from them: and secondly, self-command, by which we are enabled to abstain from present pleasure or to endure present pain, in order to obtain a greater pleasure or to avoid a greater pain in some future time. (TMS IV.2.6: 189)

Although Smith speaks of "remote consequences", it is likely that he does not mean to say that "superior reason and understanding" can predict the distant future. These virtues are associated with "self-command", that is, the capacity that, by governing our immediate passions, enables us to establish a coherent relation between present and future. When, thanks to self-command, "we restrain our present appetites in order to gratify them more fully upon another occasion", we are approved by the spectator:

> The spectator does not feel the solicitations of our present appetites. To him the pleasure which we are to enjoy a week hence, or a year hence, is just as interesting as that which we are to enjoy this moment. When for the sake of the present, therefore, we sacrifice the future, our conduct appears to him absurd and extravagant in the highest degree, and he cannot enter into the principles which influence it. On the contrary, when we abstain from present pleasure, in order to secure greater pleasure to come, when we act as if the remote object interested us as much as that which immediately presses upon the senses, as our affections exactly correspond with his own, he cannot fail to approve of our behaviour. (TMS IV.2.8: 189)

When the prudent man watches himself with the eyes of an impartial spectator, the future effects attributable to his behavior are viewed in the right perspective, and become tractable because he neutralizes the "solicitations of [his] present appetites". A correct comparison between present and future "pleasures" involves placing these pleasures ideally on the same level.[3] Thanks to this operation, the prudent man discovers that future benefits are greater than present ones. As Smith remarks,

> The impartial spectator does not feel himself worn out by the present labour of those whose conduct he surveys; nor does he feel himself solicited by the importunate calls of their present appetites. To him their present, and what is likely to be their future situation, are very nearly the same: he sees them nearly at the same distance, and is affected by them very nearly in the same manner. [...] He cannot therefore but approve, and even applaud, that proper exertion of self-command, which enables [the persons principally concerned] to act as if their present and their future situation affected them nearly in the same manner in which they affect him. (TMS VI.i.11: 215)

The temporal dimension considered by the prudent man is circumscribed and easily manageable. Graduality marks the rhythm of his life: he

[3] Bacon's words resonate in these passages: "affections principally regard a present good, whilst reason, seeing far before it, chooses also the future and capital good. And therefore, as present things strike the imagination strongest, reason is generally subdued; but when eloquence and the power of persuasion raise up remote and future objects, and set them to view as if they were present; then imagination goes over to the side of reason, and renders it victorious" (Bacon, 1868 [1623]: 236).

"is naturally contented with his situation, which, by continual, though small accumulations, is growing better and better every day" (TMS VI.i.12: 215). The dimension of time relevant to him is the one related to his capacity to build his future day after day. The future is like a succession of points that he does not contemplate in its entirety, but that he helps gradually construct. On the one hand, for him present time is functionally organized in view of the near future, while on the other hand, the near future, if correctly observed, is projected on, and compared to the present. The two dimensions of time are placed on the same level, and this makes it possible to deal with the future as a "present future". This is the view that characterizes the "practice of frugality, industry, and application", a practice much esteemed by all men "though directed to no other purpose than the acquisition of fortune" (TMS IV.8: 190).

These topics reappear in the WN, where Smith examines the circumstances which favor accumulation. "Parsimony" (or frugality), and not "industry", he maintains, is the first cause of the increase of capital (see Sect. 4.2). In particular, it is because of parsimony that "prudent" people first save and then invest: "whatever industry might acquire, if parsimony did not save and store up, the capital would never be the greater" (WN II.iii.16: 337).[4] By contrast, prodigality dissipates wealth.

Frugal and prodigal behaviors reflect alternative attitudes toward time.

> With regard to profusion, the principle, which prompts to expence, is the passion for present enjoyment; which, though sometimes violent and very difficult to be restrained, is in general only momentary and occasional. But the principle which prompts to save, is the desire of bettering our condition, a desire which, though generally calm and dispassionate, comes with us from the womb, and never leaves us till we go into the grave. (WN II.iii.28: 342)

The "desire of bettering our condition", unlike "the passion for present enjoyment", is oriented toward (the near) future, and it is at the basis of the development of society. It is "calm and dispassionate", like the calm and dispassionate behavior of the prudent man, who, by adopting the spectator's point of view, is not drawn astray by the "solicitations of [his] present appetites". Prudent people accumulate gradually and apparently

[4] Prudent behavior is based on "industry and frugality", and as such is approved by the impartial spectator, and "the representative of the impartial spectator, the man within the breast" (TMS VI.i.11: 215). For this reason, Raphael and Macfie point out in the *Introduction* to the TMS that "[t]he prudent man of TMS VI.i. is the frugal man of WN.II.iii" (TMS: 18).

do not consider the remote consequences of their behavior. As the argument of Nature's deception shows, there is a gap between what human beings do intentionally on the basis of their limited expectations and the unexpected, social consequences of their behaviors. Savings, accumulated thanks to frugal behavior, are investments in the future, and in particular in that (small) portion of the future that individuals can control.

However, individuals are not able to predict complex events which develop throughout history. The history of the "revolution" which led to the formation of market societies is an example of this. If landed proprietors probably followed their "passion for present enjoyment" when they "exchanged the maintenance" of a thousand men for "a pair of diamond buckles", "to gratify the most childish vanity", merchants were only slightly more farsighted when they "acted merely from a view to their own interest". If the former were unable to consider a temporal plane other than the immediate satisfaction of their desires, the latter considered only a slightly larger portion of the future. Merchants' horizon of expectations was limited, although less so than the landowners', and their investment in the future was inspired by "their own pedlar principle of turning a penny wherever a penny was to be got". However, in both cases, "Neither of them had either knowledge or foresight of that great revolution which the folly of the one, and the industry of the other, was gradually bringing about" (WN III.iv.10 and 17: 418–419 and 422).

A similar view had been anticipated to some extent by Hume in his *Treatise*, although he was less optimistic than Smith.

> It has been observ'd, in treating of the passions, that men are mightily govern'd by the imagination, and proportion their affections more to the light, under which any object appears to them, than to its real and intrinsic value. What strikes upon them with a strong and lively idea commonly prevails above what lies in a more obscure light; and it must be a great superiority of value, that is able to compensate this advantage. Now as every thing, that is contiguous to us, either in space or time, strikes upon us with such an idea, it has a proportional effect on the will and passions, and commonly operates with more force than any object, that lies in a more distant and obscure light. Tho' we may be fully convinc'd, that the latter object excels the former, we are not able to regulate our actions by this judgement; but yield to the sollicitations of our passions, which always plead in favour of whatever is near and contiguous.
>
> This is the reason why men so often act in contradiction to their known interest; and in particular why they prefer any trivial advantage, that is pres-

ent, to the maintenance of order of society. (Hume, 1985 [1739–40]: 586–587)

Hume pointed out the distortive effects of our preference for benefits contiguous "in space and time". We often react to the "sollicitations of our passions" (note that Smith used the phrase "solicitations of our present appetites") and "prefer any trivial advantage, that is present", although this preference opposes our real interest. By contrast,

> When we consider any objects at a distance, all their minute distinctions vanish, and we always give the preference to whatever is in itself preferable, without considering its situation and circumstances. This gives rise to what in an improper sense we call *reason*, which is a principle, that is often contradictory to those propensities that display themselves upon the approach of the object. (Hume, 1985 [1739–40]: 587–588, emphasis in original)

As in Smith, the idea of correctly evaluating advantages and disadvantages is embodied in the image of watching "objects" from a correct distance. The eyes of the mind, or reason, redefine relations among things under examination, and this redefinition is metaphorically both spatial and visual. It is spatial, because we formulate correct judgments when we organize a space in which we place ourselves at the right distance from objects. It is visual because our evaluations are phrased in observational terms. While for Smith the impartial spectator "sees" "present" and "future situation[s]" "nearly at the same distance" (TMS VI.i.11: 215), for Hume ideas strike us according to the "light" in which we look at them.

9.5 Division of Labor and Structure of Time

Although the flow of time cannot be directed, its rhythm can be governed. However, there is a relation between the flow of time that characterizes the evolution of the economic order, and the structure of time imposed in productive processes.

By means of the division of labor, Smith maintains, time is ruled in the factory, and consequently in society. The economic order is shaped by the new organizational structure of labor which prevails especially in "workshops", where the technical division of labor reduces the labor time required to produce a commodity. In particular, the increase in dexterity, "saving the time commonly lost in passing from one species of work to another", and the invention of machines (WN I.i. 5: 17) which increase the laborer's productivity have the control of labor time in common. This is a specific feature of modern societies, which we do not see in ancient communities. Smith illustrates this point in reference to the slave economies of Rome and Athens:

> Slaves [...] are very seldom inventive; and all the most important improvements, either in machinery, or in the arrangement and distribution of work, which facilitate and abridge labour, have been the discoveries of freemen. Should a slave propose any improvement of this kind, his master would be very apt to consider the proposal as the suggestion of laziness, and a desire to save his own labour at the master's expence. (WN IV.ix: 684)

Innovations that reduce labor time were possible (and "freemen" might occasionally introduce them), but if introduced by slaves, the labor savings would have been interpreted as detrimental to the "master". The distinctive feature of ancient economies was not the governance of time in productive activities, but the extensive exploitation of human force.

The more the division of labor advances, the more time acquires a social dimension for individuals. The overall labor time, which individuals in remote ages distributed among different activities (productive and unproductive), in commercial societies becomes a time which no longer can be divided according to their preferences, because now productive and unproductive activities are performed by specific professions. The division of labor in the new situation involves a social division of time. This idea is expressed in a passage in which Smith examines how leisure was reorganized over time:

> A shepherd has a great deal of leisure; a husbandman, in the rude state of husbandry, has some; an artificer or manufacturer has none at all. The first may, without any loss, employ a great deal of his time in martial exercises; the second may employ some part of it; but the last cannot employ a single hour in them without some loss, and his attention to his own interest naturally leads him to neglect them altogether. These improvements in husbandry too, which the progress of arts and manufactures necessarily introduces, leaven the husbandman as little leisure as the artificer. (WN V.i.f.15: 783)

Before the division of labor, leisure was under individuals' control. A shepherd could decide how to divide his time between productive (pasturage) and unproductive activities (martial exercises). Though with more limitations, a peasant was in a similar condition in "the rude state of husbandry", while the "manufacturer" did not have this opportunity. In other words, in ages in which the division of labor pertains not to social, but to individual organization of labor, leisure is a share of the overall time available to individuals, which can be used to develop personal qualities. By contrast, with the "division of employments" in society, the share of private leisure, formerly included in unproductive activities, is placed in a space occupied by a specific profession. Similarly, the space in which productive activities are performed is no longer private, as it is a social space occupied by a specific class of workers. Time has been socially reorganized and with it the relationship between productive and unproductive labor.

Leisure, as time spent in unproductive activities, is a feature of the work of intellectuals. In civilized societies, "philosophers or men of speculation" are members of a distinct profession (WN I.i.9: 21). They are

> those few, who, being attached to no particular occupation themselves, have *leisure* and inclination to examine the occupations of other people. The contemplation of so great a variety of objects necessarily exercises their minds in endless comparisons and combinations, and renders their understandings, in an extraordinary degree, both acute and comprehensive. (WN V.i.f.51: 783, emphasis added)

By contrast, in barbarous societies where the mind is exercised because of the "good deal of variety in the occupations of every individual" (WN V.i.f.51: 783), a certain amount of intellectual activity is not restricted to a particular class of men. In these conditions, however, intellectual abilities cannot develop beyond a certain limit, because this development requires specialization. Knowledge increases only by creating a social space for intellectual activity, although this means that most people are doomed to intellectual poverty because of the social division of labor.

With the new organization of labor, the modern subject—the individual—acquires an identity that ultimately derives from a new reorganization of time. In this situation, knowledge continues to spread in society, but this involves a social cost. The undivided personality of individuals, integrated in the community, is a condition belonging to a hypothetical age which precedes the division of labor. By contrast, it is where the technical division of labor prevails that individuals are deprived of important qualities. In this respect, Smith in a famous passage maintains:

> In the progress of the division of labour, the employment of the far greater part of those who live by labour, that is, of the great body of the people, comes to be confined to a few very simple operations; frequently to one or two. But the understandings of the greater part of men are necessarily formed by their ordinary employments. The man whose whole life is spent in performing a few simple operations, of which the effects too are, perhaps, always the same, or very nearly the same, has no occasion to exert his understanding, or to exercise his invention in finding out expedients for removing difficulties which never occur. He naturally loses, therefore, the habit of such exertion, and generally becomes as stupid and ignorant as is possible for a human creature to become. (WN V.i.f.50: 781–782)

In these circumstances individuals are less able to relate themselves to the community. While in "barbarous societies" "every man [...] is in some measure a stateman" (WN V.i.f.51: 783), in a civilized society the individual is "incapable of judging" "the great and extensive interests of his country" (WN V.i.f.50: 782). The degenerating effects of the division of labor are manifold and regard the fact that individual's "dexterity at his own particular trade seems [...]to be acquired at the expence of his intellectual, social, and martial virtues" (WN V.i.f.50: 782). This situation is irreversible, but the State, by encouraging public education, can partially mitigate the intellectual degeneration caused by the conditions in which individuals live (see Hont & Ignatieff, 1983: 8).

The individual (a term whose etymological meaning is "undivided") that the liberal tradition considers to be the pillar of the market society is described in Smith as a divided personality, who certainly follows his or her self-interest, but is at the same time cognitively limited. If so, then, one might ask how individuals know and represent their self-interest.

9.6 Self-Interest and Visibility

A problem pointed out in the previous section is that in advanced societies the divided personality of individuals prevents most of them from formulating an appropriate opinion about their country's general interest. This condition, however, can be related to the fact that social, political and economic processes become less intelligible because of the dynamism of society. The impersonal forces of the social division of labor establish a "division of employments" which is beyond the control of individuals, and this reduces their capacity to predict future events. Moreover, their subjective condition further limits this capacity. If in a civilized society "gross ignorance and stupidity [...] seem so frequently to benumb the understandings of all the inferior ranks of people" (WN i.f-g.61: 788), it is plausible to think that individuals so "mutilated" do not correctly interpret the environment in which they live. In short, two circumstances seem to reduce individual capacity to understand the social order: one is that society has become more complex, and the other is that individuals in the new circumstances show specific cognitive limits.

Given these premises, one might ask whether self-interest is fully clear to individuals. Smith maintains that laborers, capital owners and landowners, as "orders of society", have specific interests that, however, are not always correctly interpreted. In particular, landowners and workers do not understand the close connection between their "real" interest and "the general interest of the society" (WN I.xi.p. 8: 265).[5] But the problem is not limited to this relationship. The "real interest" of the two social groups consists in increasing their private wealth, but both are unable to identify the strategies that lead to this result. The distance between their real interest and what they erroneously perceive as such depends not on temporary, conceptual mistakes which in principle could be revised and corrected, but on more substantive reasons.

Landowners do not possess "a tolerable knowledge" of their real interest. This condition is not simply due to ignorance. Rather, it reflects a sort of psychological attitude which derives from the material conditions in which they live. In this respect, Smith maintains:

[5] Smith explains this relation by pointing out that "All those improvements in the productive powers of labour, which tend directly to reduce the real price of manufactures, tend indirectly to raise the real rent of land" (WN I.xi.p.4: 264). As regards laborers, he maintains: "The wages of the labourer [...] are never so high as when the demand for labour is continually rising, or when the quantity employed is every year increasing considerably. When this real wealth of the society becomes stationary, his wages are soon reduced to what is barely enough to enable him to bring up a family, or to continue the race of labourers. When the society declines, they fall even below this. The order of proprietors may, perhaps, gain more by the prosperity of the society, than that of labourers: but there is no order that suffers so cruelly from its decline" (WN I.xi.p. 9: 266).

> That indolence, which is the natural effect of the ease and security of their situation, renders them too often, not only ignorant, but incapable of that application of mind which is necessary in order to foresee and understand the consequences of any publick regulation. (WN I.xi.p. 8: 265)

"Indolence" is a distinctive trait of landowners' behavior because it is rooted in "the ease and security of their situation". This basic feature explains their inability to orient in their favor "any regulation of commerce or police" and to formulate "any plan or project of their own" (WN I.xi.p. 8: 265).

In the commercial society, landowners receive a rent which they prefer to spend for their consumption, instead of investing it with the expectation of increasing their wealth. This attitude originated with the advent of the commercial society, when landowners "bartered their whole power and authority" for "frivolous and useless" objects (WN III.iv.10: 418–419). Their subjective representation of their self-interest does not coincide with their "real" interest, because they identify their own interest with consumption. "Vanity", and not the prospect of increasing their revenue, guides their choices.

This behavior can be compared to the merchant's conduct:

> A merchant is accustomed to employ his money chiefly in profitable projects; whereas a mere country gentleman is accustomed to employ it chiefly in expence. The one often sees his money go from him and return to him again with a profit: the other, when once he parts with it, very seldom expects to see any more of it. Those different habits naturally affect their temper and disposition in every sort of business. (WN III.iv.3: 411)

The different views of merchants and landowners depend not only on their ability to rationally evaluate their self-interest but also on a more pervasive "habit", one that tacitly directs their behavior in the economic sphere. However, neither merchants nor landowners, while conceptualizing their real interest so differently, imagine what consequences their behaviors will produce on the social level.

Smith's analysis of the conditions of laborers also shows that they do not have a correct view of their real interest. Their "interest" "is as strictly connected with the interest of the society as that of" landowners (WN I.xi.p. 9: 266). Nevertheless, the laborer:

> is incapable either of comprehending that interest, or of understanding its connection with his own. His condition leaves him no time to receive the necessary information, and his education and habits are commonly such as to render him unfit to judge even though he was fully informed. (WN I. xi.p. 9: 266)

The laborers are deprived of their time. This condition makes them unable to "receive the necessary information". But the problem is not limited to the lack of information, if the organization of labor makes the laborer "stupid and ignorant", and if "his education and habits" prevent him from understanding how the increase of public wealth may improve his condition.

The condition of the "merchants and master manufacturers" is different. They are aware of their real interest because "during their whole lives they are engaged in plans and projects", and this allows them to "have frequently more acuteness of understanding than the greater part of country gentlemen" (WN I.xi.p. 10: 266). Although this reduces the gap between the subjective perception of interest and real interest, this does not necessarily favor the increase of public welfare. In fact,

> As their thoughts, however, are commonly exercised rather about the interest of their own particular branch of business, than about that of the society, their judgment, even when given with the greatest candour (which it has not been upon every occasion) is much more to be depended upon with regard to the former of those two objects, than with regard to the latter. (WN I. xi.p. 10: 266)

Capital owners' knowledge of their self-interest, however, poses a problem regarding the functioning of the invisible hand, because their interest

> in any particular branch of trade or manufactures, is always in some respects different from, and even opposite to, that of the publick. To widen the market and to narrow the competition, is always the interest of the dealers. (WN I.xi.p. 10: 267)

To "widen the market" is a behavior which promotes the increase of public welfare, but "to narrow the competition" is an operation having the opposite effect. If the capital owners' behavior is selfish, the "optimal" market order (at least partially) cannot be attained because they increase their profits by damaging the rest of society. The revenues of selfish merchants are losses for other individuals because free competition is altered. In this perspective, the invisible hand illustrates an ideal condition that is not clearly explained, although this metaphor aims to show that a harmonious coherence between private and public welfare is possible. Although it is undeniable that market society is progressing, many circumstances make this progress difficult because, for different reasons, behaviors of the three orders of society can limit the proper functioning of the market.

References

Bacon, F. (1868 [1623]). On the Dignity and Advancement of Learning. In *The Physical and Metaphysical Works of Lord Bacon*. J. Devey (Ed.), Bell and Daldy.

Condorcet, J.-A.-N. de Caritat marquis de. (1795). *Outlines of an Historical View of the Progress of the Human Mind*. Printed for Johnson.

Ferguson, A. (1995 [1767]). *An Essay on the History of Civil Society*, F. Oz-Salzberger (Ed.). Cambridge University Press.

Fiori, S., & Pesciarelli, E. (1999). Adam Smith on Relations of Subordination, Personal Incentives and the Division of Labour. *Scottish Journal of Political Economy, 46*(1), 91–106.

Foucault, M. (2008). *The Birth of Biopolitics*, Lectures at the College de France, 1978–79, M. Senellart (Ed.). Palgrave Macmillan.

Haakonssen, K. (1981). *The Science of a Legislator. The Natural Jurisprudence of David Hume and Adam Smith*. Cambridge University Press.

Hont, I., & Ignatieff, M. (1983). Needs and Justice in the *Wealth of Nations*: An Introductory Essay. In I. Hont & M. Ignatieff (Eds.), *Wealthand Virtue. The Shaping of Political Economy in the Scottish Enlightenment* (pp. 1–44). Cambridge University Press.

Hume, D. (1985 [1739–40]). *A Treatise of Human Nature*, E. G. Mossner (Ed.). Penguin Books.

Hume, D. (2007 [1748]). *An Enquiry Concerning Human Understanding*, P. Millican (Ed.). Oxford University Press.

Koselleck, R. (2004 [1979]). *Futures Past: On the Semantics of Historical Time*. New York: Columbia University Press.

Lindgren, R. J. (1973). *The Social Philosophy of Adam Smith*. Martinus Nijhoff.

Locke, J. (1980 [1690]). *Second Treatise of Government* (C. B. Macpherson, Trans. and Ed.). Hackett Publishing Company.

Meek, R. L. (1976). *Social Science and the Ignoble Savage*. Cambridge University Press.

Millar, J. (1779). *The Origin of the Distinction of Ranks* (3rd ed.). Murray.

Millar, J. (1803). *An Historical View of the English Government* (Vol. IV). Printed for J. Mawman.

Pesciarelli, E. (1977). Adam Smith: dal modo di sussistenza al modo di produzione. *Quaderni di Sociologia, 26*(3–4), 219–231.

Pesciarelli, E. (1988). *La jurisprudence economica di Adam Smith.* Giappichelli.

Rothschild, E. (2001). *Economic Sentiments: Adam Smith, Condorcet and the Enlightenment.* Harvard University Press.

Schliesser, E. (2017). *Adam Smith. Systematic Philosopher and Public Thinker.* Oxford University Press.

Skinner, A. S. (1979). *A System of Social Science. Papers Relating to Adam Smith.* Clarendon Press.

CHAPTER 10

Conclusions

Abstract Rethinking order. This is the theme that summarizes an important part of Smith's research, which we set out to analyze by considering the various sources that had led that author to formulate his ideas about the self-regulating market and social order. In particular, Smith's idea of social order has been interpreted here as the result of a combination of theoretical analyses and less structured visions, which ultimately rested on the use of metaphors.

A vast amount of literature has argued that metaphors are conceptual tools and not mere elocutionary tools. In this perspective, this study has analyzed the three main metaphors that conceptualized order in Adam Smith's thought: the machine, the body and the invisible hand.

It has also been argued that the notion of invisibility, as the expression of a logic that goes beyond the context in which the figure of the "invisible hand" was used, was the hallmark of Smith's economic theory, of life sciences and of other disciplines of his time.

Lastly, it has been shown that time became an element to take into account in analyzing the social order. In particular, in the new circumstances, the continuous reconfiguration of order made the future open and unpredictable.

Keywords Logic of modern social systems • Notion of invisibility • Visible order • Invisible order

S. Fiori, *Machines, Bodies and Invisible Hands*,
https://doi.org/10.1007/978-3-030-85206-1_10

Rethinking order. This is the theme that summarizes an important part of Smith's research, which we set out to analyze by considering the various sources that had led that author to formulate his ideas about self-regulating market and social order. In particular, Smith's idea that social order was the unintended result of the behavior of individuals driven by their own self-interest, however they represented it, has been interpreted here as the result of a combination of theoretical analyses and less structured visions, which ultimately rested on the use of metaphors.

A vast amount of literature has argued that metaphors are conceptual tools and not mere ornamental tools. They have an ostensive character, identify relationships, make it possible to represent complex phenomena in the first instance and can direct research when tools to produce a formal analysis are unavailable. Furthermore, the formal tools themselves are often simply a development of the causal relationships established by metaphors. In this perspective, the study has analyzed the three main metaphors that conceptualized order in Adam Smith's thought: the machine, the body and the invisible hand.

The idea I have attempted to sustain is that they incorporated alternative but at the same time partially overlapping visions. If the invisible hand was the metaphor that best conceptualized the self-regulatory processes of the market, on the other hand it shared several elements with the other two metaphors. The machine, the body and the invisible hand appear without any precise order in Smith's work; however, they can be interpreted as metaphorical models that with an increasing degree of complexity offered a representation of the social order of the market, as if they were aligned in an ideal succession. For this reason, in the present work they have been interpreted as heuristic tools that allowed the exploration of possible explanations for economic phenomena.

Smith's metaphors of the machine and the body revealed many novel elements compared to similar metaphors used in the seventeenth century, as we can deduce from a comparison with the economic and scientific systems that legitimized their use. In Smith the machine is represented as an evolving system rather than a system that implies a hierarchy. In this sense, he revitalized the mechanical metaphor by giving it new meanings.

Furthermore, unlike its use in the seventeenth and early eighteenth centuries, he did not employ the metaphor of the "balance" (balance of trade, balance of power, etc.) to represent the equilibrium of the economic order. This image had been exploited by the Mercantilists and, in a more elaborate form, by Mandeville. But it was Hume who had revealed its limits, and thus had tried to reconfigure it. However, despite its new elements, Smith's mechanical metaphor (like any similar metaphor) implied that changes in the system were not endogenous, and therefore could not be used to explain the nature of self-regulatory processes.

Smith also resorted to the metaphor of the body. But unlike seventeenth-century authors, he used it neither in a mechanistic sense nor to represent the hierarchy in the natural and political body via images of nourishment, circulation and distribution. Instead, he adopted it to exemplify the not yet known but observable properties of self-regulation and self-preservation of both political and natural bodies. Although the image of the body itself was quite elementary, what made it significant was that it was related to a system of discourses which, taken together, helped to identify the nature of economic orders.

However, even the metaphor of the body only partially managed to account for the processes that characterize social order. The body's equilibrium, although guaranteed by endogenous biological mechanisms, may require continuous regulatory interventions, Smith pointed out. Like a good physician for the natural body, the legislator will help the political body to heal itself, when self-regenerative properties are not sufficient to guarantee its survival. Furthermore, while the natural body dies, a political body regenerates itself and often progresses continuously. Moreover, Smith argued that the history of European societies demonstrates this tendency, since social orders tend to realize the "natural order", albeit in an irregular way. In short, natural bodies, unlike political bodies, do not progress indefinitely. They recover from diseases, but they cannot go beyond the limits imposed by nature.

Furthermore, like the mechanical metaphor, the metaphor of the body assumed that the whole, that is, the body itself, was predefined and that the parts that made it up were assigned a stable function, without which the order itself would have been unthinkable. The novelty introduced by the metaphor of the invisible hand, as a general concept that characterizes Smith's work and is not limited to the three circumstances in which it is mentioned, was that order had to be conceived starting from the not predetermined behaviors of individuals. In other words, order had to be interpreted as the "result" of decentralized movements, and not as the premise of the discourse. The invisible hand exhibited, although it did not formally explain, the self-regulating properties of economic and social systems. In this sense, it was an ostensive metaphor.

Even when Smith does not explicitly mention it, the invisible hand recalls the logic of modern social systems. This logic is at the heart of the present study. Although the invisible hand of WN encapsulated many concepts not expressed in metaphorical form in the same chapter where it appears, none of these concepts were able to demonstrate why social order and progress had to prevail, especially in the light of an empirical and historical analysis from which emerged how far we are from those optimal conditions that guaranteed the development of society.

From a theoretical point of view, the invisible hand was an innovation compared to seventeenth-century conceptual metaphors. It constituted a change from the model of "visibility as intelligibility" prevalent in the decades of the Scientific Revolution. This model was employed in various approaches, including alternative ones. The Cartesian deductive model implied that "Knowing Is Seeing" and that the intelligibility of the natural world could be deduced from the intelligibility of the machine. However, the ocular model of knowledge manifested itself in several ways. For Bacon it had to be reformulated in order to overcome the deception of the senses, because this would have made nature visible without residues. More generally, it was believed that nature could be understood by making visible parts of it that were not observable by the naked eye. Experiments and technical tools, such as microscopes and telescopes, would have served this purpose. Art could reveal nature, forcing it to show itself, and even forcing it to perform operations that it did not perform spontaneously. This occurred in the artisan workshops, but also in agriculture, where nature could be induced to multiply its products. The more manageable nature was, the less mysterious it was. The more its inconspicuous aspects were brought to the surface, the less it appeared to be a system dominated by "occult forces". The task of science seemed to be to make nature visible by improving its observational procedures. Therefore, the notion of visibility implied at least two aspects. One was empirical: it was necessary to be able to better describe nature in all its details. The other was conceptual: it was necessary to have good methods that strengthened "the mind's eye", as Boyle emphasized, also with appropriate "Similitudes, or Comparisons".

These ideas penetrated economic approaches. From Petty to Quesnay, visibility could be increased with appropriate calculations, and the idea that the task of science was to make economic phenomena visible using appropriate tools was expressed by the metaphor of anatomy, the discipline which *par excellence* was distinguished by its ability to reveal to the scientist what was not immediately observable in the body.

The notion of invisibility, as the expression of a logic that goes beyond the context in which the figure of the "invisible hand" was used, was the hallmark of Smith's economic theory, of life sciences and of other disciplines of his time. Smith's own moral philosophy can be reconsidered in this perspective. The figure of the spectator (and of the "impartial spectator") showed how it was necessary to introduce the relationship between visibility and invisibility in order to analyze the moral sphere. The mechanism of the gaze, which was activated by the presence of the spectator, led to reformulating the moral experience of individuals, and to generating an order at the base of which there were shared norms, which no one had planned but were instead the result of many independent relationships between individuals. The visible order of moral relations was based on invisible mechanisms, not observable as such, which ultimately were identified with the capacity for "sympathy" and with the work of the imagination.

For Smith, even nature's order can be interpreted as a constant relationship between an observed visible order and an invisible order that explains it, where the latter is continually reinterpreted by scientists and philosophers. Finally, the circular relationship between visible and invisible order was replicated in economic analysis. The visible is based on invisible forces, not always well defined and identifiable. But it is the observable dimension that leads us to identify and represent the forces on which it is built. This is also the point of metaphors, when few other investigative tools are available. The analysis of the division of labor, real and nominal price, natural and market prices, and the notion of productive labor showed, as Foucault says, that the analysis of the "visible" could not be based on the observation of visible interdependencies alone, as was the case in Petty and Quesnay, but had to be related to a system of invisible forces.

Life sciences in Smith's time used the word "organization" to denote invisible order. Life appeared to be a domain that could not be interpreted on a mechanistic basis, whose visible characteristics had to be related to properties not fully understood but identifiable to some extent. Buffon had advanced the idea that life was shaped by "penetrating forces" that our senses cannot perceive. The idea of invisible organization was further developed in vitalistic approaches. And with Bordeu the image of the "swarm of bees" seemed to illustrate (as in Smith in other respects) how the properties of the whole (the body) emerged from the behavior of components endowed with individuality, which in principle have autonomous behaviors.

Visible nature appeared complex due to its evolutionary processes, Diderot said. Therefore, the problem of temporalization made it difficult to explain the formation and development of the order of nature. Similarly, time became an element to take into account in analyzing the social order. The time of the market showed different characteristics compared to the time experienced in the pre-modern age.

In the new circumstances, the continuous reconfiguration of order made the future open and unpredictable. Time, so to speak, escaped the control of individuals, but at the same time its internal rhythms could be governed. How individuals could favor the impersonal processes of the creation of order, pursuing a self-interest that they themselves did not always understand, was what the "invisible hand" set out to explain … within the limits allowed by a metaphor.

Bibliographic Note

The material in this book is based on articles and a previously published Italian book of mine. However, all this material has now been rethought, reorganized and extended in the present book.

Fiori, S. (1996). Order Metaphors, and Equilibrium in Adam Smith's Thought. *History of Economic Ideas, 4*(1–2), 175–203.

Fiori, S. (2001a). *Ordine, mano invisibile, mercato. Una rilettura di Adam Smith*. UTET.

Fiori, S. (2001b). Visible and Invisible Order. The Theoretical Duality of Smith's Political Economy. *The European Journal of the History of Economic Thought, 8*(4), 429–448.

Fiori, S. (2005). Individual and Self-Interest in Adam Smith's *Wealth of Nations. Cahiers d'économie politique, 49*, 19–30.

Fiori, S. (2012). Adam Smith on Method: Newtonianism, History, Institutions, and the "Invisible Hand". *Journal of the History of Economic Thought, 34*(3), 411–435.

Fiori, S. (2014). Adam Smith and the Unintended Consequences of History. *History of Economic Ideas, 22*(2), 55–74.

Fiori, S. (2019). Nature and Labour. Theoretical Approaches and Metaphors of Wealth Before Adam Smith. *The European Journal of the History of Economic Thought, 26*(6), 1153–1186.

S. Fiori, *Machines, Bodies and Invisible Hands*,
https://doi.org/10.1007/978-3-030-85206-1

Works of Adam Smith

Smith, A. (1981). An Inquiry into the Nature and Causes of the Wealth of Nations. In R. H. Campbell, A. S. Skinner, & W. B. Todd (Eds.), *The Glasgow Edition of the Works and Correspondence of Adam Smith* (Vol. II). Indianapolis.

Smith, A. (1982a). Essays on Philosophical Subjects. In W. P. D. Wightman & J. C. Bryce (Eds.), *The Glasgow Edition of the Works and Correspondence of Adam Smith* (Vol. III). Indianapolis.

Smith, A. (1982b). Lectures on Jurisprudence. In R. L. Meek, D. D. Raphael, & P. G. Stein (Eds.), *The Glasgow Edition of the Works and Correspondence of Adam Smith* (Vol. V). Indianapolis.

Smith, A. (1984). The Theory of Moral Sentiments. In D. D. Raphael & A. L. Macfie (Eds.), *The Glasgow Edition of the Works and Correspondence of Adam Smith* (Vol. 1). Indianapolis.

Smith, A. (1985). Lectures on Rhetoric and Belles Lettres. In J. C. Bryce (Ed.), *The Glasgow Edition of the Works and Correspondence of Adam Smith* (Vol. IV). Indianapolis.

Bibliography

Ahmad, S. (1990). Adam Smith's Four Invisible Hands. *History of Political Economy, 22*(1), 137–144.

Anonymous. (1997). Organic and Mechanical Metaphors in Late Eighteenth-Century American Political Thought. *Harvard Law Review*, 1832–1849.

Anstey, P. R. (2000). *The Philosophy of Robert Boyle*. Routledge.

Aristotle. (1936). *Physics*, a Revised Text with Introduction and Commentary by W. D. Ross. Clarendon Press.

Arrow, K. J. (1983). *General Equilibrium*. Elsevier.

Arrow, K. J., & Hahn, F. H. (1971). *General Competitive Analysis*. Holden-Day.

Aspromourgos, T. (1996). *On the Origins of Classical Economics: Distribution and Value from William Petty to Adam Smith*. Routledge.

Aspromourgos, T. (2009). *The Science of Wealth. Adam Smith and the Framing of Political Economy*. Routledge.

Aspromourgos, T. (2012). The Machine in Adam Smith's Economic and Wider Thought. *Journal of the History of Economic Thought, 34*(4), 475–490.

Bacon, F. (1625). *The Essays or Councils, Civil and Moral*. Printed by Iohn Haviland.

Bacon, F. (1868 [1623]). On the Dignity and Advancement of Learning. In J. Devey (Ed.), *The Physical and Metaphysical Works of Lord Bacon*. Bell and Daldy.

Bacon, F. (1999 [1627]). New Atlantis. In S. Bryce (Ed.), *Three Early Modern Utopias. Utopia, New Atlantis, The Isle of Pines* (pp. 149–186). Oxford University Press.

Bacon, F. (2000 [1620]). *The New Organon*, L. Jardine & M. Silverthorne (Eds.). Cambridge University Press.

S. Fiori, *Machines, Bodies and Invisible Hands*,
https://doi.org/10.1007/978-3-030-85206-1

Bailer-Jones, D. (2002). Models, Metaphors and Analogies. In P. Machamer & M. Silberstein (Eds.), *The Blackwell Guide to the Philosophy of Science* (pp. 108–127). Blackwell.

Banzhaf, S. H. (2000). Productive Nature and the Net Product: Quesnay's Economies Animal and Political. *History of Political Economy, 32*(3), 517–551.

Barbon, N. (1859 [1685]). An Apology for the Builder. In J. R. McCulloch (Ed.), *A Select Collection of Scarce and Valuable Economical Tracts* (pp. 3–26). Printed for the Political Economy Club.

Barbon, N. (1905 [1690]). A Discourse of Trade. In J. H. Hollander (Ed.), *A Reprint of Economic Tracts* (pp. 9–43). John Hopkins Press.

Bazerman, C. (1993). Money Talks: The Rhetorical Project of the *Wealth of Nations*. In W. Henderson, T. Dudley-Evans, & R. Backhouse (Eds.), *Economics and Language* (pp. 173–199). Routledge.

Bentham, J. (1791). *Panopticon or, the Inspection-House*. T. Payne.

Bentham, J. (1983). *Panopticon*, M. Foucault & M. Perrot (Eds.). Venezia.

Berkeley, G. (2017 [1732]). An EssayTowards A New Theory of Vision. In *Saggio su una nuova teoria della visione. Trattato sui principi della conoscenza umana*, Facing English Text. Bompiani.

Bernardi, W. (1995). La conquista del mondo invisibile: modelli epistemologici e teorie della vita nella rivoluzione scientifica. In *Storia della filosofia, storia della scienza. Saggi in onore di Paolo Rossi* (pp. 59–75). La Nuova Italia.

Berry, C. J. (2006). Smith and Science. In K. Haakonssen (Ed.), *The Cambridge Companion to Adam Smith* (pp. 112–135). Cambridge University Press.

Besomi, D. (2011). Crises as a Disease of the Body Politick. A Metaphor in the History of Nineteenth-Century Economics. *Journal of the History of Economic Thought, 33*(1), 67–118.

Bicchieri, C. (1988). Should a Scientist Abstain from Metaphor? In A. Klamer, D. N. McCloskey, & R. M. Solow (Eds.), *The Consequences of Economic Rhetoric* (pp. 100–114). Cambridge University Press.

Bittermann, H. J. (1940a). Adam Smith's Empiricism and the Law of Nature. *Journal of Political Economy, 48*(4), 487–520.

Bittermann, H. J. (1940b). Adam Smith's Empiricism and the Law of Nature. *Journal of Political Economy, 48*(5), 703–734.

Black, M. (1962). *Models and Metaphors. Studies in Language and Philosophy.* Cornell University Press.

Black, M. (1993 [1979]). More About Metaphor. In A. Ortony (Ed.), *Metaphor and Thought* (2nd ed., pp. 19–41). Cambridge University Press.

Botero, G. (1606). *A Treatise, Concerning the Causes of the Magnificencie and Greatnes of Cities.* Richard Ockould and Henry Tomes.

Bourke, J. (2012). Pain, Sympathy and the Medical Encounter Between the Mid Eighteenth and the Mid Twentieth Centuries. *Historical Research, 85*(229), 430–452.

Boyd, R. (1993). Metaphor and Theory Change: What Is "metaphor" a Metaphor For. In A. Ortony (Ed.), *Metaphor and Thought* (2nd ed., pp. 481–532). Cambridge University Press.

Boyle, R. (1772a [1666]). The Origin of Forms and Qualities, According to the Corpuscular Philosophy. In *Works* (Vol. 3). Johnston et al.

Boyle, R. (1772b [1690]). The Christian Virtuoso. In *Works* (Vol. 5). Johnston et al.

Boyle, R. (1772c [1690]). The Christian Virtuoso. The Second Part. In *Works* (Vol. 6). Johnston et al.

Brewer, A. (1992). Petty and Cantillon. *History of Political Economy, 24*(3), 711–728.

Brewer, A. (2009). On the Other (Invisible) Hand .... *History of Political Economy, 41*(3), 519–543.

Brown, V. (1994). *Adam Smith's Discourse. Canonicity, Commerce and Conscience.* Routledge.

Brown, T. L. (2003). *Making Truth: Metaphor in Science.* University of Illinois Press.

Buffon, G.-L. Leclerc de. (1749). *Histoire naturelle, générale et particulière*, nouvelle édition, tome I. Imprimerie Royale.

Buffon, G.-L. Leclerc de. (1750). *Histoire naturelle, générale et particulière, avec la description du Cabinet du Roi*, tome II. Pierre le Hondt.

Caffentzis, G. C. (2003). Medical Metaphors and Monetary Strategies in the Political Economy of Locke and Berkeley. *History of Political Economy*, Annual Supplement, *35*, 204–233.

Campbell, T. D. (1971). *Adam Smith's Science of Morals.* Allen & Unwin.

Cantillon, R. (2015). *Richard Cantillon's Essay on the Nature of Trade in General. A Variorum Edition* (R. van den Berg, Trans. & Ed.). Routledge.

Caravale, G. (1992). Alcune considerazioni sulla nozione di equilibrio nella teoria economica. *Studi economici., 47*(2), 5–44.

Carey, T. V. (2017). Adam Smith's Invisible Hand: A Brief History. In F. Forman (Ed.), *The Adam Smith Review* (Vol. 9, pp. 88–104).

Casini, P. (1980). *Introduzione all'illuminismo*, 2 voll. Laterza.

Cassirer, E. (1968). *The Philosophy of Enlightenment.* Princeton University Press.

Chamberlayne, E. (1683). *The Third Part of The Present State of England.* Printed for William Whitwood.

Christensen, P. P. (1989). Hobbes and the Physiological Origins of Economic Science. *History of Political Economy, 21*(44), 689–709.

Christensen, P. P. (1994). Fire, Motion, and Productivity: The Proto-Energetics of Nature and Economy in François Quesnay. In P. Mirowski (Ed.), *Natural Images in Economic Thought* (pp. 249–288). Cambridge University Press.

Cipolla, C. M. (1996). *Le macchine del tempo.* Il Mulino.

Clément, A. (2003). The Influence of Medicine on Political Economy in the Seventeenth Century. *History of Economics Review, 38*(1), 1–22.

Clericuzio, A. (2015). Le forme e i moti della materia. Trasformazioni del meccanicismo nel Seicento. In P. Pecere (Ed.), *Il libro della natura* (Vol. I, pp. 67–107). Carocci.

Close, A. J. (1969). Commonplace Theories of Art and Nature in Classical Antiquity and in the Renaissance. *Journal of the History of Ideas, 30*(4), 467–486.

Cohen, B. I. (1980). *The Newtonian Revolution. With Illustration of the Transformation of Scientific Ideas.* Cambridge University Press.

Cohen, B. I. (1993). Analogy, Homology, and Metaphor in the Interaction Between the Natural Sciences and Social Sciences, Especially Economics. In N. de Marchi (Ed.), *Non-Natural Science: Reflecting on the Enterprise of More Heat than Light. History of Political Economy* (pp. 7–44)., Annual Supplement to volume 25.

Cohen, B. I. (1994). Newton and the Social Sciences, with Special Reference to Economics, or, the Case of the Missing Paradigm. In P. Mirowski (Ed.), *Natural Images in Economic Thought* (pp. 55–90). Cambridge University Press.

Coleman, W. O. (2001). The Significance of John Locke's Medical Studies for the History of Economic Thought. In P. Groenewegen (Ed.), *Physicians and Political Economy. Six Studies of the Work of Doctor-Economists* (pp. 36–55). Routledge. https://play.google.com/books/reader?id=At15ArwgfQUC&hl=it&pg=GBS.PT71.w.6.8.0

Condillac, E. B. (2014 [1749]). Treatise on Systems. In *Philosophical Writings of Etienne Bonnot, Abbé de Condillac* (Vol. 1). Routledge.

Condorcet, J.-A.-N. de Caritat marquis de. (1795). *Outlines of an Historical View of the Progress of the Human Mind.* Printed for Johnson.

Cook, H. J. (1999). Bernard Mandeville and the Therapy of "The Clever Politician". *Journal of the History of Ideas, 60*(1), 101–124.

Cremaschi, S. (1984). *Il sistema della ricchezza. Economia politica e problema del metodo in Adam Smith.* Franco Angeli.

Cremaschi, S. (2002). Metaphors in the *Wealth of Nations.* In S. Boehm, C. Gehrke, H. D. Kurz, & R. Sturn (Eds.), *Is There Progress in Economics? Knowledge, Truth and the History of Economic Thought* (pp. 89–114). Edward Elgar.

Cremaschi, S. (2009). Newtonian Physics, Experimental Moral Philosophy and the Shaping of Political Economy. In R. Arena, S. Dow, & M. Klaes (Eds.), *Open Economics: Economics in Relation to Other Disciplines* (pp. 73–94). Routledge.

Cremaschi, S. (2017). Adam Smith's Irony and the Invisible Hand. *Iberian Journal of the History of Economic Thought, 4*(1), 43–62.

Dascal, M. (2006). Adam Smith's Theory of Language. In K. Haakonssen (Ed.), *The Cambridge Companion to Adam Smith* (pp. 79–111). Cambridge University Press.

Davenant, C. (1771a [1698]). Discourses on the Public Revenues, and on the Trade of England. In *The Political and Commercial Works* (Vol. I). Printed for R. Horsfield.

Davenant, C. (1771b [1699]). An Essay Upon the Probable Methods of Making a People Gainers in the Balance of Trade. In *The Political and Commercial Works* (Vol. 2). Printed for R. Horsfield.

Davidko, N. (2013). Metaphoricity in the History of Economic Thought (on the Basis of the 17th Century Economic Discourse). *Kalbų Studijos/Studies about Languages, 22*, 86–97.

Davidson, D. (1978). What Metaphors Mean. *Critical Inquiry, 5*(1), 31–47.

Davis, J. B. (1989). Smith's Invisible Hand and Hegel's Cunning of Reason. *International Journal of Social Economics, 16*(6), 50–66.

de Bolla, P. (1996). The Visibility of Visuality. In T. Brennan & M. Jay (Eds.), *Vision in Context: Historical and Contemporary Perspectives on Sight* (pp. 65–81). Routledge.

de Bordeu, T. (1751). Recherches anatomiques sur la position des glandes et leur action. In *Œuvres complètes de Bordeu*, tome I. Caille et Ravier.

de La Mettrie, J. O. (1748). *L'homme machine*. Elie Luzac, fils.

De Marchi, N. (2001). Exposure to Strangers and Superfluities: Mandeville's Regimen for Great Wealth and Foreign Treasure. In P. Groenewegen (Ed.), *Physicians and Political Economy. Six Studies of the Work of Doctor-Economists* (pp. 73–95). Routledge. https://play.google.com/books/reader?id=At15ArwgfQUC&hl=it&pg=GBS.PT71.w.6.8.0

Dear, P. (1995). *Discipline and Experience. The Mathematical Way in the Scientific Revolution*. University of Chicago Press.

Dear, P. (2006). *The Intelligibility of Nature. How Science Makes Sense of the World*. University of Chicago Press.

Deleule, D. (1979). *Hume et la naissance du libéralisme économique*. Aubier Montaigne.

Demeter, T. (2016). *David Hume and the Culture of Scottish Newtonianism: Methodology and Ideology in Enlightenment Inquiry*. Brill.

Des Chene, D. (2001). *Spirits and Clocks. Machine and Organism in Descartes*. Cornell University Press.

Descartes, R. (1985a [1647]). Principles of Philosophy. In *The Philosophical Writings of Descartes* (Vol. 1). Cambridge University Press.

Descartes, R. (1985b [1662]). Treatise on Man. In *The Philosophical Writings of Descartes* (Vol. 1). Cambridge University Press.

Desmedt, L. (2005). Money in the "Body Politick": The Analysis of Trade and Circulation in the Writings of Seventeenth-Century Political Arithmeticians. *History of Political Economy, 37*(1), 79–101.

Diderot, D. (1996 [1769]). Le Rêve de D'Alembert. In *Il sogno di D'Alembert*, Facing French text. Rizzoli.

Diderot, D. (1999 [1753]). *Thoughts on Interpretation of Nature*. Clinamen Press.

Endres, A. M. (1996). Security' and Capital Formation. *The Wealth of Nations. History of Economic Ideas, 4*(1–2), 149–173.

Eriksen, C. B. (2017). Circulation of Blood and Money in Leviathan – Hobbes on the Economy of the Body. In J. Bek-Thomsen et al. (Eds.), *History of Economic Rationalities: Economic Reasoning as Knowledge and Practice Authority*. Springer.

Ferguson, A. (1995 [1767]). *An Essay on the History of Civil Society*, F. Oz-Salzberger (Ed.). Cambridge University Press.

Finkelstein, A. (2000). *Harmony and the Balance: An Intellectual History of Seventeenth-Century English Economic Thought*. University of Michigan Press.

Fiori, S. (1992). Persuasione e mercato. Note su un problema lasciato aperto da Adam Smith. *Trimestre, 25*(1–2), 41–53.

Fiori, S. (2019). Nature and Labour: Theoretical Approaches and Metaphors of Wealth Before Adam Smith. *The European Journal of the History of Economic Thought, 26*(6), 1153–1186.

Fiori, S., & Pesciarelli, E. (1999). Adam Smith on Relations of Subordination, Personal Incentives and the Division of Labour. *Scottish Journal of Political Economy, 46*(1), 91–106.

Fleischacker, S. (2004). *On Adam Smith's* Wealth of Nations. *A Philosophical Companion*. Princeton University Press.

Flew, A. (1987). Social Science: Making Visible the Invisible Hands. *The Journal of Libertarian Studies, 8*(2), 197–211.

Foley, V. (1973). An Origin of the Tableau Economique. *History of Political Economy, 5*(1), 121–150.

Foley, V. (1976). *The Social Physics of Adam Smith*. Purdue University Press.

Fontenelle. (1998 [1686]). *Entretiens sur la pluralité des mondes*. Flammarion.

Force, J. E. (1987). Hume's Interest in Newton and Science. *Hume Studies, 13*(2), 166–216.

Forget, E. L. (2003). Evocations of Sympathy: Sympathetic Imagery in Eighteenth-Century Social Theory and Physiology. *History of Political Economy*, Annual Supplement, *35*, 282–308.

Forman-Barzilai, F. (2010). *Adam Smith and the Circles of Sympathy. Cosmopolitanism and Moral Theory*. Cambridge University Press.

Foucault, M. (1995 [1975]). *Discipline and Punish: The Birth of the Prison* (A. Sheridan, Trans.). Vintage Books.

Foucault, M. (2005 [1966]). *The Order of Things. An Archeology of the Human Sciences*. Routledge.

Foucault, M. (2008). *The Birth of Biopolitics*, Lectures at the College de France, 1978–79, M. Senellart (Ed.). Palgrave Macmillan.

Freudenthal, G. (1981). Adam Smith's Analytic-Synthetic Method and the 'System of Natural Liberty'. *History of European Ideas, 2*(2), 135–154.

Freudenthal, G. (1986). *Atom and Individual in the Age of Newton. On the Genesis of the Mechanistic World View*. Reidel.

Galilei, G. (1960 [1590]. *De Motu*, EN (Vol. I, pp. 251–419); *On Motion* (I. E. Drabkin, Trans.). University of Wisconsin Press.

Galilei, G. (1967 [1632]). *Dialogue Concerning the Two Chief World Systems—Ptolemaic & Copernican* (2nd ed.). University of California Press.

Gervaise, I. (1954 [1720]). *The System or Theory of Trade of the World*, with a Foreword by J. Viner, and an Introduction by J. M. Letiche. Johns Hopkins Press.

Gilardi, R. (1988). Hume e il "principio di analogia". *Rivista di Filosofia Neo-Scolastica, 80*(1), 63–104.

Grampp, W. D. (2000). What Did Smith Mean by the Invisible Hand? *The Journal of Political Economy, 10*(3), 441–465.

Griswold, C. L., Jr. (1999). *Adam Smith and the Virtues of Enlightenment*. Cambridge University Press.

Groenewegen, P. (2001). From Prominent Physician to Major Economist: Some Reflections on Quesnay's Switch to Economics in the 1750s. In P. Groenewegen (Ed.), *Physicians and Political Economy. Six Studies of the Work of Doctor-Economists* (pp. 96–116). Routledge. https://play.google.com/books/reader?id=At15ArwgfQUC&hl=it&pg=GBS.PT71.w.6.8.0

Haakonssen, K. (1981). *The Science of a Legislator. The Natural Jurisprudence of David Hume and Adam Smith*. Cambridge University Press.

Haakonssen, K. (1996). *Natural Law and Moral Philosophy: From Grotius to the Scottish Enlightenment*. Cambridge University Press.

Harcourt, G. C., & Kriesler, P. (2012). *Introduction* (To Handbook of Post-Keynesian Economics. Oxford University Press), Australian School of Business Research, Paper No. 2012 ECON 33: 1-70.

Harris, J. G. (1999). The Canker of England's Commonwealth': Gerard de Malynes and the Origins of Economic Pathology. *Textual Practice, 13*(2), 311–327.

Harrison, J. R. (1995). Imagination and Aesthetics in Adam Smith's Epistemology and Moral Philosophy. *Contributions to Political Economy, 14*, 91–112.

Harrison, P. (2011). Adam Smith and the History of the Invisible Hand. *Journal of the History of Ideas, 72*(1), 29–49.

Hayek, F. A. (1978). Dr Bernard Mandeville. In *New Studies in Philosophy, Politics, Economics and the History of Ideas* (pp. 249–266). Routledge and Kegan Paul.

Heath, E. (2014). Metaphor Made Manifest: Taking Seriously Smith's 'Invisible Hand'. In D. F. Hardwick & L. Marsh (Eds.), *Propriety and Prosperity New Studies on the Philosophy of Adam Smith* (pp. 169–197). Palgrave Macmillan.

Henderson, W. (1994). Metaphor and Economics. In R. E. Backhouse (Ed.), *New Directions in Economic Methodology* (pp. 343–367). Routledge.

Herzog, L. (2013). *Inventing the Market: Smith, Hegel and Political Theory.* Oxford University Press.

Hesse, M. (1966). *Models and Analogies in Science.* University of Notre Dame Press.

Hesse, M. (1987). Unfamiliar Noises: Tropical Talk: The Myth of the Literal. *Proceedings of the Aristotelian Society,* Supplementary Volumes, *61*, 297–311.

Hetherington, N. S. (1983). Isaac Newton's Influence on Adam Smith's Natural Laws in Economics. *Journal of the History of Ideas, 44*(3), 497–505.

Hirschman, A. O. (1977). *The Passions and the Interests. Political Arguments for Capitalism Before Its Triumph.* Princeton University Press.

Hobbes, T. (1991 [1658]). On Man. In B. Gert (Ed.), *Man and Citizen.* Anchor Books.

Hobbes, T. (1996 [1651]). *Leviathan,* J. C. A. Gaskin (Ed.). Oxford University Press.

Hobbes, T. (1998 [1642]). *On the Citizen.* Cambridge University Press.

Hodgson, G. M. (1999). *Evolution and Institutions. On Evolutionary Economics and the Evolution of Economics.* Edward Elgar.

Hont, I., & Ignatieff, M. (1983). Needs and Justice in the *Wealth of Nations*: An Introductory Essay. In I. Hont & M. Ignatieff (Eds.), *Wealth and Virtue. The Shaping of Political Economy in the Scottish Enlightenment* (pp. 1–44). Cambridge University Press.

Hooke, R. (1665). *Micrographia or some Physiological Descriptions of Minute Bodies Made by Magnifying Glasses, with Observations and Inquiries Thereupon.* Printed by Martyn andAllestry.

Hooke, R. (1705). *The Posthumous Works of Robert Hooke,* Published by R. Waller. Printed by S. Smith and B. Walford.

Hoselitz, B. F. (1968). Agrarian Capitalism, the Natural Order of Things: François Quesnay. *Kyklos, 21*(4), 637–664.

Howell, W. S. (1975). Adam Smith's Lectures on Rhetoric: An Historical Assessment. In A. S. Skinner & T. Wilson (Eds.), *Essays on Adam Smith* (pp. 11–43). Clarendon Press.

Hume, D. (1985a [1739–40]). *A Treatise of Human Nature,* E. G. Mossner (Ed.). Penguin Books.

Hume, D. (1985b [1777]). Whether the British Government Inclines More to Absolute Monarchy, or to Republic. In E. F. Miller (Ed.), *Essays Moral, Political, and Literary* (pp. 47–53). Liberty Fund.

Hume, D. (1985c [1777]). Of Commerce. In E. F. Miller (Ed.), *Essays Moral, Political, and Literary* (pp. 253–267). Liberty Fund.

Hume, D. (1985d [1777]). Of Refinement in the Arts. In E. F. Miller (Ed.), *Essays Moral, Political, and Literary* (pp. 268–280). Liberty Fund.

Hume, D. (1985e [1777]). Of the Balance of Trade. In E. F. Miller (Ed.), *Essays Moral, Political, and Literary* (pp. 308–326). Liberty Fund.

Hume, D. (1985f [1777]). Of the Balance of Power. In E. F. Miller (Ed.), *Essays Moral, Political, and Literary* (pp. 332–341). Liberty Fund.

Hume, D. (1985g [1777]). Of the Populousness of Ancient Nations. In E. F. Miller (Ed.), *Essays Moral, Political, and Literary* (pp. 377–464). Liberty Fund.

Hume, D. (2007a [1748]). *An Enquiry Concerning Human Understanding*, P. Millican (Ed.). Oxford University Press.

Hume, D. (2007b [1779]). *Dialogues Concerning Natural Religion*, D. Coleman (Ed.). Cambridge University Press.

Hundert, E. J. (1994). *The Enlightenment's Fable: Bernard Mandeville and the Discovery of Society*. Cambridge University Press.

Hurtado Prieto, J. (2004). Bernard Mandeville's Heir: Adam Smith or Jean Jacques Rousseau on the Possibility of Economic Analysis. *The European Journal of the History of Economic Thought, 11*(1), 1–31.

Iacono, M. (1982). *Il borghese e il selvaggio. L'immagine dell'uomo isolato nei paradigmi di Defoe, Turgot e Adam Smith*. Franco Angeli.

Jacob, F. (1973). *The Logic of Life. A History of Heredity*. Pantheon Books. Trans. from French Edition: *La logique du vivant. Une histoire de l'hérédité*. Gallimard, 1970.

Johnson, E. A. J. (1960 [1937]). *Predecessors of Adam Smith*. Augustus M. Kelley.

Johnson, M. (2008). Philosophy's Debt to Metaphor. In R. W. Gibbs Jr. (Ed.), *The Cambridge Handbook of Metaphor and Thought* (pp. 39–52). Cambridge University Press.

Jonsson, F. A. (2010). Rival Ecologies of Global Commerce: Adam Smith and the Natural Historians. *American Historical Review, 115*(5), 1342–1363.

Kames, L., & Home, H. (1751). *Essays on the Principles of Morality and Natural Religion*. Fleming.

Keller, V. (2012). Mining Tacitus: Secrets of Empire, Nature and Art in the Reason of State. *The British Journal for the History of Science, 45*(2), 189–212.

Kennedy, G. (2008). *Adam Smith. A Moral Philosopher and His Political Economy*. Palgrave Macmillan.

Kennedy, G. (2014). The 'Invisible Hand' Phenomenon in Economics. In D. F. Hardwick & L. Marsh (Eds.), *Propriety and Prosperity New Studies on the Philosophy of Adam Smith* (pp. 198–222). Palgrave Macmillan.

Kennedy, G. (2017). *An Authentic Account of Adam Smith*. Palgrave Macmillan.

Khalil, E. L. (2000). Beyond Natural Selection and Divine Intervention: The Lamarckian Implication of Adam Smith's Invisible Hand. *Journal of Evolutionary Economics, 10*, 373–393.

Klamer, A., & Leonard, T. C. (1994). So What's an Economic Metaphor? In P. Mirowski (Ed.), *Natural Images in Economic Thought* (pp. 20–51). Cambridge University Press.

Koerner, L. (1999). *Linnaeus: Nature and Nation*. Harvard University Press.

Koselleck, R. (2004 [1979]). *Futures Past: On the Semantics of Historical Time.* Columbia University Press.

Kövecses, Z. (2010). *Metaphor. A Practical Introduction* (2nd ed.). Oxford University Press.

Koyré, A. (1968). *Newtonian Studies.* University Chicago Press.

Kuhn, T. S. (1993 [1979]). Metaphor in Science. In A. Ortony (Ed.), *Metaphor and Thought* (2nd ed., pp. 533–542). Cambridge University Press.

Lagueux, M. (1999). Do Metaphors affect Economic Theory? *Economics and Philosophy, 15*, 1–22.

Lakoff, G. (1993). The Contemporary Theory of Metaphor. In A. Ortony (Ed.), *Metaphor and Thought* (2nd ed., pp. 202–251). Cambridge University Press.

Lakoff, G. (2008). The Neural Theory of Metaphor. In R. W. Gibbs Jr. (Ed.), *The Cambridge Handbook of Metaphor and Thought* (pp. 17–38). Cambridge University Press.

Lakoff, G., & Johnson, M. (1980). *Metaphors We Live By.* University of Chicago Press.

Lakoff, G., & Johnson, M. (1999). *The Philosophy in the Flesh. The Embodied Mind and Its Challenge to Western Thought.* Basic Books.

Lakoff, G., & Núñez, R. (2000). *Where Mathematics Comes From: How the Embodied Mind Brings Mathematics into Being.* Basic Books.

Lawrence, C. (1979). The Nervous System and Society in the Scottish. In B. Barnes & S. Shapin (Eds.), *Natural Order: Historical Studies of Scientific Culture* (pp. 19–40). Sage.

Lecaldano, E. (1995). Introduzione. In A. Smith (Ed.), *Teoria dei sentimenti morali.* Rizzoli.

Letwin, W. (1975). *The Origins of Scientific Economics.* Greenwood Press.

Lewis, P. (1999). Metaphor and Critical Realism. In S. Fleetwood (Ed.), *Critical Realism in Economics. Development and Debate* (pp. 83–101). Routledge.

Lindgren, R. J. (1973). *The Social Philosophy of Adam Smith.* Martinus Nijhoff.

Linnæi, C. (1748). *Amoenitates Academicae.* Cornelium Haak.

Locke, J. (1980 [1690]). *Second Treatise of Government* (C. B. Macpherson, Trans. & Ed.). Hackett Publishing Company.

Locke, J. (1997 [1690]). *An Essay Concerning Human Understanding.* Penguin Books.

Lovejoy, A. O. (1936). *The Great Chain of Being.* Harvard University Press.

Macfie, A. L. (1967). *The Individual in Society.* Allen & Unwin.

Macfie, A. L. (1971). The Invisible Hand of Jupiter. *Journal of the History of Ideas, 32*(4), 595–599.

Machamer, P. (1998). Galileo's Machines, His Mathematics, and His Experiments. In P. Machamer (Ed.), *The Cambridge Companion to Galileo* (pp. 53–79). Cambridge University Press.

Maclaurin, C. (1748). *An Account of Sir Isaac Newton's Philosophical Discoveries*. Millar and Nourse.

Magner, L. N. (2002). *A History of the Life Sciences*. Marcel Dekker.

Magnusson, L. (2015). *The Political Economy of Mercantilism*. Routledge.

Malebranche, N. (1700 [1674–5]). *Treatise Concerning the Search After Truth*. Bowyer.

Malynes, G. (1622a). *The Maintenance of Free Trade [...]*. Printed by *I. L.* for *William Sheffard*; available at: https://quod.lib.umich.edu/e/eebo/A06789.0001.001?rgn=main;view=fulltext. Accessed 14 June 2020.

Malynes, G. (1622b). *Consuetudo, Vel Lex Mercatoria*. Adam Islip.

Mandeville, B. (1924a [1723]). A Search into the Nature of Society. In F. B. Kaye (Ed.), *The Fable of the Bees: Or, Private Vices, Publick Benefits* (Vol. 1). Clarendon Press.

Mandeville, B. (1924b [1723]). An Essay on Charity, and Charity-Schools. In F. B. Kaye (Ed.), *The Fable of the Bees: Or, Private Vices, Publick Benefits* (Vol. 2). Clarendon Press.

Mandeville, B. (1924c [1724]). The Fable of the Bees, or Private Vices, Publick Benefits. In F. B. Kaye (Ed.), *The Fable of the Bees: Or, Private Vices, Publick Benefits* (Vol. 1). Clarendon Press.

Marshall, D. (1984). Adam Smith and the Theatricality of Moral Sentiments. *Critical Inquiry, 10*, 592–613.

Marx, K. (1976 [1867]).*Capital. A Critique of Political Economy* (Vol. 1), Introduced by E. Mandel. Vintage Books.

Maupertuis, P. L. Moreau de. (1965a [1745]). Vénus physique. In *Oeuvres* (Vol. II). Georg Olms.

Maupertuis, P. L. Moreau de. (1965b [1754]). Sistème de la Nature. Essai sur la formation des corps organisés. In *Oeuvres* (Vol. II). Georg Olms.

Mayr, E. (1982). *The Growth of Biological Thought. Diversity, Evolution, and Inheritance*. The Belknap Press of Harvard University Press.

Mayr, O. (1986). *Authority, Liberty and Automatic Machinery in Early Modern Europe*. Johns Hopkins Press.

McCloskey, D. (1998). *The Rhetoric of Economics* (2nd ed.). University of Wisconsin Press.

McKenna, S. J. (2006). *Adam Smith. The Rhetoric of Propriety*. State University of New York Press.

Meek, R. L. (1976). *Social Science and the Ignoble Savage*. Cambridge University Press.

Millar, J. (1779). *The Origin of the Distinction of Ranks* (3rd ed.). Murray.

Millar, J. (1803). *An Historical View of the English Government* (Vol. IV). Printed for J. Mawman.

Mirabeau, (V. Riqueti, marquis de). (1763). *Philosophie Rurale*. Libraires Associés.

Mirabeau, (V. Riqueti, marquis de). (2003 [1763]). Extract from 'Rural Philosophy'. In R. L. Meek (Ed.), *The Economics of Physiocracy. Essays and Translations* (pp. 57–64). Routledge.

Mirowski, P. (1989). *More Heat than Light. Economics as Social Physics: Physics as Nature's Economics*. Cambridge University Press.

Misselden, E. (1623). *The Circle of Commerce*. Printed by J. Dawson.

Moravia, S. (1978). From Homme Machine to Homme Sensible: Changing Eighteenth-Century Models of Man's Image. *Journal of the History of Ideas, 39*(1), 45–60.

Moscovici, S. (1956). A propos de quelques travaux d'Adam Smith sur l'histoire et la philosophie des sciences. *Revue d'histoire des sciences et de leur applications, 9*(1), 1–20.

Moyle, W. (1727 [1698]). An Essay on the Lacedæmonian Government. In *The Whole Works of Walter Moyle*. Printed for Knapton, A. Bettesworth, E. Curll, J. Pemberton, and J. Batley.

Moyle, W. (1969 [ca 1699]). An Essay Upon the Constitution of the Roman Government. In C. Robbins (Ed.), *Two English Republican Tracts*. Cambridge University Press.

Mun, T. (1664). Mun, T. (1664). England's Treasure by Forraign Trade or The Ballance of Our Forraign Trade Is the Rule of Our Treasure. In J. R. McCulloch (Ed.), (1856), *A Select Collection of Early English Tracts on Commerce from the Originals of Mun, Roberts, North, and Others* (pp. 115–209). Printed for the Political Economy Club.

Myers, M. L. (1983). *The Soul of Modern Economic Man. Ideas of Self-Interest, Thomas Hobbes to Adam Smith*. University of Chicago Press.

Newman, W. R. (2004). *Promethean Ambitions. Alchemy and the Quest to Perfect Nature*. University of Chicago Press.

Newton, I. (1952 [1704]). *Opticks*. Fourth English Edition (1730). Foreword by A. Einstein, Introduction by Sir E. Whittaker, Preface by I. B. Cohen. Dover Publications.

Newton, I. (1999 [1687]). *The Principia. Mathematical Principles of Natural Philosophy*. University of California Press.

Nicholson, D. J. (2014). The Machine Conception of the Organism in Development and Evolution: A Critical Analysis. *Studies in History and Philosophy of Biological and Biomedical Sciences, 48*, 162–174.

Núñez, R. (2008). Conceptual Metaphor, Human Cognition, and the Nature of Mathematics. In R. W. Gibbs Jr. (Ed.), *The Cambridge Handbook of Metaphor and Thought* (pp. 339–362). Cambridge University Press.

Olson, R. (1975). *Scottish Philosophy and British Physics 1750–1880. A Study in the Foundation of the Victorian Scientific Style*. Princeton University Press.

Onions, C. T. (Ed.). (1973). *The Oxford Universal Dictionary Illustrated on Historical Principles* (Vol. 1, 3rd ed.). Clarendon Press.

Oslington, P. (2011). Divine Action, Providence and Adam Smith's Invisible Hand. In P. Oslington (Ed.), *Adam Smith as Theologian* (pp. 61–76). Routledge.

Pack, S. J. (1995). Theological (and Hence Economic) Implications of Adam Smith's "Principles which Lead and Direct Philosophical Enquires". *History of Political Economy, 27*(2), 289–307.

Pack, S. J. (1996). Adam Smith's Invisible/Visible Hand/Chain/Chaos. In L. S. Moss (Ed.), *Joseph A. Schumpeter Historian of Economics. Perspectives on the History of Economic Thought* (pp. 181–195). Routledge.

Packham, C. (2002). The Physiology of Political Economy: Vitalism and Adam Smith's Wealth of Nations. *Journal of the History of Ideas, 63*(3), 465–481.

Packham, C. (2012). *Eighteenth-Century Vitalism. Bodies, Culture, Politics.* Palgrave Macmillan.

Pascal, B. (1995 [1670]). *Pensées and Other Writings.* Oxford University Press.

Pepper, S. C. (1942). *World Hypotheses: A Study in Evidence.* University of California Press.

Perelman, C., & Olbrechts-Tyteca, L. (1969). *The New Rhetoric. A Treatise on Argumentation.* University of Notre Dame Press.

Perrotta, C. (2004). *Consumption as an Investment: I. The Fear of Goods from Hesiod to Adam Smith.* Routledge.

Persky, J. (1989). Adam Smith's Invisible Hands. *Journal of Economic Perspectives, 3*(4), 195–201.

Pesciarelli, E. (1977). Adam Smith: dal modo di sussistenza al modo di produzione. *Quaderni di Sociologia, 26*(3–4), 219–231.

Pesciarelli, E. (1988). *La jurisprudence economica di Adam Smith.* Giappichelli.

Petty, W. (1963a [1690]). Political Arithmetick. In C. H. Hull (Ed.), *The Economic Writings of Sir William Petty* (Vol. 1). Augustus M. Kelley.

Petty, W. (1963b [1691]). The Political Anatomy of Ireland. In C. H. Hull (Ed.), *The Economic Writings of Sir William Petty* (Vol. 1). Augustus M. Kelley.

Petty, W. (1963c [1662]). Treatise of Taxes and Contributions. In C. H. Hull (Ed.), *The Economic Writings of Sir William Petty* (Vol. 1). Augustus M. Kelley.

Petty, W. (1967 [1928]). *The Petty Papers. Some Unpublished Writings of Sir William Petty* (Vol. II). Marquis of Lansdowne (Ed.), reprint. Augustus M. Kelley.

Prigogine, I., & Stengers, I. (1984). *Order out of Chaos: Man's New Dialogue with Nature.* Bantam Books.

Purcell, W. M. (1986). A Reassessment of Adam Smith's Lectures on Rhetoric and Belles Lettres. *Central States Speech Journal, 37*(1), 45–54.

Quesnay, F. (1888 [1743]). Mémoires de l'Académie Royale de Chirurgie – Préface. In A. Oncken (Ed.), *Œuvres économiques et philosophiques.* J. Baer & C., Libraires Éditeurs.

Quesnay, F. (1958a [1756]). Évidence. In *François Quesnay et la physiocratie* (Vol. II). I.N.E.D.

Quesnay, F. (1958b [1763]). Chapitre VII de la "Philosophie Rurale". In *François Quesnay et la physiocratie* (Vol. II). I.N.E.D.

Quesnay, F. (1958c [1767]). Despotisme de la Chine. In *François Quesnay et la physiocratie* (Vol. II). I.N.E.D.

Raphael, D. D. (1985). *Adam Smith*. Oxford University Press.

Raphael, D. D., & Skinner, A. S. (1980). General Introduction. In A. Smith (Ed.), *Essays on Philosophical Subjects*, In W. P. D. Wightman, & J. C. Bryce (Eds.), *The Glasgow Edition of the Works and Correspondence of Adam Smith*. Oxford University Press.

Rashid, S. (1998). *The Myth of Adam Smith*. Edward Elgar.

Reill, P. H. (2005). *Vitalizing Nature in the Enlightenment*. University of California Press.

Rescher, N. (1991). *G.W. Leibniz's Monadology. An Edition for Students*. University of Pittsburgh Press.

Richards, I. A. (1965 [1936]). *The Philosophy of Rhetoric*. Oxford University Press.

Rizzolatti, G., & Sinigaglia, C. (2006). *So quel che fai. Il cervello che agisce e i neuroni specchio*. Raffaello Cortina.

Roe, S. A. (1981). *Matter, Life, and Generation. Eighteenth-Century Embryology and the Haller-Wolff Debate*. Cambridge University Press.

Roger, J. (1997). *Buffon: A Life in Natural History*. Cornell University Press.

Rorty, R. (1987). Unfamiliar Noises: Hesse and Davidson on Metaphor. *Proceedings of the Aristotelian Society*, Supplementary Volumes, *61*, 283–296.

Rosenberg, N. (1963). Mandeville and Laissez-Faire. *Journal of the History of Ideas, 24*(2), 183–196.

Rosenberg, N. (1965). Adam Smith on the Division of Labour: Two Views or One? *Economica, 32*(126), 127–139.

Rossi, P. (1968). *Francis Bacon: From Magic to Science* (S. Rabinovich, Trans. & Ed.). Routledge and Kegan Paul.

Rothschild, E. (2001). *Economic Sentiments: Adam Smith, Condorcet and the Enlightenment*. Harvard University Press.

Rousseau, J.-J. (1932). *Correspondance Générale de J.-J. Rousseau*, T. Dufour (Ed.), Tome 17. Librairie Armand Colin.

Sabbagh, G. (2016). Cantillon in French and English. Two Editions by Richard van den Berg and Antoin E. Murphy: New Facts and Hypotheses. *Contributions to Political Economy, 35*(1), 91–125.

Samuels, W. J. (2011). *Erasing the Invisible Hand: Essays on an Elusive and Misused Concept in Economics*. Cambridge University Press.

Sawday, J. (2007). *Engines of the Imagination. Renaissance Culture and the Rise of the Machine*. Routledge.

Schabas, M. (2001). David Hume on Experimental Natural Philosophy, Money, and Fluids. *History of Political Economy, 33*(3), 411–435.

Schabas, M. (2005). *The Natural Origins of Economics.* University Chicago Press.

Schliesser, E. (2017). *Adam Smith. Systematic Philosopher and Public Thinker.* Oxford University Press.

Schumpeter, J. A. (1997 [1954]). *History of Economic Analysis.* Routledge.

Searle, J. R. (1993 [1979]). Metaphor. In A. Ortony (Ed.), *Metaphor and Thought* (2nd ed., pp. 83–111). Cambridge University Press.

Shapin, S. (1996). *The Scientific Revolution.* University of Chicago Press.

Sheehan, J., & Wahrman, D. (2015). *Invisible Hands. Self-Organization and the Eighteenth Century.* University of Chicago Press.

Sivado, A. (2017). Resurrecting the Body Politic – Physiology's Influence on Sir William Petty's Political Arithmetick. *Early Science and Medicine, 22*, 157–182.

Sivado, A. (2019). The Ontology of Sir William Petty's Political Arithmetic. *The European Journal of the History of Economic Thought, 25*(5), 1003–1026.

Skinner, A. S. (1979). *A System of Social Science. Papers Relating to Adam Smith.* Clarendon Press.

Solinas, G. (1967). *Il microscopio e le metafisiche. Epigenesi e preesistenza da Cartesio a Kant.* Feltrinelli.

Steiner, P. (1998). *La "science nouvelle" de l'économie politique.* Presses Universitaires de France.

Stewart, D. (1980 [1793]). *Account of the Life and Writings of Adam Smith.* In A. Smith (Ed.), *Essays on Philosophical Subjects* (pp. 269–332). In W. P. D. Wightman & J. C. Bryce (Eds.), *The Glasgow Edition of the Works and Correspondence of Adam Smith.* Oxford University Press.

Swift, J. (1701). *A Discourse of the Contents and Dissensions Between the Nobles and the Commons in Athens and Rome.* Printed for John Nutt.

Théré, C., & Charles, L. (2008). The Writing Workshop of François Quesnay and the Making of Physiocracy. *History of Political Economy, 40*(1), 1–42.

Thomson, H. F. (1965). Adam Smith's Philosophy of Science. *Quarterly Journal of Economics, 79*(2), 212–233.

Tobin, J. (1992). The Invisible Hand in Modern Macroeconomics. In M. Fry (Ed.), *Adam Smith's Legacy. His Place in the Development of Modern Economics* (pp. 117–129). Routledge.

Trincado, E. (2019). *The Birth of Economic Rhetoric. Communication, Arts and Economic Stimulus in David Hume and Adam Smith.* Palgrave Macmillan.

Tucker, J. (1774). *Four Tracts, on Political and Commercial Subjects* (2nd ed.). Printed by R. Raikes.

Turner, B. P. (2016). Mandeville Against Luxury. *Political Theory, 44*(1), 26–52.

Vaggi, G. (1987). *The Economics of François Quesnay.* Macmillan.

Vaggi, G. (1995). The Limits of Physiocracy and Smith's Fortune. In *Economies et Sociétés*, Série Œconomia, Histoire de la Pensée économique, P.E., *22–23*(1–2), 59–77.

Vaughn, K. I. (1989). Invisible Hand. In J. Eatwell, M. Milgate, & P. Newman (Eds.), *The New Palgrave. The Invisible Hand* (pp. 168–172). Norton.

Versieren, J. (2016). The Moral Foundations of Adam Smith's Transitional Society: Reappraising Foucault's Representations of Wealth and Marx's Reconstruction of Value Theory. *Capital & Class, 40*(3), 1–22.

Vigo de Lima, I., & Guizzo, D. (2015). An Archaeology of Adam Smith's Epistemic Context. *Review of Political Economy, 27*(4), 585–605.

Viner, J. (1972). *The Role of Providence in the Social Order.* Princeton University Press.

Voltaire. (1951 [1733]). *Lettres philosophiques ou lettres anglaises.* Garnier.

Walraevens, B. (2010). Adam Smith's Economics and the *Lectures on Rhetoric and Belles Lettres.* The Language of Commerce. *History of Economic Ideas, 18*(1), 11–32.

Wennerlind, C. (2006). David Hume as a *Political* Economist. In A. Dow & S. Dow (Eds.), *A History of Scottish Economic Thought* (pp. 46–70). Routledge.

Wight, J. B. (2014). Instincts and the Invisible Order: The Possibility of Progress. In D. F. Hardwick & L. Marsh (Eds.), *Propriety and Prosperity New Studies on the Philosophy of Adam Smith* (pp. 223–239). Palgrave Macmillan.

Wolfe, C. T. (2017). Models of Organic Organization in Montpellier Vitalism. *Early Science and Medicine, 22*, 229–252.

Wolfe, C. T. (2018). Smithian Vitalism? *Journal of Scottish Philosophy, 16*, 264–271.

Wootton, D. (2006). Liberty, Metaphor, and Mechanism: "Checks and Balances" and the Origins of Modern Constitutionalism. In D. Womersley (Ed.), *Liberty and American Experience in the Eighteenth Century* (pp. 209–274). Liberty Fund.

Wootton, D. (2015). *The Invention of Science: A New History of the Scientific Revolution*. Harper.

Worland, S. T. (1976). Mechanistic Analogy and Smith on Exchange. *Review of Social Economy, 34*(3), 245–257.

Index[1]

[1] Note: Page numbers followed by 'n' refer to notes.

S. Fiori, *Machines, Bodies and Invisible Hands*,
https://doi.org/10.1007/978-3-030-85206-1

The manufacturer's authorised representative in the EU is Springer Nature Customer Service Centre GmbH, Europaplatz 3, 69115 Heidelberg, Germany. If you have any concerns regarding our products, please contact ProductSafety@springernature.com

Printed and bound by CPI Group (UK) Ltd, Croydon, CR0 4YY
30/09/2026
02225499-0006